PERSPECTIVES IN POLITICAL THEORY

PERSPECTIVES IN POLITICAL THEORY

edited by

J.S. BAINS
R.B. JAIN

HUMANITIES PRESS
ATLANTIC HIGHLANDS, N.J.

First Published 1980 in the United States of America by
Humanities Press Inc.
Atlantic Highlands
N. J. 07716

ISBN 0-391-01900-7

Printed in India

CONTENTS

CONTRIBUTORS

J.S. BAINS is Professor of Political Science, University of Delhi. He was formerly Professor of Political Science, Guru Nanak University, Amritsar and Editor of *Indian Journal of Political Science*. He has published *Domestic Jurisdiction and the Law of the United Nations*, *Studies in Political Science*, *India's International Disputes*, *The Administration of Indian Foreign Policy through the United Nations* (with C. Schleicher), and *Political Science in India*.

ISAIAH BERLIN was formerly Fellow of New College, 1938-50, and of All Souls, 1950-67 and 1975 onwards. He has been a Professor of Social and Political Theory, University of Oxford, 1956-65; President of Wolfson College, Oxford, 1966-75; President of the British Academy, 1974-78; and Visiting Professor at a number of American universities. His published works include *Karl Marx*, *Four Essays on Liberty*, *Fathers and Children*, *Vico and Herder*, *Russian Thinkers*, and *Concepts and Categories*.

D.C. GROVER is Reader in Political Science, Kurukshetra University and has publised *M. N. Roy: A Study of Revolution and Reason in Indian Politics*.

R.B. JAIN is Professor and Head, Department of Public Administration, Punjab University, Patiala. He was formerly Reader in Political Science, University of Delhi He has been a Visiting Research Scholar at the Columbia University, New York and has worked with the US Civil Service Commission and the US Agency for International Development. He has also been a British Council Fellow in Public Administration at the London School of Economics and Political Science (1967-68), and a Senior Fulbright Fellow and Visiting Professorial Lecturer at the Georgetown University, Washington, D.C. (1975-76). He is the author of *Contemporary Issues in Indian Administration*, *Indian Parliament: Innovations, Reforms and Development*, and *Comparative Legislative Behaviour: Research Perspectives*.

SUDIPTA KAVIRAJ is Assistant Professor of Political Science,

Centre for Political Studies, Jawaharlal Nehru University, New Delhi. He is the co-author of *The State of Political Theory: Some Marxist Essays*.

SUBRATA MUKHERJEE is Reader in Political Science, University of Delhi.

ZEHEER MASOOD QURAISHI is Reader in Political Science, University of Delhi. He was formerly Professor of Political Science and Dean of the Faculty of Social Sciences, University of Kashmir. He has published *The President of India, Patterns of Western Domination in Africa, Liberal Nationalism in Egypt, Struggle for Rashtrapati Bhawan*, and *Election and State Politics in India*.

L.S. RATHORE is Professor and Chairman, Department of Political Science, University of Jodhpur and Editor of *The Indian Journal of Political Studies*. He was formerly Senior Fulbright Fellow and Vice President, All India Political Science Association (1978). He has published *Political and Constitutional Developments in the Princely States of Rajasthan, 1920-49* and *The Changing Bhutan*.

BIBEKBRATA SARKAR is Lecturer in Political Science, Kirori Mal College, University of Delhi and is the author of the forthcoming *Left Politics in India, 1920-1947*.

V.P. VERMA is Senior Lecturer, Bhagat Singh College, University of Delhi and is the author of *Political Philosophy of Hegel* and *Sociology of Thought*.

PREFACE

The essays in the present book are grouped in two parts—the Western Tradition and the Indian Perspective. The five essays in Part I analyse various themes in Western political thought in the modern perspective. In the first essay, "Social Contract and Contractual Society," Sudipta Kaviraj deals with the theme of "social contract," interpreting it in an altogether new way through the use of Marxian categories of interpretation of cultural objects. He suggests that although the social contract theorists spoke a language different from that of our times, they still shared our concern about capitalism, instrumentalist politics, representation, and forms of democracy.

In the next essay, "Rousseau's General Will," Zaheer Masood Quraishi contends that although the concept of General Will is full of many ambiguities, Rousseau's influence is, in a general sense, universal and transcends all boundaries of space and time.

V.P. Verma in his piece "Marxism: The Eternal Dimensions," argues that political science today has become a miracle creed; for none of its developments can claim immunity from the Marxian view of social existence. He thus tries to unfold some of the fundamental aspects of Marxism which have the necessary potentialities to generate a continuum. Marxism reinforced with metaphysical dialectics has both negative and positive dimensions which contribute to its eternal validity.

Subrata Mukherjee in his contribution "Poems of Karl Marx" gives an insight into some of the little-known aspects of Marx such as his work as a poet. He tries to show how Marx's poems, though written in the formative period of his life, yet do not lie outside the mainstream of his thought.

In the last of the essays in this part, L.S. Rathore evaluates Hannah Arendt's contribution to political theory. Referring to the normative legacy left behind by Arendt, which, he suggests, is of major importance and durability, he shows how, with the help of extensive and carefully structured argument, she supports the view that politics provides the only guarantee of our sanity, that political activity alone confers meaning upon life, and that in it the highest form of happiness is to be found.

The first of the essays in the second part is a study of Guru Gobind Singh's ideas on religion, politics, and society by

J.S. Bains. It starts with the assumption that the Sikh view of life regards the activities of the individual and society as amenable to spiritiual influence and as capable of making a significant impact on the social, political, economic, and other aspects of man's life. It then shows how Guru Gobind Singh believed that all authority—secular and spiritual—flows from God, who is omnipotent and the final determinant of all things. Even then he rejected the doctrine of the divine right of authority claimed by despotic rulers. In order to bring into existence an ideal society, the Guru laid emphasis on the regeneration of both the physical and spiritual aspects of the personality of the individual. He was the first Indian leader to practise as well as to advocate the principles of equality, fraternity, and democracy. He sought to ensure that ethical and spiritual values formed the foundations of all human activity—political, social, and economic.

In the next essay, "Tagore and the Consciousness of Nationality," Isaiah Berlin contends that Rabindranath Tagore, a great master of words, spoke about language and its connection with social and political life with great insight, and that what he said has great interest for us even today. During his long and marvellously fruitful life, Tagore was absorbed more in creative work of a literary type than in social or political acitivity. He sought to make only what was beautiful and say only what was true. This, Berlin concludes, entailed self-discipline and exceptional patience and integrity.

In the same vein, writing on "Nationalism, Marxism, and Gandhi," Bibekbrata Sarkar emphasizes the point that the Congress-led freedom struggle was not a simple, straight, onward movement. The interaction of Gandhian and Marxian ideological thought currents brought into existence a number of movements that ran parallel to the struggle for freedom. As a result, the character of the anti-colonial struggle also changed. It ceased to be a struggle exclusively concerned about political freedom and became transformed into a wider search for the true foundations of freedom.

The next contribution by D.C.Grover deals with the viability of the New Left in India as a theory of social and political change. He attempts to show that the struggle of the New Left in India is the struggle to create and strengthen people's organs of power as centres of parallel polity so that the State does not operate as the only instrument of social and political change.

The essays in this volume thus provide an overview of some of the main currents of Western political thought from Rousseau to Marx. They also throw light on certain aspects of Indian political thought which have not received adequate scholarly attention so far.

The editors take this opportunity to express their sincere thanks to the contributors who responded to their request at short notice. They have felt vastly encouraged by the co-operation they have received all round.

J.S. BAINS
R.B. JAIN

Part I
The Western Tradition

SOCIAL CONTRACT AND CONTRACTUAL SOCIETY

Sudipta Kaviraj

I

This essay is about 'social contract'. This is obviously one of the most traditional subjects for interpretation. Yet, I think it is one that can be interpreted in a different, altogether new way—through use of Marxian categories or interpretation of cultural objects.

In this essay I shall make three unusual suggestions. These are not unusal in a logical sense. On the contrary, I think they are perfectly plausible. In fact, I shall go further and suggest that if traditional interpreters of political thought had been more conscious of the *historical* dimension of their problem besides the purely logical dimension,[1] their studies would have been less flawed. But these hypotheses are still unusual in a simple statistical sense. This style of 'reading' of political theory is still not common. I personally believe that it is a lot more reasonable.

Traditional interpreters, to text books, emphasise that there is a certain sense in which theorists who are called contractualists share basic attitudes and theoretical tools. I shall contest this. It appears to me that apart from some general methodological[2] and epistemological[3] postulates (necessarily on a very high level of generality) they had little in common. At least, as far as their preferences of political forms and views about the origin, structure and exercise of power are concerned, I am struck more by their stark differences than by the superficial similarity. This similarity consists, to my mind, in their use of a fashionable current metaphor. All else differed.

Though social contract is not the common focal point of their three theories, I think there was such a focal point nonetheless. This is the more fundamental unity of a historically constituted problem, and not, as commonly supposed, of a shared problem. All three of the great contractualists registered the fact that a new kind of society had risen in Europe in the seventeenth and eighteenth centuries. It structured human relationships in new, unfamiliar forms. Since the relations in which men found themselves placed were new, it gave rise to new types of basic conflicts, which, in turn, called for new institutions and legal frames for sorting them out and of explaining them. Taken as a whole, as a kind of shorthand, we can call this - a new *structure of political experience*, and an answering *structure of theoretical sensibility*—patterned expectations about whether science is possible, and if so, in what sense, how exactly. In a sense, there is a deep underlying connection between this new structure of experience, and the new structures of thinking— through which thinkers interpreted their experience. It seems to me that this critically significant conjunction—of a new structure of lived experience and a new way of interpreting world— is what caused the development of the new type of social theory—theory of the social contract. Other ways of looking at them undervalues their originality. We may not agree with any of the thinkers. But we must not miss the shattering originality of what they suggested—both collectively (i.e. in posing the problem of possibilities of politics in the context of capitalism) and vis-a-vis each other (in each posing the problem of power in early capitalism in a distinctive way, and suggesting a highly original institutional framework for solving it). This is what is really common to them—a problem that they define, articulate and tackee differently, but one that is common enough for them for them to recognise that they are conceptually engaged with the same thing.

The third proposition is that in analysing the political possibilities in early capitalism, they not only suggested different positions; these in a sense represent the three fundamental possibilities that are likely. In other words, there are, one might say, three ideal-type positions that men could take up about early capitalism. In the rest of this paper I shall argue out my case, giving marginal propositions in support of the main thesis : reading social contract theories not in the traditional way, but through the problematic of rising capitalism.[4] For the sake of symmetry, and clarity in polemic, I shall state the various positions in structured forms so that both the continuities and the differences stand out sharply.

Il

The Position of Divine Right Theorists

If one judged Hobbes by his conclusions, one would be disappointed. Hobbes suggested little that was entirely new about what should be the preferred political arrangement in a society. After all he came down on the side of an irresponsible, monarchical government; but so had the divine right theorists. However it would be wrong to think that there was nothing new in Hobbes's theory. His conclusions about preferred governmental form may have been similar to the divine rightists. What were utterly new were his ways of arriving at these conclusions, what he considered to be adequate grounds for a political theory of absolution. The conservative clergy of Oxford had decided that it was not enough to burn copies of the Leviathan; for added security, one must burn the author with it. They were not, from their point of view, far wrong. Hobbes's thought converged with established orthodoxies on a secondary or marginal point, after destroying its most fundamental premises. They had instinctively sensed this.

The theorists who believed in divine right of kings were deeply suspicious of Hobbes's doctrines. I think in this they displayed a basically correct historical sense. Political theories lose their cutting edge with the passing of time, and still more, by the passing of old and entry of newly-constituted structures. Since fundamental questions get differently constituted, the older theories and suggested solutions lose their meaning their topicality, their ability to rouse people emotionally, to excite partisanship and anger. Most of social contract theories have lost their edge of meaning, and their ability to excite in this sense. We have to recreate those typical situations of rising capitalism and its politics—to recapture their meanings, and to understand why they were, quite rightly, considered seditious.

If one starts from this simple observation—that Hobbes's theory, after all, arrived at conclusions very similar to the divine right doctrine, one has already created a 'problem' to be explained. One has to explain the deep hostility between the two positions in that case. Two factors explain this. Contractualists offered a political theory that was non-metaphysical. It can be described 'quasi-historical'[5] from a modern point of view. Still, it started from the basic premise that the grounds or sources or authority, its structure, its mode of exercise, and the calculations or those who are the objects of state-power vis-a-vis its weilders, are all human, rational and therefore rationally explicable questions. The source of power is a human act, and not divine grace or ordainment. The implications of this general statement are significant. The only conceivable attitude towards an act of God (unless, of course, one is talking of a Cartesian God, i.e. a mathematician whose major function is to set mathematical problems through nature) is submission. It is wrong even to ask where or why a divine right to rule has originated. It has an axiomatic, self-evident, non-rational origin. But, if the source or power is a human act—it becomes knowable. Human beings are rational creatures. When they do something as decisive as founding a political authority, it is unlikely that they would do this without rational calculations and motives. And since these calculations are human, and therefore, *rational*, these must be rationally explicable too. A second rule of renaissance scientific theory also becomes logically applicable to the case of political knowledge. You can easily know what you have yourself created—an artifact. Social contract makes the states literally an artifact in this sense, although the artifact of a human collective. Since it is created by human beings, by a second logical argument, it becomes explicable through national knowledge. So, though conclusions of the divine right theorists and Hobbes, sometimes converge, but this is misleading. The methodological distances are enormous.

Medieval epistemological conceptions were symmetrical and logically consistent. Concisely, these were the exact reverse of the renaissance pastulates. For the native optimism of the renaissance theorists, although everything was not known, everything was knowable.[6] This was very abstractly qualified by the obvious constraints of Cartesian dualism; a certain sanctuary reluctantly left to the 'spirit', after carefully defining all significant phenomena into the realm of the 'material' or as Hobbes would put more abrasively and defiantly, 'the body' Medieval conceptions were fundamentally different: a nature that is largely random; therefore, ruled by a God who is a capricious tyrant, not a mathematical question—setter. And if things are intrinsically random, is follows that they are not subject to rational procedures of knowledge. A randomly behaving nature can be logically opposed only by a random kind of knowledge: a sort of knowledge that comes by 'revelation' (that is, by random and mysterious, *rationally inexplicable* processes) not by rationalist methodologies. Nature and society are both, in principle, unknowable in significants. respects. The epistemological significance of having the state founded by a contract, becomes more understandable this way. The myth of the contract was certainly a-historical. That did not trouble the contractualists excessively. This is because they were trying to make a logical, and not a historical point. Though there could well have been individual theorists who believed that their propositions were both logically and historically valid. Anthropological research did dot exist. Even modern historiography was in its infancy. Under these circumstances, it was quite excusable if a theorist like Hobbes or Locks did actually suppose that what they described in their 'state of nature' was actually very likely to have happened in primitive tribes intending to set up states. For us, however, the logical point is for more significant. Whether a social contract had been considered to have occurred or not. it was in the logical necessity of the new type of political theory. The internal logic of these theories demanded a conceptual construct like that. Given their epistemological presuppositions, a conrtact suited them perfectly. The instrumentality of the contract helped them to make two related theoretical suggestions—but in a dramatic and popular form—which could, in Gramsci's terms, make the crucial transition from abstract 'theory' to 'common sense'. There two interconnected propositions were: (i) that the creation of political authority was a collective human act, and therefore, subject to rational knowledge; and (ii) that the calculations which led to the institution of political power were rational calculations of probable gains and losses—very much like the mental operations a businessman would have to go through before undertaking a risk-involving commercial enterprise. It was, therefore, an act of a familiar cast, a thing that is done by ordinary individuals everyday—with of course obvious differences of gravity. (government was more serious than property). This particular decision affects *very life,* not some men's property. And Hobbes was enough of a renaissance man still to consider life more fundamental than property. For him property is meaningless, is not worth having, without life. There would be others who would suggest that life is not worth having without property. Still, this does make a lot of difference to the way we look at the political process. From a primordial and mysterious process, it turns, at one stroke, into something that is human and *knowable*. One can understand the latent passion of the contractualists' debate with divine right theorists'. They were essentially defending the *epistemological possibility* of political theory. Only under these conditions, what they called political theory (description and purely instrumental or rational analysis of the ways of power as a rational activity) had a right to exist. This way one can understand the scathing, intolerant, malicious, bitter tone of Hobbe's critique. He was situated in the midst of a living debate-vicious, embittering and violent. He lived it—his every sentence dripped poison. Hobbes was committed to the radicalism of his age. In fact, he narrowly escaped a martyrdom that is rarely expected of modern radicals.

III

Hobbes's Position

Hobbes's intellectual project, then, was a combination of two intellectual propositions that were previously considered irreconcilable: a substantive pro-absolutist doctrine, and a comletely rationalist epistemology. How one 'reads' Hobbes depends on what one considers more fundamental—the substantive conclusions or the basic method. Hobbes and his contemporary critics thought it was his method. Later interpreters (those I have generally called 'the traditionalists') thought it was his conclusion, evidently, because they thought the main business of political theory was to speculate about the relative advantages of various constitutional forms. Power had receded from their vision.

All theories which followed the deductive style of discourse necessarily concealed a difference between the *logic of enquiry* (which the author had gone through) and a *logic of presentation* (which he constructed for his reader, and which by no means duplicated his own knowledge process). The second was considerably more petified. An author, particularly if he is a deductivist, does not take his reader through his own puzzlements, hesitations, false leads, bad hypotheses. It is all tidied up, given the impressiveness and finality of a completed logical process. It is offered to readers in that finished, recreated, or rethought form. The presentation is a series of certainties. It inevitably conceals the series of doubts which must have gradually and untidily led to each of them.[7] Its deductive form tends to conceal the complexity and the contradiction (by prevailing intellectual standards) of Hobbes's project. His project sought to reconcile feudalist political conclusions with the logical and ontological necessities of a rationalist discourse. He succeeded in this unusual project. And as an unintended consequence, he also succeeded in alienating his two political class—audiences—the feudals and the early bourgeois. Feudals rejected his method, the bourgeoisie his conclusions, Machiavelli was at least celebrated as a great figure in the Italian cultural tradition.[8] Continental interpreters, occasionally, though not as a rule, admired him even as a political theorist. Hobbes was less fortunate. He was finally and inexorably rejected by English liberal political theory. Once more it had good reason. Whatever else Hobbes was, he certainly was not a liberal.[9]

Let me state in relatively modern terms, what I consider to be Hobbes's position on bourgeois politics.[10] A word first about what 1 have Summarily called 'bourgeois politics'. Elsewhere I have termed it 'the possibilities of politics in the context of an early capitalist society'. This unqainly phrase is used to denote some fairly widely accepted political problems. Schematically these are:

i) an organic conception of the quality of relations in which men are placed, and by which society is structured; a society gives rise to typical, recurrent patterns of interests and conflicts between them; in a particular society one can expect certain recurrent types of conflicts; the function of political authority is to manage these conflicts;

ii) an early capitalist society, because of the nature of men and groups who constitute it, would give rise to a certain measurable range of typical conflict situations;

iii) a certain specific type of governmental organisation or form of state-power, or a few of them (arranged in a hierarchy) would be able to best respond to these conflictual needs, and would be therefore considered the more preferable (I shall speak of preferred state-forms strictly in this sense).

iv) This state-form would have a finite range of 'options' or 'strategies' to subjects in their dealing with the state.

Let us see now what would be Hobbes's position on these questions, if we render it in modern equivalents. I think Macpherson has convincingly shown that Hobbes's state of nature was a logical abstraction[11]. It portrayed men who were very inadequate savages. They understand the advantages of contract too easily. They singlemindedly search for 'commodious living'. This is not how men had actually behaved in an original stateless condition, at a primitive stage of human development. It is not a picture of the past, but of the present. It describes how Hobbes's contemporaries would most probably behave had there been no central authority. In other words, it is Hobbes's own society minus the state. The anarchy in the state of nature is, then, an imaginative intensification, to a pure or limit-case, of the already prevalent qualified anarchy of early English capitalistic.

Sociological structures and the stable configuration of interests determine political outcomes : an inexorable and honestly mechanical materialist determinism[12]. Hobbes's society is an unmistakably capitalist society, and his men are bourgeois men[13]. This comes out clearly in his purely economic, market-oriented and contract-ridden analysis of power.[14] Hobbes probably had ideas of lateral isomorphism-the feeling, quite unfounded, that if a certain pattern of explanation (or, more loosely, a model) was useful in one sector (say, the economy) there was a high likelihood of its being so in contiguous fields (say, in politics). For Hobbes, the economy is axiomatically market-oriented and determined by contractual relations.[15] He tries a contractual device, and a market-like structural analysis in explanation of political life as its logical counterpart. As a legal form, contract anyway dominates capitalist social relations. Hobbes tries a logical extension of this to sort out political experiences under early capitalism.

We can read Hobbes on two levels—a formal level and a substantive—modernised level.   On the formal level the sequence is the following. Because of equally shared extreme insecurity[16] in the state of nature, men decide to set up a state. Living conditions in the state of nature are so bad that men are prepared to exchange it for even the most irrevocable and irremediable absolutism. Read *historically*, Hobbes's argument is more plansible. A capitalist society is based on purely rational calculation of self-interest.   Such calculation leads to a situation of extreme, unqualified individualism, aggression, competitiveness. Hobbes could not see how a society of unqualified individualists could exist for long without a modicum of order imposed from outside. Capitalism would explode, or, if you prefer modern terminology, break down out of sheer unrestricted individual competition. The political form most suited to managing such conflicts between such monsters is obviously a cruel authoritarian state.   What Hobbes thought about the likely state-form was thus derived from the probable behaviour of men, i.e. from what Hobbes thought of the sociology of capitalism.

Here is the central paradox of Hobbes's theory. He was a *political* theorist.   Curiously, however, almost all that he said about the capitalist state turned out to be misleading. As a compensation, nearly all that he said about the sociology of early capitalism was right.   This was because of his excessive reliance on logic, There was in the else he could do.   I have argued elsewhere that Hobbes misunderstood the capitalist state so radically because he understood the capitalist society so well.[17]

What were the things that Hobbes did not adequated grasp? Macpherson mentions two flaws in Hobbes's analysis of early capitalism. I shall add a third. Of Macpherson's two criticisms, one is, strictly speaking, a flaw in his understanding of capitalist **society**, the second of the capitalist **state**.   The two wrong visions were, of course, related.

The First Error

Hobbes was certainly observant about the way people behaved in his kind of society. It goes without saying that he did not work with a modern, that is, a post-Hegelian sense of history. Consequently, the whole problem of society-making and state making were, for him, time-lessly constant. Marx noted this eternity reflex, a feature of social theory of the entire pre Hegelian period : It is not a reproach to the physiocrats that, like all their successors, they thought of these material factors... in isolation from the social condition, in which they appeared in capitalist production ... and thereby made of the capitalist form of production an eternal, natural form of production. For them the bourgeois forms of production necessarily appeared as natural forms. It was their great merit that they conceived these forms as physiological forms of society : as forms arising from the natural necessity of production itself, forms that are independent of anyone's will or politics etc. They are material laws, the error is only that the material law of a definite historical stage is conceived as an abstract law governing equally all forms of society.[18] I think this can be applied without any modification whatsoever to Hobbes's very similar equation of capitalist-natural=eternal, conflating a logical necessity with histrorical timelessness. Problems of politics were for him, derived from an eternal unchanging human nature. Hobbes's categories are fixed and static. Still, one can apply a modern historical sense to Hobbes's absence of it, and draw interesting lessons. Hobbes certainly confused the historical problem, and transposed historically created characteristics of 'human nature' into 'eternal' ones. But, subject to this, he was an excellent observer. From his empirical observation of human behaviour in capitalist contexts, he was struck by the aggressiveness, competitiveness, acquistiveness and unrestricted individualism based on national-instrumentalist calculation. As a methodological individualist, he developed a highly simplified picture of capitalist society—a simple totality that admits of the possibility of just two terminal units—individual unit and the secial whole. There were no intermediate structures or configurations in the middle-no classes, no groups, and no permanent clusters of interest, nothing beyond the purely opportunist, and therefore, utterly temporary, combinations between predatory individuals.[19] This society is not likely to appeal to an anthropologist, for there is little likelihood of its actually existing anywhere. But it can delight the logician—one can prepare beautiful aesthetically satisfying, deductive generalisations with it. So it appealed to Hobbes who frankly declared his ambition to be the geometrician of political behaviour.

The basic flaw of Hobbes's analysis lies in his incapacity to 'see' and then conceptualise the existence of classes.[20] Hobbes's capitalism is a highly simplified abstract model of capitalism—a capitalism that is perfect in all respects, *except the registration of class*. It is this which leads Hobbes off on a wrong scent. It is this too that makes for that strange sense of a mixture of a mixture of truth and inadequacy that one feels in Hobbes's descriptions of what we call capitalism. Hobbes was right in characterising the capitalist society as one principally based on contradiction, but wrong in believing that this conflict is exclusively among individuals. Actually, conflict goes on in capitalist societies on several levels—fundamental conflicts of classes and other organised groups, sometimes expressed through, and sometimes parallel to the general conflict among individuals. Since aggression and conflict among acquisitive individuals is a major apparent fact in bourgeois society, a large part of Hobbes's section 'of Man' has startling relevance in any capitalistic setting—even today.[21] In as much as the central conflict in a capitalistic structure is class-conflict, Hobbes was in error about three things : the level of conflict, the units involved in the conflict, and its mode of articulation. His first error was to miss the existence of class;

The Second Error

A second error logically followed from the first. In actual fact, despite Hobbes's analytical talent, an existing capitalist state would function closer to Locke's model, not his. Hobbes was concerned, as Macpherson shows, with the problem of reproduction and perpetuation of political authority. He thought the best way to ensure self-perpetuation of sovereign authority was through a version of dynastic succession, or what Macpherson calls the 'self-perpetuating sovereign'. Power is transmitted through a straight and ordinarily undisputed line of individuals. Hobbes had not seen class as an economic or sociological figure. Therefore, he could not have inferred the *political implications* that class had. Stability of the Power-configuration is a condiction that a bourgeois ruling class would always seek. But it seeks that in a way very different from the one Hobbes suggested. Stability of power is actually achieved—not by fixing power in an individual, but in seeing to it that it *may*, or indeed *does* move from one set of men to another, but stays within the outer circle of the class.[22] This creates the ideological magic of representation—the genuine appearance that politics or power is being 'bargained for' in an open market place, instead of being locked up and strictly guarded in a castle. It creates the objective basis for the appearance of 'openness' of the capitalistic power system. This goes in the plausible, but misleading name of representation; and creates the objective logical nexus between a capitalist economic system and political democracy. Locke, as was his style, saw this clumsily and untidily. Hobbes who saw everything clearly if he saw it, missed this point altogether.

The Third Error

Hobbes also, I think, committed a third error. An actual capitalist state does not function as a mechanism of pure force. Its coercive apparatus functions with the support provided by the legitimatizing-process, through the consent-manufacturing mechanisms of the 'civil society'.[23] Even this in Hobbes's case, is a derivative of the failure to see class. Hegemony is exercised by a ruling *class*. Personal authoritarianisms depend exclusively on force. Stable class-rule depends on structures creating hegemony for the ruling class, predominantly through non-coercive means. Hobbes thought that the enterprise of taming aggressive, unrestricted individualists would be exclusively an affair of coercison. Occasionally, he verges on the thresholds of surprisingly modern themes—like seeing the nexus between knowledge and interest in social sciences.[24] But he under estimated the role of recurrent encounters with constituted reality, and crystallised ideas in the entire scheme of ruling. He missed what Marx called 'ideology'.

Still, Hobbes insights were invaluable. One can, at least, arrange a series of extenuating circumstances for his errors— these peculiar cases of 'non-vision' in a thinker who could see so much that was hidden to others. A basic reason was, I think, historical. Hobbes lived rather early in the process of transition from feudalism to capitalism in Europe. Capitalist enclaves had grown within the general effective framework of a feudal structure. The capitalist class had not yet attempted to capture state-power; and had not become, in a political sense, a class 'for itself'. His picture of capitalism was fatally flawed, because of its intellectual derivation. It was not based on historical observation of the dynamics of a complete structure. It was logically extrapolated from the behaviour of men in very inadequate and fragmented capitalist settings As a methodological individualist of a particularly aggressive but also rather naive kind, Hobbes believed this was all right. What was true of the 'elements' must also be true of the 'whole'. Society was, in any case, a mechanical and additive totality. But this involved another subtle error. The transition from a fragmented and politically-repressed capitalism to a full-blooded formation that has captured statepower is not a simple transition from a part to a whole. It was the—rather different—transition from a cribbed and flawed realisation of an organising principle of society to a full and unencumbered one. It was a qualitative transition, and not as Hobbes believed, a quantitative one. That is why his logic went wrong. Marx had not done systematic study of political theories. But in *Theories of Surplus Value*, he makes an interesting comment on the Physiocrats which, I think, applies perfectly to Hobbes's political theory: "All these are contradictions of capitalist production as its works its way out of feudal society, and *interprets feudal society itself in a bourgeois way*, but has not yet discovered its own peculiar form—somewhat as philosophy first builds itself up within the religious form of consciousness, and in so doing, on the one hand, destroys religion as such, while on the other hand, in its positive content, it still moves onls within this religious sphere, idealised and reduced to terms of thought."[25]

Hobbes was above all a *critical* theorist. He conceived as the main function of theory a consistent rationalist demystification of social relations and reality in general. Naturally, part of his intellectual project was *objective* reporting of things as they are : since this is a first and fundamental step towards demystification. But Hobbes did not discriminate in his objectivity. He was not merely objective in his critique of feudal arragements, but also in his presentation of capitalism. He presented capitalism in the raw—without embellishments or ideological *cosmetics*, making for eternal embarassment of later bourgeois intellectuals. Precisely because he thought capitalist conditions are anyway natural and immutable, he did not see any need to touch them up. Anyway, men had to accept them. That is how things are. Consequently, we get a picture of capitalism that is highly objective—cynical, mocking, to the point of being fintal in its frankness. This I believe explains why Hobbes could never be a part of the liberal orthodoxy. He belongs to a tradition of unqualified critique-continuously, and without exception, subversive. It mercilessly subjects everything to the scrutiny of rational thought. All totems are broken. All sacral symbols are ridiculed. The world of thought is shown to be completely open. There is no conclusion that is precluded. No possibilities are barred. Thinking affects the constituted world as a most violent radical force. Thinking is equated with doubting. Rational thought is always, in principle, subversive. Nothing is 'given' for it.

Locke's Position

Locke represents the second point of our theoretical triangle. Hobbes was a radical, a revolutionary—though, of the intellect.[26] Locke is a liberal. These two positions are irreconcilable. Of all possible positions in intellectual debate, the one that is the furthest from the radical is the liberal one. One can go even further and argue that critical radicalism is the theoretical attitude of capitalism in the 'storm and stress' of the revolution; liberalism is a reflex of its consolidation and stability. There is a second characteristic distinction. Revolutionary bourgeois theory is typically concerned with the larger question state-power-the transition from feudal class-power to bourgeois class-power. It is less concerned with the specific institutional *form* that, this power would take. Liberalism is typically concerned with governmental forms. Viewed from this angle, a large part of revolutionary bourgeois political theory (Machiavelli Hobbes, Rousseau, Hegel) is illiberal.

Locke was a liberal in his tone, a liberal in his style of argument and argued for a proto-liberal state—persuasive, tolerant, sympathetic, pedestrian, commercial and reasonable. He never raises his voice. He is devoid of humour He is usually uninspiring, often ambiguous, except of course on the question of property which brought him to the verge of lyricism. He was the intellectual prototype of what the romantics called the 'unheroic bourgeois.' Locke's position, as Marx said clearly in a cryptic note in the *Theories of Surplus value*, was a "classical expression of bourgeois society's idea of right as against feudal society"[27]

Locke did not derive the foundation of society from a threat of universal extinction, but from rational calculation. Men in his state of nature are not driven by fear or destination and an intolerably anarchic situation. They are moved, rather, by the calculation of self-interest and the attraction of a political gain. In a modernised form, the moments of his theory of society are highly interesting. As a legimising theorist, he started from original propositions that were far more 'reasonable', that is, ones that made many more compromises with a feudal sensibility, but went on to get round each of them.

First Economic Model

In the first stage of Locke's, state of nature the earth and all its fruits are given to humanity in common. This is one basic egalitarian postulate. Locke is also careful in seeming to go by a second current postulate-again of an egalitrarian sort that human being are, by nature, rational. There exists, therefore, in a rather abstract sense, a certain kind of equality among men. In Locke's theory, however, the starting points are uniformly misleading. The ingenuity of Locke as a theorist lies precisely in his elegant transcending of the postulates he had started with. Given this biblical injunction, the initial stage of the 'state of nature' has a universal regime of limited property. Macpherson specifies three essential limitations on property in this initial condition.[28] The first, spoilage limitation, requires that no one should have more from the common natural-social fund than he can properly use. Nothing that nature has given must be wasted. In modern terms, this is a strict consumption limitation, and resembles an imaginative reconstruction of feudal, domestic unit economy, Methodologically, this is close to what Hobbes does in his 'state of Nature'. It derives a feudal situation through logic and what they would have called imaginative reasoning, instead of through historical investigation. A second restriction is based on sufficiency. True to the communitarian inspiration, noone can take away from the common natural-social fund utterly egotistically. He must keep 'enough and as good' for others. The third limitation is about labour. One can claim as one's property only such things as he has removed by his 'own' labour from nature.[29] A piece of land enclosed from the commons is property. Metal extracted from nature through labour is property. The implicit rule for making of property, therefore, is your mixing labour with something. Locke gives us his criterion for property along with three excellent examples in a single sentence. "Thus the grass my horse has bit, the turfs my servant has cut, and the ore that I have digged in any place where I have a right to them in common with others, become my property without the assignation or consent of anybody. The labour that was mine, removing them out of that common state they were in has fixed my property in them."[30]

This, in a sense, is the critical sentence, if he meant it rigorously, as I think he did. It gives us two, as we shall find rather dissimilar, examples. It also gives us his criterion for fixing property on things.

The criterion is simple. A man's title to his property is fixed by his mixing labour with natural objects. By itself this is an anti-capitalist principle. At least, it is an antibis capitalist principle. It is interesting to note that for Locke this is basically an ideal construct having the same function in his theory as simple commodity production has for Marx's—a way of arriving at more complex and concrete propositions about the nature of capitalism as it exists in historical reality.

The Second Economic Model

Surprisingly, however, Locke has already created the logical conditions for transcending this idyllic order of limited property-holding. The socalled limitation of labour, as Macpherson carefully shows, is at bottom, only supposed: it simply does not exist. Locke's two example are openly discondant. The ore that I have dug at some place certainly belongs to me as 'my property', by Locke's labour rule. For I have quite obviously 'mixed my labour with it.' The same is not true of the second case. My servant has cut the turf, after all; not me. It would be rather curious if it still belongs to me-unless we explicate an unstated assumption in Locke's thinking: the 'naturalnees' of wage labour and wage-relationships. Wage-labour is 'natural' in the characteristic double meaning in which the contractualists used the term: natural, in the sense of being independent of social and political arrangements, being present in pre-political and presocial nature. Natural: also in the sense of flowing out of the very nature of things and relations, out of the most elemental, nonsubstitutible drives of human character. Both senses, one can immediately see, are logically related, and support one another. Precisely because these are men's most elemental drives, they would appear and predominate in the temporally-meant state of nature, because there are no artificial social curbs on them. The two senses are distinct, but mutually supportive. And all the three contractualists made masterful use of these related but distinct meanings, often creating 'slides' from one meaning to another—creating a typical 'rolling concept'.

Transcending of the limiting principles is done simply. These are corollaries of the introduction of money. 'The state of nature', for the first two contractualists at least, is a truly elastic idea. A state of nature, ironically, can even include a full-grown money-economy. We shall soon see the logical necessity of this historically implausible proposition. Men's life in nature is divided into two clear stages—before and after the introduction of money, which means, also, inequality. Money removes the limitations on the scale of property or accumulation. The spoilage limitation is obviously removed. Gold and silver do not spoil. Therefore, a man can, after the introduction of money, accumulate more than he can consume. Use-values cannot be accumulated, once exchange-value comes into existence, men can exceed the consumption-limit. The second restriction—of sufficiency for others—is removed more ingeniously. Locke establishes in the process a style of argument that would become typical of later bourgeois political economy. Introduction of unrestricted accumulation with the coming of money disturbs the evenness of the earlier property distribution. In the first stage, though natural inequalities exist, they are not yet amounting to qualitative differences in the relations of production. In a group, X may have more ability to labour and acquire property than Y; Y may have a similar superiority over Z. But they are limited surperiorities. The logic of wage-labour and unrestricted accumulation does not yet apply. X can have more than

Y, and Y more than Z. But they cannot have too much more because of the inherent limits of labouring capacity; and much more, because they must leave things that are 'enough and as good' for Z. Under the dispensation of the first stage, it is the responsibility of X and Y to ensure that Z is not reduced to destitution; to marxianise the language, they have to see that he has some control over means of production.

Money magically alters all this. Since X can, now, acquire property without the spoilage limitation, this would naturally at some stage squeeze Z out of any control over his resources or means of production. Already, two classes have emerged. Locke has imaginatively derived the actual class-structure of bourgeois society, and its logic of unrestricted accumulation. X is already different from the non descript equality of stage 1. And a condition for X becoming a new class is Z's becoming a new class too, in a less fortunate way. X becomes an unrestricted accumulator organising production on an ever-larger scale. He has to move beyond the pool of his own labour. By providence, or if you prefer, by the laws of motion of capitalism, precisely at the same moment Z comes to a position where he can (or must) sell his labour to X. The organic connection between the capitalist and the wage-worker is seen and legitimised. It follows of course that it would be increasingly unlikely for Y to keep up as an independent producer in face of the superior organisation of X (Z). The tendency is towards concentration and a consequent greater polarization of class relations. Is his not disturbingly like Marx? No, it is only disturbingly like capitalism. And to the extent Marx is a most sensitive observer of its dynamics, only by that transition, like Marx. Locke however needed all these arguments for his own political theory. Besides, any functioning capitalism would have told Locke the same things.

Let us return to how the sufficiency limitation is transcended. One must not however miss a difference here, for the somewhat confusing terminology that Macpherson used. To Macpherson, both are 'transcendences'. Actually, this hides a small logical difference. Restrictions of spoilage are *cancelled* by money; they simply no longer apply. By contrast, the sufficiency limitations are not axiomatically cancelled. Locke *gets round* them. (There is a difference between a case when an argument falls or does not apply, and a second case in which it does not fall; but you find a way of getting past it). The way Locke got past this objection was to be historic. This would form a foundation of legitimising political-social-economy theory for all times to come, until Keynes. By the new arrangement of production, if X can show that he has made greater productivity possible, then this transition from unproductive equality to productive inequality is rationally justified. If, in other words, the production of x', y', z', the production of x, y, z, then this is obviously justified, from a social point of view. But what about Z? Is he not adversely affected? Can we say that the sum of individual utility-maximization has led to 'common good' in a methodologically individualist sense? Locke would say yes, for the common pool has increased, and, therefore, also, the logical, or hypothetical possibility of Z getting a larger share than he previously had. In a sense, therefore, even Z gains by losing his former equality.[30] He can lose by a reckoning in *class*-terms; he profits by a reckoning in terms of standards of living as an *individual*. If we keep this is mind, we would understand the seventeenth and eighteenth century lyricism about property and accumulation—the automatic and purely aesthetic symmetry between personal gain and social good; the impeecably rational demonstration that by ruining a person and forcing him into wage-labour you are not merely serving your own interest, but, in a beautiful logical scheme, even his. Under such circumstances, these people displayed what could be called the 'happy consciousness' in political theory.

The Political Model

But aren't we talking of economics and commerce? How do we get to the state? And how does this all fit into a *political* theory? For one thing, the classicals were far more clear-sighted on these questions than the fashionable short-sightedness of the behavioural 'scientists'. For them, these highly unrealistic boundaries did not exist. There can also be a more strictly logical answer. Locke was a rationalist: he sought to generate a strictly rationalist theory of politics. A rationalist theory had to be developed around the central category of rationality or reason. Rationality is a unitary concept. It has varying 'applications' both in economics and politics. These were simply two types of decisions made in two different fields. But they called for the application of the same ability in men for their solution. Locke was, through these interesting preliminaries, establishing what exactly be meant by 'rationality'. It was simpler to show what rationality meant in economics and commerce. And, in any case, definition of rationality and establishment of a secure rational ranking among men is neccessary before we enter the field of politics, or so he thought.

In the second-stage model of the state of nature, we have a number of significant features. An economic hierachy has been established—with clear, realistic definition of classes. How is this differentiation between X and Z possible? After all, they had started with equal portions from nature. How did X husband his belonging, and expand it, and Z lose whatever he had? Because of something that X had and Z had not. This is rationality. Already, in the state of nature, rationality differentials are firmly established. Property and unlimited acquisition are introduced. Finally, these are all sanctified as being 'natural'—independent of the state. A state defends them. It does not create them. In fact, if a state cannot defend property, it has to be replaced by another that can. Here too, as in Hobbes, and in most other classicals, economics is prior to politics; property to government; political inequality a logical outgrowth of natural economic difference.

This view accomplished a second wonder. Property differentials are based on differentials of rationalist and willingness to work. It is, therefore, a justification in seemingly rationalist terms of the puritan view of poverty. Poverty is seen as a justified retribution against laziness; riches as an equally justified reward for industry. So poverty is not a structural phenomenon. It is a deserved individual fate. It is not pretty. But to help a man out of it is still worse. It is to help in his moral degeneration. Poverty was his only incentive to be become industrious. You cannot take away his last chance by giving him government subsidy. No wonder the earliest rationalists were against better social legislation. For that would remove whatever chance of correction of these people there was. "This primitive accumulation plays in political economy about the same part as sin in theology In times . . . gone by there were two types of people; one the diligent, intelligent and above all frugal elite; the other lazy rascals, spending their substance, and more, in riotous living."[31] Locke quite openly introduced this apologetic argument into political theory.

Let us skirt the technical aspects of Locke's contract : the two contracts and their purely legalistic implications. Let us go straight into his political programmes, and his so-called theory of democracy. Locke then, takes it as established that there are rationality differentials among men. His quality as a legitimising theorist lies in that he has derived this happy result without offending some basic semi-egalitarian premises, or, rather, in showing that these could be obtained by getting past and reinterpreting propositions that were wrongly considered fundamentally egalitarian. One example was the intitial condition of equality in terms of reason; "all men are rational". Locke's legitimising genius lies in showing that this does not necessarily lead to an egalitarian social theory. It could serve and justify inequality, with a little ingenuity of interpretation. All men are rational, but they are not rational in an equal degree. This is demonstrated by the transition from the first to the second economic model in the state of nature itself. Once artificial restrictions are removed by introduction of money, some people prove their superior rationality by the commercial and free transactions. Locke's argument is the exact obverse of the one given by Wycliff, "The man who makes money out of the turn of the market, the man who must be wicked, or he could not have been poor yesterday and rich today". Locke's point is just the reverse. If a man had enjoyed equality (i.e. a certain portion of the means of production) and lost it, this must prove that he is deficient in rationality. The poor are poor because they are less rational. It is just one step to the belief that the poor are poor because they deserve to be poor. How do we know that they deserve to be poor? Because they are poor in fact. This is certainly a circular argument, but one that contemporary puritans found quite convincing. They resisted, successfully, the growth of better poor laws on the grounds of such self-evident axioms. No wonder, Locke considered any remission of the horrors of poverty, a license to the lazy.

Locke's political theory seems to me to be based on this general supposition. The poor are less rational, or less than rational. The difference between classes is not based on accidents of fortune, but, more fundamentally, based on a naturally unequal distribution of rationality. This is a point that need not be argued. Like the axiomatic justification of wage labour as natural, this is taken for granted. Rationality and irrationality are demonstrated on the market. No further proofs are necessary. Fortunes in the market place or in a market-like society creates an infallible order of rationality shading off into irrationality. Let us see the consequences of this for directly political arrangements. These are not exactly democratic sentiments or preferences. Locke has a repute for being one of the first democratic political theorists. If he is, then his political theory would be at considerable variance with his views of economic behaviour. He will, then, be inconsistent, though in a way that will be rather nice. I am afraid we shall find such views largely unfounded. Locke was as little democratic in his political views as in his economic. This is a myth created by the illegitimate hopefulness of the later liberal tradition. Locke, to our great disappointment, was quite logical.

Differential rationality is established in the sphere of commerce. It is then carried over to the field of political institutions. This is done by means of two arguments. The first is that both economic activity and political require rational calculation—the political sphere, if anything, more than the commercial. For what is being decided in commercial decisions is the single fate of the single economic individual. What is decided in politics is the fate of the whole community. These are, in other words, critically important decisions. It follows therefore that such vital things cannot be left to those who have already proved the unsoundness of their decisions by their failure on the economic market.

From here Locke cannot go in the direction of any democratic preference in any real sense. What he derives, out of this, however, is a form of oligarchic constitutionalism. Government is too important a thing to be left to any single individual. Besides, others have proved that they too have rationality in the market operations in the second stage of the state of nature. Differential rationality simultaneously prevents democracy and autocratic government. After all, it is all a question of numbers. On the showing of what happens in the state of nature, this critical number is much more than one and also much less than the whole population of the Lockean State. The obvious logical solution of the problem then is a form of constitutionalism: different from both "extremes" prevalent in political theory of Locke's times—monarchical absolution and democracy.

Now it is much easier to see the grounds of Locke's preferences in political arrangements. It is a constitutional monarchy: a happy coincidence of Locke's theoretical preferences and actualities of late seventeenth century English politics. Or probably not entirely a coincidence. Locke was explicitly a legitimist. His political theory, on his own admission, sought 'to make good the claim of his king in the loyalty of his subjects'. The arrangements are by now clear, by implication. There are, as it were, four layers in the political pyramid—an executive, a legislature, an electorate of the propertied, and the rest of the subject people. Macpherson has shown how the 'fourth estate' were under the control of the state machinery without being part of the machinery for representation. The propertied are the *citizens;* the propertyless are *subjects*. This is the strange concept that Locke leaves behind for later democratic adaptation. It is undoubtedly of great use to later theorists of democracy. For Locke wins for them—not the principle of *democracy* as such, but the principle of *responsibility*. But the all important question is not representation in the abstract, but representation for whom ? Is it to the whole people, because the whole people would in any case be affected by what the goverment does? Or is it only to the propertied, with the right to representation restricted by high fences of property qualifications? Locke is not a democrat. Yet he is a precondition for democratic theory of later times. After all, the difference between constitutionalism and democracy is basically a difference in scale. At the same time, this was a vital difference. Democracy could come only after a lot of struggles by those who were kept out of this charmed circle and wanted to break in.

As theorists, Hobbes and Locke were exact antitheses. Hobbes was the typical—I am tempted to say, paradigmatic—representative of the critical intellect—corrosive, cynical, radical, destructive, irreverent of everything, not afraid to take up unpopular causes, against current opinion—but doing it aggressively and brilliantly, unreasonable, arrogant and so unconventional that as a high-quality radical theorist he was characteristically mistrusted by the comparatively dogmatic practicalists who were really on the same side. Locke is his logical opposite— legitimist, cautious, unambitious, nonstartling, pedestrain, reasonable, persuasive, tolerant—everything that a good liberal ought to be. The bitterness, the originality, the mistrustful, concealed ·humour, the unremitting cruelty and malice of Hobbes's prose is missing in him. Political theory is on way to becoming respectable. In many things, they belonged to the same side. But even in these, they give off this basic difference between aggression and tolerance—the two attitudes of society when rising and rebelling and thinking through the tenseness of a revolutionary period; and the same society in the quiet after the victory, relaxed and victorious, self-satisfied and flabby. Locke's style already lacks the urgency, the cutting edge and the heat of Hobbes's rationalism which had to raise it's voice precisely because others did not consider its self-evident truths. Locke's tone is marred by the certainty of an advance consent, a general acquiescence in what he was pressing for. In Gramsci's terms, Hobbes's rationalism is striving to overthrow the hegemony of feudal epistemological values; Locke's is already the society's constituted common sense. The differences, though heightened by individual temperaments, are, I think, rooted in history. The historical function of rationalist political theory had changed. From a weapon of attack, it had become a weapon of self-defence. Between Hobbes and Locke, political theory had taken the fatal turn that Hegel would call 'tragic'. From a principle of radical, unconditional doubt, it had become rationalisation, a mode of distribution of certainties : afunc tion that is institutionally more significant, but intellectually far less colourful.

Rousseau's Position

We have already found enough material to doubt the traditional supposition—that the significant thing to study in Hobbes and Locke were the technical legalistic variations in their use of social contract. The central point, I suggested, was to find the variations in their attitude towards capitalism as a historical question, as a social formation. Rousseau too shares this problem with Hobbes and Locke, but he does something unprecedented and audacious. Radicalism is simpler when the contradictions of a society have already unfolded fully. It is a far more difficult proposition when they have not. A critic of a society that is still on the ascendant has to content with the structure at its best: this is its period of hope, its happy consciousness, when ambitious promises are made and believed, when the disillusionment and cynicism and defiance have not yet set in. Rousseau established the possibility of an authentically radical, socially dissenting position, in the face of the constituted common sense of his age, against the manifest plausibility of bourgeois claims in the eighteenth century. Rousseau therefore completes our triangle. I wish to call it the basic triangle. For, I believe, the theoretical positions articulated by Hobbes, Locke and Rousseau were not simply differences in individual perceptions and attitudes towards their age. I think they are far more, and quite uniquely significant. These are not just three positions. These are the three fundamental positions, that it is possible for men to take about the politics of rising capitalism and its most likely political outcomes. As positions about bourgeois political theory, they are therefore archetypes.

Since I have written elsewhere[32] about a possible Marxian reading of Rousseau, I shall be brief. I shall simply mention the principal elements of a Marxian modernisation of his theory. All elements of his theory constitute the material for a non-Lockean vision of politics and society—primarily a rejection of two of Locke's ideas. First was Locke's twist into the conventional proposition of rational equality of men. Rousseau detested its Lockean subversion by the proviso added on to it. In fact, though he never celebrated feudalism, he was surprisingly true to a few of the principles of medieval ethics. This was one such point where his preferences squared essentially with the nonindividualistic ethic of the earlier ages. By contrast, he was far more critical of the ethic of 'civil society'. Lucio Colletti has shown a beginning of anticapitalist radicalism in Rousseau.[33] I believe his position is fundamentally correct. And in any case, Colletti is not alone in finding this tendency in Rousseau. Others have done this from the most diverse theoretical angles. Those who regarded Rousseau as a radical included the German idealists, the classical scholar Gierke, in an implied manner Engels[34] himself. Of the more modern commentators one can mention Talmon[35] and Colletti. Rousseau made no secret of his heterodoxy. He did not believe in the age of reason. It is not very difficult therefore to understand that Rousseau was somewhat different from his average contemporaries. There were difficulties however in *situating* him in two ways, against two significant coordinates: to situate him in a certain relation to the significant bourgeois tradition that went before him—that is, basically, with Hobbes and Locke; and in relation to the anticapitalist radicalism that developed afterwards, that is, with utopian socialists and Marx. In essence, these are not two relations, basically two sides of the same relation.

I shall confine myself to comments on two points in Rousseau's theory. The first would be the nature of class-power under capitalism, and the second—his theoretical relation with Hobbes and Locke. Rousseau had seen much more of real capitalism than Hobbes had. Yet his response was entirely different. Hobbes, as I said, thought capitalist patterns of behaviour self-evident. So he wrote them into the basic constitution of his 'human nature'. Hobbes, in a sense, sees the inevitability of capitalism, and takes it for granted. Rousseau saw its inevitability equally clearly. This made him reject it with greater vehemence.

Critique of Bourgeois Society

I think the question of capitalism in history is central to all the three areas of Rousseau's thinking—where Rousseau had something significant and unusual to say—the fields of sociology (in our modern sense), history and politics. The polemical character of his work is obvious. But what is often missed is that it was not an assorted polemic, against individual authors, expressing disagreement with views that Rousseau did not approve of. I think this idea—of a chaotic, anarchic tendency in Rousseau's selection of targets—is misleading. Certainly, Rousseau was anarchic and unsystematic in many ways. This was part of his being romantic. But his target is fixed. Through all his work, despite the variation in themes, and subtle shifts in emphasis, Rousseau was attacking an integrated structure of the mind that he recognised as common. In himself, Rousseau was not coherent. The system of views that he continuously attacked, however, was. And the coherence of the rationalist vision—expressed symmetrically in its scientific methodology, rationalist-individual apologetics of capitalist society, its naive confidence about progress, its advocacy of representation on rationality differentials—through a negative transposition, imposed a latent coherence in Rousseau's critique. Let us see what were these antinomies on the three central questions in Rousseau : (i) the quality of capitalist society as a social formation; (ii) the 'logic' or tendencies in history—again, in the context of the inevitable coming of capitalism through its evolution; (iii) the political structure that capitalist society seemed most logically to produce.

Capitalist society was most obviously based on competitive individualism. This was true in a purer form about early capitalism. Late capitalism invents arrangements to counteract the most damaging effects of such trends. No objective observer of early capitalism could miss this. In their rather different ways, most of the theorists of 17th and 18th centuries registered this —both as a *fact* of objective economic life, and as a fact of effective *values* that motivate men's actions. A kind of dialectic between these two moments of individualism was assumed in early bourgeois social and political literature. Hobbes, Locke, Mandeville, Rousseau, Adam Smith, Bentham—all noted this, without exception. But this also gives us, incidentally, a most interesting example of how fundamental critical or legitimist attitudes enter into and interfere with observation of social life and the constitution of what are given the deceptively unproblematic name of 'facts'. That men acted rationally, which meant egotistically, was a 'fact' for all observers. There were certain effects that were supposed to follow from this, and which were both items of logic and items of observation. Paradoxically the theorists were sharply divided on this question—on what *obviously* followed from extreme egotism. There were two ways of looking at it. Locke, Smith and Bentham formed one tradition—one that was canonised into the main trend of legitimist social and economic theory.[36] Rational-individualist egotism, for them, led always to beneficial results for the collectivity—the market or the state. Pursuit of individual self-interest leads somehow to 'common good'. Locke tried to justify this belief by the simple device we have seen before. It was probably an intellectual reflex of an observed fact—productive superiority of capitalism

—a society based on extreme egotism—over feudalism—a society founded on more communitarian morals. Each individual pursued his own self-interest, to the detriment of all others. A logically extreme case of this would be one in which everyone is trying to harm everyone else's interest. Yet, somehow, they are promoting them. Additional trouble was created by the fact that for all these theorists, methodological individualism was a self-evident axiom. What held for the elements, held for the totality. And given a negative form, the position was even more surprising, logically. Society was nothing more than the individuals composing it. And, therefore, the effects, on the level of the social totality, could only be the effects of individual actions, magnified in scale or added in numbers. Methodological individualism made this curious transformation of private vices into public benefits impossible. For it meant, then, what had not existed in the elements would have existed in the whole. Curiously, Locke and Bentham did not see this difficulty. For them, pursuit of individual self-interest (which meant, in a competitive setting, working for the ruin of everyone else) caused, surprisingly, and happily, prosperity or common good for everyone. Locke evidently thought he had given a purely rationalist demonstration of how this happened. Bentham had not gone much beyond Locke, and introduced a still more vulnerable concept of the greatest good of 'the greatest number'. Adam Smith's position was more sophisticated. He did not take this as a logically unproblematic transition, and introduced an external element of the 'hidden hand'. The 'hidden hand' is an index of this logical embarassment. Still, Smith believed in the myth of this translation—as factually good, if not logically. Mandeville takes a rather curious and mixed position. He accepts it as observed 'fact', but ridicules its latent principle—'private vices', 'public benefits'; the curious process in which to create an economically virtuous society, you need a population of sinners of avarice.

There was a second tradition. Both Hobbes and Rousseau rejected this myth. Hobbes did this for primarily logical reasons; Rousseau for sociological ones. Hobbes admitted only of rational and deductive proof. Given the ordinary-language meaning of competition and acquisitiveness, he could not see how it could—instrumentally—like a machine, without any arbitrary injection of qualities or outcomes from outside—produce a situation of harmony. Order, harmony, predictability are necessary for a society. But these could not arise naturally out of all possible combinations and permutations of the elements and relations of which a capitalist social model was composed. Hobbes did not share in this mythology of harmonious individualism in which effects are always pleasant. As a logician, he could not accept it. A society based exclusively on the principle of unrestricted individualism must, logically, lead to threats of common ruin through a 'war of all against all'. Hobbes rejected this essential legitimising myth of bourgeois ideology. Still, he accepted capitalism. And even today, any capitalist society in which legitimation structures do not function effectively, would gravitate towards a Hobbesian solution of political conflicts. Th's is also why Hobbes has such an uneasy, curious relation with later bourgeois theory, full of embarassments and paradox.[37] Hobbes gave later bourgeois political theory some of its indispensable tools: the demonstration that a secular, materialist, rationalist political theory is possible and necessary; a basic mode of rationalist political enquiry; instrumentalism; the essential psychological presuppositions that Benthamites would build on later; even, for a fleeting moment, the logical derivation of sovereignty from the people. Still, he could not be canonised in the liberal tradition. I think this was for the essential reason that he symbolised—in both what he saw and what he did not see as part of the structure of his vision—a critical intellectualism. In the strictest and widest possible sense, it doubted eveything; it exposed unstated assumptions, subjected everything to scrutiny, refused to believe in old myths, and more troublesomely, to set up new ones. It decided not to take existing social relations for granted and to justify them. Such critical rationalism is perfect in the period of revolution, when the historic need is to destroy the intellectual bases of the earlier order. It becomes increasingly uncomfortable in the period of stablity and consolidation. Others, who have diametrically opposite ideological goals, can also utilise it against the new society. This is not something that was merely logically possible. This is what actually happened. Rationality ceased to be the predominant slogan by the nineteenth century. Critical rationalism remained a weapon of attack. But those who defended themselves more and more lamely now were not the feudals. This were the bourgeoisie.

Rousseau shared with Hobbes his scepticism about this mythology of happy composition. Colletti has shown how Rousseau, Adam Smith and Mandeville 'see' the same things; yet there is a critical part of their seeing that is quite discordant.[38] 'Seeing' means not only seeing the objective or physical features or associations but also their meanings, or, in a different sense, their effects. There is a fundamental level of contradiction that they all admit—antagonism of potential interests: between buyer and seller; consumer and producer; owners and workers. But they see what happens at another level quite differently. At a higher level, the legitimists see a spontaneous effect of harmony; critics a heightened or magnified contradiction. This difference probably consists in their referring to two distinct things when they speak of the common good. In one case, it is the fact that there is increased production, and abstractly, a possibility of covering greater needs. This is 'common good'. On the other hand, there is the fact of how this product is produced, through what specific human effects and relations; and the added fact that what is produced, and what, only hypothetically, represents a promise of satisfaction of greater human needs, is a promise that is never realised—leading to accumulation on one end and a stability of deprivation on the other. This is the absence of 'common good'. In one case, the criterion is the economy seen as a machine—as a purely instrumental construction. In the other, the criterion is felt human effects, or society in human perception as a non-technologic, primarily humanistic construction. In the language of the Frankfurt School, one can already see as the basis of this conflict a rupture in the meaning of rationality itself—a 'technological rationality', and a human rationality of the end.[39]

Rousseau's position is in this context, very curious and also significant. His intervention in theoretical debates played a critical role in this rupturing of the rationality concept, in bringing into doubt the formerly accepted narrow means oriented definition of what is rational. But positively, Rousseau did not work out a redefinition or a recoordination of the concept of rationality. It was mainly the work of others. He was its precondition, not its author. Kant was mainly responsibile for the new theory. But the problems, to solve which Kant suggested the new definition of rationality were perceived by Rousseau.

Rousseau had no sense of proportion. Locke had an excess of it. And strangely both benefited from their fault. This turned Locke into a careful objective reporter of social relations and their basic inter-connections. Rousseau profited from his flaw in a different way. It made him bolder, more radical, capable of questioning certainties that were considered the coordinates of all sensible discourse. Occasionally, this also pushed him into absurdity. But it helped him to pose his questions effectively and dramatically. It is essential in interpreting his theory, to seek the secular outlines of his questions rather than the rhetoric or the form in which they were expressed.

The quality of Rousseau's social and political doctrines is determined by his sense of history, or rather by his lack of it. Rousseau, in a curious fashion, could see the inexorability of the historical laws which brought in capitalist transformation of European societies. Still, he rejected this logic. Since believing in history means eventually accepting the inevitability of capitalism, logically, a rejection of capitalism would get transformed into a rebellion against history. For it imposes capitalism as a destiny on mankind. The romantic rejection of history is rooted in this particular complex of sensibilities: a rejection of the capitalist order, troubled by a feeling that it was probably inevitable. The finality of existence, the historical reality of capitalism forced them into this utopian and romantic channel—creating dream worlds that could be counterposed to the apparent imbecility of the existent world, and finally to a stage where the real and ideal change meaning as words. The existent appears as unreal, because it does not square with human essensce. Only the ideal, or what does so, is to be called real; a counterempirical definition of reality that flowed into the idealist political theory. The real is what I desperately wish existed, but which does not. What does exist is an inferior order of things contemptuously called sheer existence. Real is a name that is reserved for what should exist in its place. We are already approaching the sensibility of German idealism, and even its language. Though as idealists, they would add this extra proposition that an order that exists in people's minds as a superior order of things is already on its way to being realised in history.

History appears, not surprisingly, as a continuous process of degeneration. Once more, we should not take Rousseau's language too seriously. Apparently, this would imply that Rousseau was celebrating medieval society compared to capitalism. Yet, though he misleadingly uses a quasi-historical language, what he has in mind is not a historical contrast. It is, once more, a logical contrast between the given, the present, historical moment, and a logically abstracted condition of nature. Human nature is, as Cassirer pointed out, the nature of man, not man in nature, in the sense of any historically existent presocial condition.

Though Rousseau was the first romantic, all romantics did not take his view on this question. A part of the later romantic movement had a seriously meant reactionary theory of history. Such later romantics really preferred medieval society to early capitalism, though in most cases a highly beautified version touched up against evidence of historical facts. But romantics in any case were not people who could be cowed down by prosaic things like historical facts. But in Rousseau what we find is a preference for nature over history; not of a particular point or stage in history over another. Historically this was much less sensible than a straightforward reactionary vision—criticising an existing, functioning social order that had the "rationality" of simple existence on its side, not from the point of view of another constituted structure, but from wholly utopian positions, beautiful coloured ideas about how things ought to be. Historically, this was worse than weak. But this is also, at the same time, quite typical of Rousseau. Rousseau is certainly a radical. But he personifies a somewhat tragic kind of radicalism, one without a sense of history. Only those who believe in history can believe in the future. Rousseau did not look even at the future hopefully. His world is therefore a tortured vision of a timeless squalidness unrelieved by hope. There is no hope held out by history. You are hemmed in literally from all sides—in a literal and magnified prison from which even the relief of a future has been taken away.

Curiously, it is precisely this gloom that brings out Rousseau's theoretical creativity; this is its proper setting. This gloom of history is relieved only by the improbably colourful utopia that men ought to strive for. In the sphere of political theory it is an image like some of the incredible beautiful romantic sunsets. Their beauty is enhanced by the distance from squalor and filth and the colourlessness of ordinary scenery of industrial society. Rousseau's utopia, I shall argue, has a very similar function in the field of political theory. Given the existent arrangements, those things simply cannot exist. But in the peculiar contrary logic of the romantics, there precisely lies their value. Their business is make a negative point by way of a utopian discourse. They are protests against reality.[40]

I shall argue that the general will is a utopian concept in this specific sense. Only if we do not look at it this way, and expect other things from it, does it appear pointless and muddled. There is a duality of reasoning in Rousseau's idea of the general will.[41] General will refers to a quality[42] of policies that should be followed by governments that are constituted by the contract. This quality subsumed two analytically distinct critical propositions. All of Rousseau's arguments are directed against Locke or a Lockean understanding of the principles of politics. This considerably simplifies the situation and gives Rousseau a coherent and personal target. But criticising Locke is, at bottom, criticising two things at once: Locke's theoretical ideas and the English political system (or from our point of view, an average early capitalist system) which meant basically the same thing.

There is a last point about Locke that must be rendered explicit. Locke had rationalised a scheme of constitutional, and within restrictive limits, a kind of responsible government. But in his theory the problem of representation was treated very differently. Strictly speaking, in Locke, there is no problem about representation. Representation was simple, direct and complete. The group from which representatives were chosen was also the group that excercised real power. It is not surprising that mandatory representation was popular as long as the electorate and the rulers came from the same class. Or, in other words, as long as there were no fundamental class differences between the formal repositories of power (the electorate) and the actual ones (the ruling class). It is only when universal suffrage is instituted that problems of a different sort appear—giving power to the people in the most abstract level of excercise of authority (elections) and ensuring its alienation, or gradual filtering on more concrete levels (real decision-making on issues, or ruling). Still the principles of representation had anticipations of this latter arrangements.

The idea on a general will argues against the cornering of political power in two senses. In a first, simple sense, it means that decisions of the ruling body must take into account all interests without exception. It is interesting to note that this does not square logically with his vision of capitalist society as one of irreconcilable and opposed interests. If interests are irreconcilable, they could not all be ensured at the same time, and composed into a "general will". If they can be so composed, they were not so irreconcilable in the first place. Given that, he was expecting the impossible out of government. It was in other words, utopian. Rousseau's two images—of capitalism, and of acceptable political authority—were logically contradictory. But I shall defend Rousseau.

The idea of a general will also makes a second point. This is about representative democracy. The rhetoric of democracy is based on the principle of political equality; the reality of representation is based on its denial. Interpreted as a point on representation, general will implies that Otto von Gierke had called "permanent revolution".[43] Purely in terms of participation revolutions represent peak periods in the political process. During a revolution normal fences that kept decisions away from the common people, and vest them in far smaller cricles of instituted authority, are destroyed. People take part, in a literal sense, indeciding the most fundamental of all political questions: what society or its political authority should be like. Obviously, all other questions and their answers are contingent upon how this particular question is decided. After democratic revolutions, representative arrangements frustrate continued highlevel participation, and install new structures of alienation of political power from the people. In this sense, continuous participation, direct democracy and permanent revolution are three expressions of the same thing.

I believe this, was the point Rousseau was trying to make if one renders it into modern terms. If one looks at the actual exercise of political power, one immediately finds two rhythms: one at times of political stability when structures of institutionalised authority are intact. Institutional authority means that

there are people who specialise in, or more realistically, mono-
polise the making of the vital political decisions. Ordinary men
are as a rule kept out of it. They are given the imperfect
compensation of being collectively called the sovereign. But the
concept of a contract, particularly the form that Rousseau gives
to this critical fiction, adds credence to this claim. People
"create" sovereign authority in a literal sense. For those who
genuinely believe in an idea of social contract, the ordinary
political situation, the lack of effective power of the common
people must have looked much more directly as alienation—
taking away through institutional arrangements somthing that
they actually did have, or ought to have. This is, therefore,
alienation in a literal sense.

The contrasting case is of a revolution. In these periods political authority is redistributed and vests in the whole people. It
is they who through their action and inaction make possible
what comes to happen. Revolution is, therefore, the high point
of participation. And Rousseau's had to put forward their
demands they had to do it through bourgeois liberal structures
and in its terms, because that had become accepted as the only
admissible language of legal disputes. Partly also because tolerant and genuinely democratic liberalism was in a large part a
"creation" of the victims of the new society. This sounds paradoxical, but it is historically true. Liberalism was for long
pulled in two directions. The victors wanted it to symbolise the
rights of the propertied alone. The defeated naturally fought for
an inclusion in aformal, universalistic framework of the rights
of the propertyless. Real liberal democracy, with universal suffrage and a universalistic, impersonal definition of rights (as
distinct from the idea that the rights of the propertied could not
be rationally excercised by the poor) was a historically evolved
compromise. Though it perfectly protected the rights of the
propertied, it gradually came to protect those of the less well to
do. This was a result of proletarian upheavals throughout the
nineteenth century starting with the Chartist movement and the
French 1848. Democracy was fought for and won by a rising
violent submerged population from a reluctant, suspicious and
repressive ruling class; not, as textbooks imply, by their grace
and enlightenment. Throughout this turbulent period when
people were fighting on the barricades, about how democracy

ought to be defined, there were those who instinctively sided with Rousseau. They were showing their resentment against the definitions imposed by the new social order in surprising and often unintellectual ways. They stole wood from enclosed forests in England. They smashed machines and burned ricks. They barricaded the streets of Paris in 1848, and fought confusedly all over Europe. They set up the Commune. They used all the ingenious and creative methods by which common people make a fundamental theoretical point. They were all participants of the great debate in political theory. This debate frequently went on the streets. They all sided with Rousseau.

To me the traditional debates about whether Rousseau was a totalitarian or a democract do not seem to make sense. No one is a democrat in the abstract. The question of democracy is a historical question. His age saw the introduction of a new social order, men were still trying to come to terms with it intellectually. People could take three basic positions regarding it: reject it from a feudal point of view; or accept it, with or without enthusiasm; or again reject it from a utopian angle and take the consequences. Since no historical alternative was in sight, the third intellectual alternative could only be one of a deep gloom about history being a colossal error, or trying to break out of history's prison by demoniacal bursts of energy, or passionate and colourful dreams. One could of course combine the gloom with the dreams, as Rousseau did.

He lived in an age of hope which had unlimited faith in everything. It believed in wonders of natural and social engineering. Nothing was considered impossible. Characteristically, Rousseau does not see the historical logic of the capitalist social formation. In his romantic and logically flawed vision, he only sensed its inequalities and contradictions. He considered representation a conspiracy against the sovereign people. He therefore rejected it with a violence and a finality that is possible only in one who refuses to see things historically. Conception of the general will seems to suggest that this level of participation should be continued indefinitely. Representative democracy is a very imperfect form of democratic government. It includes in itself a new alienation of political power. But purely in terms of practical arrangements, continuous government through direct democracy in large national states is an impossible preposition. Still, Rousseau argues that the quality of decisions in a direct democratic form must somehow be carried over into the quality of decision making in national states. This is rule by the general will. General will is clearly then not a constitutional or operational concept. It does not describe a possible political arrangement. Rousseau was entirely vague on this vital practical question. His theory simply describes the quality of a will that can claim to stand for common good. As a practical concept I think the concept of the general will cannot be operationalised. And in this second sense too, ·the concept of the general will is as utopian as in the first one. It is basically a statement of the order : 'I wish the political world were like this'. Rousseau does not take the responsibility of making the related statement : 'I think this is how the political world can be made like that'. This precisely is the quality of romantic and utopian thinking. Against real structures it sets up dream structures. These dream structures almost always have a misleading positive presentation. Nearly all utopian political projects share this quality—More's *Utopia*, Campanella's *City of the Sun*, also Rousseau's *Social Contract*. The positive form is misleading because their essential thesis is negative and critical. They are significant not because of what they say about what society can be like is valuable, or practical or even plausible. They are significant because they render explicit, by implication, the contradictions and imperfections of the present order. They speak, characteristically, more of the future than of the present. But they are valuable because of what they obliquely say about the present while pretending to talk of the future. Rousseau's general will is a utopian idea of this sort. In the form of a blueprint for nonrepresentational democracy, it is a critique or representative arrangements.

Rousseau was, on this view, the first significant critic of representative democracy. That does not however make him a 'totalitarian'. This is a shallow empiricst-liberal reflex which thinks of democracy not as a quality but as a form of government, formalised and fetishised into one of its various possible forms. One would immediately condemn Rousseau if one thinks there is one, irrefutable, self-evident way of being democratic. Any other suggestion is, in principle, aberrent. This reveals an interesting paradox of liberal theories of democracy. Liberalism is, in principle, based on tolerance. Liberal interpreters of politics, however, work with a narrow, exclusive definition of democracy as domesticated and then recognised by the liberal tradition. There can not be several degrees of democracy. Whoever tries to be democratic in any other manner than the liberal is by definition a totalitarian.

If however one concedes other ways and "degrees" of being democratic, one can have a different view of the case. And this again is not doing anything fanciful. Thinking of other, counterliberal ways of democracy was not surprising. The whole of the eighteenth and early nineteenth centuries debated this question. Certainly, the liberals emerged the victors. Liberal democracy was the victorious bourgeoisie's answer to the problem of political conflict in capitalism. It was consequently forced on the vanquished and gradually institutionalised against their weakening resistance. Through its institutionalisation the defeated also got absorbed into it by degrees. This was partly because the questions of political theory were decided militarily, and other solutions were defeated.

Conclusion

Social contract theorists spoke a language different from ours. Still they shared our concerns: capitalism, instrumentalist politics, representation and forms of democracy. Traditional ways of interpreting them clouds our vision. They appear to us as strangers. They speak a different language. They seem to bother about hopelessly false things like the origin of the state through a social contract. This immediately creates a sense of distance, unreality and a ritual form of respect mixed with neglect—'those political philosophers' who depended on 'speculation' and who did not know how wrong they were. I consider this approach unfortunate. It creates artificial distances on top of real ones. It makes strangers of generations who can speak to and understand each other. Under the somewhat unfamiliar forms one can, I think, distinguish familiar concerns. Contractualists are talking of capitalism, not just a state of nature; of structures of political authority, not a social contract; of democracy, not of political obligation. This way of seeing immediately makes them our historical contemporaries, our neighbours in the history of capitalism. Hobbes, Locke and Rousseau are significant for this reason. They represent a primordial triangle of possible intellectual attitudes towards rising capitalism and its politics. They represent three archetypal visions: acceptance of capitalism with an objective, critical presentation; an acceptance with a legitimist, rationalising proto-liberal presentation; a worried feeling that it may be inevitable but a violent rejection of it all the same, including a romantic readiness to reject history which imposes on humanity this cruel system as a fate.

Distances in language should not blind us to this interesting structure in theories of the three contractualists. After all it was not their responsibility to anticipate our idiom. It is our responsibility to understand theirs. They were not talking about fantastic unreal questions. These were all questions of history though reflected in a theoretical distorting mirror. Those were not problems of the past. These are elements that constitute the present.

REFERENCES

1 By these two shorthand phrases I shall try to differentiate between two fundamentally divergent types of interpretation that are possible. The first—which I shall call the traditional mode—looks mainly for logical coherence and the fit between concepts, statements and middle-range theories. The second type of interpretation tries to understand the social forces, or social structurations that give rise to and sustain a particular way of looking at problems and facts. The second tendency of interpretation is not theoretically homogeneous. There are two very different ways of relating theoretical systems and social structures. One is derived from the hermeneutic school which looks at cultures as objectified mind; the other way of finding out this relation is through Marxism. Personally, I think there is no necessary exclusivity between the traditional and the sociological modes of interpretation. The second mode—looking for a sociology of political theory—does not preclude tests for logical coherence. It is simply that the second goes beyond the questions with which the first stops.

2 Even methodological continuities are difficult to establish. Hobbes alone, out of these thinkers, was a self-conscious and compulsive methodologist. He followed the partly Galilean, partly Cartesian

methodological rules like the resoluto-compositive process quite scru-
pulously. Locke is less conscious of a methodological lay-out and
therefore less neat. Rousseau, with typical romantic perversity, system-
atically flouts the idea of a rational methodology.

[3] At a high level of abstraction, epistemological certainties were certainly
shared between Hobbes and Locke; for example, naive materialism, a
sensationalist empiricist theory of knowledge, methodological individualism, mechanicism, etc.

[4] This enterprise is not altogether new. Machpherson looks at Hobbes
and Locke in the context of early capitalism; so does Colletti about
Rousseau. But I have two propositions on this. I have, first, some
criticisms against Macpherson's reading of Hobbes and Colletti's about
Rousseau. Macpherson's treatment of Hobbes is probably a trifle too
marxianised. Colletti similarly overmarxianises Rousseau. If Rousseau
had really said or implied what Colletti makes him say, one would have
to speak of Rousseauanism-Marxism-Leninism. Marxism as a distinct
system would be entirely redundant. This is not to take away from
Rousseau's originality. I think Rousseau inaugurated a new tradition
of anti-capitalistic radicalism in political theory. It would be unfair
not to see Rousseau as a theoretical precondition for Marx. On the
other hand, it will be equally misleading to think that Rousseau implied
or prefigured all of Marx, or even Lenin. Strictly speaking, Rousseau
is a precursor of utopian socialism, not of Marxist historical theory.
Secondly, neither Colletti nor Macpherson looks at them comparatively
—taking their common problem as capitalism, and seeing how their
understanding of early capitalist society differs.

[5] Modern commentators like Macpherson have shown a systematic difference between an apparent logic and an essential logic in social contract theories. This is an especially valuable contribution to the debate.
It argues that the state of nature was a logical and not a historical
abstraction. To arrive at their specific conclusions each of these writers
needed a state of nature exactly of that order. Anthropological and
historical research were anyway non-existent. Therefore nothing pre-
vented men of the 17th century from believing that this myth may have
been acted out in reality. It may have been quasi-historical in this
sense. This, however, does not take away from the argument that what
was called the state of nature was not a credible historical community,
but contemporary society minus some features of the current situation.
This was considered quite the proper thing to do. Renaissance scientists had worked on these lines, through controlled experiments. They
could not see why political theorists should not do so too. C.f. J.W.N.
Watkins, *Hobbes's System of Ideas* (London, 1963); and Jurgen Ha-
bermas, *Theory and Practice* (London 1973).

[6] This is **obviously** an overstatement. Cartesian dualism assumed, for
instance, that there was an entire field of "the spirit" that was not, or
may not be, amenable to these laws and methods. However, they were
careful to see that significant scientific and epistemological problems

fell on this side. This simplification therefore does not affect my argument materially. Perhaps this allowed them to continue to be good Christians and buy them a somewhat opportunistic reprieve from religious persecution.

7 Extreme dogmatism, Hobbes said, can be based only on extreme scepticism. As he was not a modern social scientist, and therefore less conscious of problems of design and presentation, he did not add that the author goes through both moments of this process. He takes his reader only through the sequence of extreme dogmatism. To take a random example, Descartes's *Discourse on Method* is written in a very different design from Hobbes's *Leviathan*. Descartes's argument goes through the two act process. Hobbes's presentation is basically one act.

8 For an example, see Federico Chabod, *Machiavelli and Renaissance* (trans. David Moore) (New York, 1965).

9 I have discussed these problems in two papers: "Interpreting Rousseau", *Socialist Perspective*, December 1975; and "Concept of Man in Political Theory", Paper for seminar on Concept of Man, Institute of Advanced Study, Simla, October 1976 (mimeographed).

10 Bourgeois politics is of course a large and imprecise term. The 'possibilities of politics'—in terms of typical conflicts and typical answers that power wielders have to them—differ from one stage of capitalism to another. Since, however, in this paper we are concerned exclusively with theorists working in the context of early capitalism (the pre-industrial setting between mid-seventeenth to mid-eighteenth century) it means possibilities of politics (in the sense defined earlier) of early capitalist society.

11 C.B. Macpherson, *Political Theory of Possessive Individualism* (London, 1962), 17 ff.

12 Marx and Engels saw this tendency quite clearly:
"If power is taken as the basis of right as Hobbes, etc. do, then right, law etc. are merely a symptom, the expression of other relations upon which state power rests. The material life of individuals, which by no means depends merely on their "will", their mode of production and form of intercourse which mutually determine each other, this is the real basis of the state and remains so at all the stages at which division of labour and private property are still necessary, quite independently of the will of individuals. These actual relations are in no way created by state power; on the contrary, they are the power creating it."
German Ideology (Moscow, 1976), p. 348. From the Marxist point of view, one can therefore talk of an uninterrupted critical tradition in political theory as much as in political economy. The tendency to look at politics constitutionally, through a form of legal positivism, is what introduces a fundamentally new method. It creates the possibility of greater self-assertion of political science as a discipline, while simultaneously trivialising its cognitive content.

13 Macpherson, n 11.; and his "Hobbes's Bourgeois Man", in Keith C. Brown (ed), *Hobbes Studies* (Oxford 1965).

14 Macpherson, n.11.

15 Even the simple textbook reading of Hobbes is now modified by this new, more historicised view, c.f. Thorson's reworked version of Sabine's textbook, Sabine and Thorson, *A History of Political Theory* (Delhi, 1975).

16 The argument by which Hobbes establishes equality of insecurity is interesting. He is conscious of the possible objection that the physical and mental abilities vary. But he is interested in a negative propositions. No one is so extraordinarily powerful that others cannot join and destroy him. So, some men are more powerful than others, but all are equally vulnerable.

17 In my "Concept of Man in Political Theory", n. 9.

18 Marx, *Theories of Surplus Value*, Part I (Moscow, 1975), p. 44.

19 From Hobbes's angle, one such example would be the combination of weaker individuals to destroy the strongest. But logically, this must be a constantly shifting configuration. It is fundamentally different from a stable interest combination in politics.

20 Macpherson, introduction to *Leviathan* (Harmondsworth 1968), pp. 53-60.

21 As one telling example: "Desire of riches, Covetousness: a name always used in signification of blame; because men contending for them are displeased with one another attaining them." p.123
Or his celebrated initial postulate:
"I put for a general inclination of all mankind a perpetual and restless desire for power after power that ceaseth only in death. And the cause of this is not always that a man hopes for a more intensive delight than he has already attained to; or that he cannot be content with a moderate power, but because he cannot assure the power and means to live well, which he hath present, without acquisition of more."
Hobbes, *Leviathan* (Harmodsworth, 1968), p. 161.
Without suggesting a strict parallel between Hobbes and Marx, one still remembers the analysis of accumulation in *Capital I*. The only 'correction' required would be to write "bourgeoisie" for mankind, and capital instead of power. The transposition is helped by Hobbes's definition of power as "present means to obtain some future apparent good." Perhaps the most interesting postulate, described elsewhere, is: "continuously to outgo others before is felicity; continuously to be out gone by others is misery; and to foresake the course is to die". Quoted in Alasdair MacIntyre, *A Short History of Ethics* (London, 1966),

22 Macpherson, Introduction to *Leviathan*, n.20, pp. 53-56.

23 Elsewhere I have tried to present the view that Marxist characterisation of the bourgeoisie state is not one of "pure force" but of a constantly shifting equilibrium of force and legitimation, in my "The Subtler Side of Domination", *Teaching Politics*, vol. 1, no. 2, 1977.

[24] As in the closing section of the *Leviathan*.

[25] Karl Marx, *Theories of Surplus Value*, Part 1, p. 52. Of course one can also cite some potentially anti-Hobbesian passages in Marx's analysis of early bourgeois social theory. This was neither surprising, nor inconsistent. Marx's way of looking at structures of intellectual history was determined by the complex Hegelian system of "reading". Marx said on occasions that he asked three interrelated questions in his study of theories: (i) what the theorist had said; (ii) whether what he had said was right or wrong; (iii) why, though he had been wrong, it was natural for him to think the way he did. Here is an example of a potentially anti-Hobbesian line of reasoning: "Speaking exactly and in the prosaic sense, the members of civil society are not atoms. . . . Every activity and property of his being, every one of his vital urges, beccmes a need, a necessity, which his selfseeking transforms into seeking for other things and human beings outside him. But since the need of one individual has no self-evident meaning for another egoistic individual capable of satisfying that need, and therefore no direct connection with that satisfaction, each individual has to create this connection; it thus becomes the intermediary between the need of another and the object of this need. Therefore it is natural necessity--the essential human properties however estranged they seem to be—and interest that hold the members of civil society together; civil, not political life is the real tie.' Marx and Engels, *The Holy Family*, (Moscow, 1975), p. 142. For a general discussion of seventeenth and eighteenth century materialist thought, see Chapter 6, section B.

[26] I have argued this in greater detail in "Concept of Man in Political Theory", n. 9.

[27] Karl Marx, *Theories of Surplus Value*, Part I, p. 367.

[28] Macpherson, n. 11. pp. 197-222.

[29] As Macpherson points out, this is not a real limitation, only a supposed one. While postulating that one cannot take away from nature what one has not 'mixed one's labour with', Locke was assuming that wage labour was allowed. This alters the situation. So instead of one's own labour, one can also use that one has paid for. Labour is not seen naturalistically as attaching to the person who does it. It is seen under circumstances of commercial and wage transactions—as alienable and saleable, in other words as a "commodity". Ibid., pp.214-19. Marx, curiously, thinks that "the limit of personal labour remains". *Theories of Surplus Value*, Part 1, p. 367.

[30] This is not an unprecedented argument at all. There is an almost exact equivalent in Aristotle when he argues that being a slave is good for the slave because he gets the opportunity of living in proximity to his more rational master.

[31] R.H. Tawney, *Religion and the Rise of Capitalism* (Harmondsworth, 1969), p. 52.

[32] "Interpreting Rousseau", *Socialist Perspective*, December 1975.

[33] Lucio Colletti, *From Rousseau to Lenin* (London, 1972).

[34] Engels notes that for Rousseau "each new advance of civilisation is at the same time a new advance of inequality. All institutions set up by the society which has arisen with civilisation change into their opposite of their original purpose."

"Already in Rousseau therefore we find not only a line of thought which corresponds exactly to the one developed in Marx's *Capital*, but also, in details, a whole series of the dialectical turns of speech as Marx used; processes which in their nature are antagonistic, contain a contradiction; transformation of one extreme into its opposite, and finally as the kernel of the whole thing, the negation of the negation. And though in 1754 Rousseau was not yet able to speak the Hegelian jargon, he was certainly sixteen years before Hegel was born, deeply bitten with the Hegelian pestilence, the dialectics of contradiction". Engels, *Anti Duehring* (Moscow, 1969), p. 167. Plekhanov does not add anything to Engel's remark that Rousseau thought dialectically. Plekhanov, *Selected Philosophical Works*, I (Moscow, 1974), pp. 556-60.

[35] J.L. Talmon, *The Origins of Totalitarian Democracy* (New York, 1961).

[36] Strictly speaking, there was a misunderstanding hidden in this debate. The two sides were equally right, depending on the level of the argument. On the plane of logic, it is very difficult to fault Hobbes's notion that, other things remaining the same, a situation of extreme individualism could not, by itself, generate harmony. Locke and the liberals however noted a historical fact; but wrongly transposed it into a logical proposition: unrestricted search for individual benefit leads to common good. What was undeniable was that under certain historical conditions, a society based on ethics of unrestricted individualism (but made up of much else) led to the phenomenon of economic growth (which was for them axiomatically equal to common good). The second was a question of productive efficiency, the former of distributive justice. This is why this proposition was never argued out; it was used as a cheerful unstated assumption of the dismal science.

[37] I have discussed this in "Interpreting Rousseau", and "Concept of Man in Political Theory", n. 9.

[38] "Mandeville, Rousseau, and Smith", in Colletti, n. 33.

[39] For typical Frankfurt school discussions see Herbert Marcuse, *One Dimensional Man* (London, 1964) ; Max Horkheimer and Theodor Adorno, *The Dialectic of Enlightenment* (London, 1973). To talk of the Frankfurt school while discussing Rousseau is particularly apt. In many ways they are the inheritors of the romantic rejection of technology and science. On this point there is a strange tension between "critical theory" and classical Marxism. Their approaches to technology and industrialism are antithetic.

40 For various possibilities in utopian discourse, see Engels, *Socialism, Utopian and Scientific;* Karl Mannheim, *Ideology and Utopia* (London, 1949); Herbert Marcuse, *Reason and Revolution* (London, 1941); A.L. Morton, *The English Utopia* (London, 1952).

41 Technically, we can distinguish between the concept of general will' and the theory of the general will, meaning the determinate logical procedures leading up to the concept.

42 This was noted by traditional interpreters: general will was a qualitative, not a quantitative concept; it was determined by the quality of the will, not by the quantity of the wills backing it. C.f. Ernest Barker, introduction to *Social Contract: Locke, Hume and Rousseau* (London, 1952).

43 Otto von Gierke, *The Development of Political Theory*, quoted in Colletti, n. 33, p. 183.

ROUSSEAU'S GENERAL WILL

Zaheer Masood Quraishi

Though central to the political philosophy of Jean Jacques Rousseau, the concept of General Will is loaded with many ambiguities and equivocations. That is why it has been interpreted by many commentators to imply diverse and even contradictory meanings. However, one feels that it has not been exhausted of fresh interpretations. For long Rousseau suffered for he was read in the narrow historical perspective of the decades preceeding the French Revolution. It is only during the recent days that he has come to be evaluated within a larger perspective of developments since 1789. What is the precise meaning of the General Will for Rousseau? This is, of course, the central question before his interpreters, but other questions follow in train. Whether or not Rousseau has a self-consistent thought which can be regarded as a plausible contribution to the volume of political philosophy? Does he uphold the revolutionary tradition or conservative? Is the import of his General Will essentially individualistic or collectivistic or a judicious combination of the two? If the last possibility is conceded, what is the mechanics he adopts to combine what apparently seem to be mutually contradictory? This paper presumes that the interpretors of the General Will base their arguments on sound logic as well as on substantial support from his texts and, then, highlight the nature of his General Will against its relevant background with a view to evaluating its merits and limitations.

Rousseau's Self-Consistency

It has been pointed out that Rousseau is a mass of contradictions and there is hardly any idea of significance which he himself has not contradicted. "The defiant individualism of

Discours sur l'inegalite" (1758) is presented in contrast with "the equally defiant collectivism of the *Contrat social*".[1] As *Emile* (1761) is associated with the first trend and the *Economie politique* (1757) is classed with the *Contrat social*, similar conflict has been noted between these two works also.[2] In his *Projet de constitution pour le Corse* (1767) he closely follows his principles. But his idealistic temperament has been reversed in his *Consideration sur le government de Pologne* (1772) wherein he is prone to compromise with the actual conditions obtaining in Poland and will conceed exceptions to his ideal state.[3] This attitude has been clearly set out in Rousseau's letter to Mirabeau where he defines the science of government as "a science purely of combinations, applications and exceptions which are determined by time, place and circumstance".[4]

Moreover, critics have discovered contradictions in the *Contrat social* itself. They present the individualism of the earlier chapters in contradiction to the collectivism of the latter ones.[5] In the opening chapters, he displays himself as a passionate devotee of anarchism. In the latter chapters, he pleads for complete collectivism that will allow the unqualified authority of the state to prevail.

It is further alleged that Rousseau states the general problem of political philosophy in the form of a paradox in the earlier chapters of the *Contrat social*.[6] The problem, he states, is

> to find a form of association which would defend and protect with the whole common force the person and goods of each associate, and in which, each, while uniting himself with all, may still obey himself alone, and remain as free as before.[7]

The paradox is well illustrated in a similar passage in the *Economie politique*: "By what inconceivable art has a means been found of making man free by making them subject."[8]

In fact, there are innumerable contradictions in Rousseau's. views on the State of Nature, education, property and religion. He depicts a pleasant picture of the State of Nature, but is doubtful of its historicity. He tells us both that "property" is root of all evils and that it is a sacred institution. He advocates for toleration of all religions, but banishes atheism from his own Republic.[9]

This is really a serious charge. A colossal mass of contradictions is not historically significant. The critics, nevertheless, realize that the assumption is not well-founded. Hence, they seek further evidence from the life of Rousseau to supplement their arguments.

It is by analysing Rousseau's personality in the light of the *Confessions* (1770) that his critics most easily establish his inconsistency. He denounces arts, Hearnshaw points out,[10] yet writes operas. He emphasizes the fundamental importance of the family life in the growth of human personality, but in his own life, he had a scant regard for his family. Hence it is argued, Rousseau presents a picture of dichotomy of actions and convictions.

No doubt, Rousseau's inconsistencies in this respect is patent. But it does not help us much in understanding his ideas. However, the argument has serious implications that deserve some attention. Rousseau had a deeply divided personality, in which morbidities of sex and religion played significant roles. He admits that he developed "a heart at once proud and affectionate, a character at once effiminate and inflexible, which by always wavering between self-indulgence and virtue has throughout my life set me in conflict with myself."[11] It is this split personality that is reflected in his paradoxical works. "Rousseau projected," Sabine explains, "the contradictions and maladjustments of his own nature upon the society about him and sought an anodyne for his own painful sensitivity".[12] He, therefore, betrayed at least two coexisting trends in his social philosophy. As Faguet thinks, "Il y a en deux Rousseau: le Rousseau sociologique qui a ete anti-societaire et anarchique, le Rousseau politique qui a ete ultra-societaire et ultra-archaique."[13]

It is, however, difficult to projects this dichotomy in his life into his political writings. Rousseau himself rejects such a view in anticipation when he says, "*The Social Contract* has previously appeared in the *Essay on Incquality* : all that is challenging in *Emile* was previously in *Julie*."[14]

Writers have tried to explain Rousseau's inconsistencies in terms of his personal nature. It is said that Rousseau had "a rhetorician's liking of paradoxes"[15] or that he was "an omnivorous reader with underdeveloped power of assimilation".[16] These explanations appear unconvincing at the first sight. When one discovers that the *Discours* and the *Economie politique*, appeared within eighteen months of one another and the *Emile* and the *Contrat social* were simultaneously worked out, one is forced to examine the allegation a little more closely instead of taking it for granted.[17]

Vaughan, having realized the difficulty, worked upon it rather carefully. He attempted an interpretation which is convincing at least at first sight. If the *Discours* and the first few chapters of the *Contrat social* are put aside, he argues, the individualism of Rousseau will seem to be a myth. He explains that Rousseau, beginning as a follower of Locke, came under the influence of Plato when he was writing the *Contrat social*, to fall subsequently under the influence of Montesquieu, which can be clearly discerned in his *Considerations sur le gouvernement de Pologne.*[18]

It is, however, difficult to accept his explanation. Rousseau does not undergo a mental evolution, the manner in which, as Jaeger notes, Aristotle does.[19] Neither individualism nor influence of Plato is limited to a particular period. The influence of Montequieu is, of course, written large all over his political works.[20] Hence, it is safer to begin a study of Rousseau without such a preconceived notion.

If Rousseau is a political thinker worth studying, he has a central argument in all his works. Whatever is inconsistent with and contrary to the central theme must be considered a departure from the argument in course of its elaboration. Such a distinction between the central thesis and ideas on the peripheries is essential for the study of Rousseau's political philosophy.

The strain of the departure from the main argument must be noticed and explained utilizing history as the frame of reference. As Cole rightly observes:

> Rousseau on the strength of what he says in the Social Contract has been interpreted in a great many different ways, usually without much attempt to refer to his other writings in the hope of elucidating his meaning.[21]

There is more in Rousseau's political thought than the *Contrat social* alone gives us and there are many ideas in this work that can be interpreted in the light of other works. Nevertheless, it should be conceded that the feeling of paradoxical character of Rousseau's political ideas is not absolutely unfounded. A careful persual even of *Contrat social* reveals a strain on the main argument of the book. It is certain that Rousseau was working under some sort of restraint or constraint of which he was fully aware. In a footnote, he made an appeal to "the attentive reader"

> Do not be in a hurry to charge me with contradicting myself. The terminology made it unavoidable considering the poverty of the language.[22]

This strain persists in all his philosophical writings.

Rousseau's difficulty arises from a conflict between the substance of his argument and the prevalent mode of expression, which he was obliged to utilize as a communicational compulsion. Substance of his works represents a current completely divorced from the main streams of thought in the Age of Reason and Enlightenment. Diderot described this gulf as "the vast chasm between heaven and hell."[23]

The Encyclopaedists constituted the dominant school of thought in the decades preceding the FrenchRevolution. They believed in the supremacy of reason. Rousseau, on the other hand, stressed the role of sentiments in human life. He pronounced that "thinking man is a depraved animal".[24] The rationalists imbibed the spirit of science. Rousseau laid emphasis on the community, whereas individualism characterized the political thinking of the Age of Enlightenment. Rousseau was the standard-bearer of traditions; the Encyclopaedists aimed at destroying traditionalism in order to build a new world based on rational values.   In a famous passage, Rousseau denounced all that the Encyclopaedists believed:

> These vain and futile disclaimers go forth on all sides armed with their fatal paradoxes to sap the foundations of our faith and nullify virtue. They smile contemptuously at such old names as patriotism and religion and consecrate their talents and philosophy to the destruction and defamation of all that men hold sacred.[25]

The basic tenets of Rousseau's political theory arise from his critical attitude towards the rationalist sprit of the *philosophes*. But in building up the edifice of his own philosophical system, he used the vocabulary in vogue with his philosophical opponents. The Natural Law, the State of Nature, the Social Contract etc. are concepts of liberal school of thought and do not cope with the central thesis of Rousseau. However, Rousseau presuming that political speculation should begin with these notions, used them and bestowed upon them new signification. Thus, in his bid to rise above his intellectual environment, he was swayed by its diction. In fact, the methodology that Rousseau selected was speculative.[26] This is why he was not able to appreciate the significance of his own digression from the fashionable ideas in the Age of Reason. Blending of sentimentalism, traditionalism and communal solidarity in political thinking with terminology of rationalism, enlightenment and individualism is certianly a contradiction which Rousseau had indulged in. But this is an inconsistency which is fundamentally different from the ones noted by most of the commentators or Rousseau.

Rousseau and Geneva

In two significant respects, Rousseau was alien to the sophisticated society of Paris. He was not a Frenchman and had adopted Paris as his new head quarter. He was born in the city-state of Geneva and was deeply attached to its simple life. He used to sign as 'Jean-Jacques Rousseau, *citoyen de Geneve*' and took pride in himself as the citizen of a free state and member of a sovereign community.[27] He dedicated his second *Discours* to the Republic of Geneva. Even his *Contrat social* is not completely free from marks of his Genevan origin. In fact, he envisages an ideal state after the pattern of social life in his birth-place and could be feasible in a country with that sort of life.

But, as Spink argued at length, Rousseau had little idea of the form of government prevailing in Geneva.[28] A comparative study of Rousseau's ideal state and the Constitution of Geneva stands enough testimony to confirm that he had little knowledge of political affairs of his country.[29] Nevertheless, it is also beyond doubt that he had assumed Geneva as an ideal community for which a constitution could be devised on the lines of his political ideas. In his critique of governments of his time, he always seeks to set out Geneva as an ideal community where popular sovereignty existed.[30] He always refers to it as a living example of simple life.[31] Indeed, Rousseau's political ideals presuppose a simple community. This is evident in his unreserved tribute to Plutarch.[32] His ideal community is founded on virtue and simple morality,—a common ground with Plato, Seneca and Tacitus. His social protest is directed against a society "carried along by the flavour of riches, the seduction of curiosities and the charm of new things".[33] His preference obviously is for a small community, because a large community induces a sense of loneliness among citizens. In a way he was anticipating Existentialists in raising the problem of loneliness in the crowd, a problem, we know, so characteristic of highly industrialized societies.

But Rousseau's defence of a small community is not so much derived from his observation of human psychopathology as on other considerations. He defends the small community, because he feels that a large community is bound to develop a stronger government and limited liberty.[34] Rousseau will consider such a development as usurpation of sovereignty by the capital whereas it ought to belong to the people in a democratic set-up.[35] He believes that the surest guarantee of the rights of citizens is the principle of popular sovereignty.[36]

The second factor that gives his philosophy a distinct colour in contradistinction to other thinkers of enlightenment in France is his plebeian background. His father was a watch-maker and a dance master and his mother a Savoyard. He was flung on the world at the age of sixteen, when his father fled the country to escape his creditors. His plebeianism presents a sharp contrast to the intellectual arrogance of the *philosophes*. He seeks to solve the problems of people rather than those of the intellectual elite. He is a republican; and he is a republican because he is Genevan.[37] And it is his republicanism that is mainly responsible for his originality both in France and in his epoch.[38] He represents the interests of the masses, who took shelter under utopia.[39]

Both these elements are vital to the understanding of the political ideas of Rousseau.[40] Rousseau was the originator of the Romantic spirit. Things go to Rousseau's heart before they penetrate into his mind. It is the success in putting forth his emotions that assured the future achievement of the Romantic movement.[41]

Philosophical Lineage of Rousseau

The eighteenth century France was characterized by an intense intellectual activity. The new elite drew inspiration from wherever it could in a bid to demolish the traditional notions, whereas the traditionalist left no stone unturned in defending the old values and assaulting the new ones. In such an intellectual atmosphere, the task of tracing Rousseau's philosophical lineage is not an easy one. Rousseau was considerably indebted to Greek Idealism, Christian Theology, the Naturalism and to his own contemporary individualism. But it would be a gross distortion of Rousseau's central thesis, if by way of over-simplified analysis, we attribute to him too heavy indebtedness to any one specific school of thought.

The impact of Greek Idealism is written large on all of his political writings. He depicted a picture of his own birth-town as an embodiment of simple life which, he thought, existed in Greek city-states. Now that Spink has decisively shown to us that Rousseau had little acquaintance with the political affairs in Geneva,[42] one can say without hazard that he looked towards Greek city-states, rather than to Geneva as a state approximating to his ideals. His appreciation for Plato's educational system is well-known.[43] He regarded Plato's *Republic* as the "finest treatise on education ever written".[44] Most of all, it is from Plato that he came to know of the predominent role which community plays in the life of an individual.[45]

In the history of political philosophy, Rousseau's idealism can be shown as a movement of revivalism of Greek Idealism. From Plato, he learns that the individual and the state constitute two closely inter-related universes. He recognizes that the state has a moral existence. He endorses Plato's view that both internal and external justice can be attained if man comes to understand his own nature.[46] But freedom continues to be Rousseau's main concern. It is important to note that he does not think in terms of metaphysical freedom. The problem of tyranny was too concrete for him to be resolved by verbiage.

Thus, while indebted to Greek Idealism, he charts his own course of idealism.

Similarly, Rousseau's indebtedness to Christian theology is also beyond doubt. Hearnshaw has pointed out the close analogy that exists between his description of man and that of the Bible.[47] Browowski and Mazlish have suggested that Rousseau's civil religion can be interpreted as a stream of fervent religious revival of eighteenth century alongwith Pietism and Methodism. These movements attempted to spark 'a religion of heart' as a reaction to what are known as 'latitudinarian bishops'.[48] There is, no doubt, a Protestant spirit in him.[49] Hendel has appropriately argued that the idea of the General Will was not Rousseau's own invention; he discovered it in Malebranche directly and through Father Lamy.[50] However, it should be noted that Rousseau's General Will was an attribute of the state in contradistinction to the one of Malebranche, which was the general will of God.

Rousseau was influenced by the jurists of the Natural Law school to a considerable extent. But Derathe has tried to demonstrate that the impact of Hobbes, Grotius, Pufendorf, Burlamanqui and Barbeyrac on Rousseau was not restricted to the extent of conjectural influence of one writer over the other. It was far more profound and far-reaching. As a matter of fact, the development of the Natural Law school in eighteenth century, he argues, was heading straightaway from the conclusions of Hobbes, Grotius and Pufendorf in the direction of Rousseau. "The political thought of Rousseau issues out from reflection under juristic theories which were authoritative."[51] Derathe arrived at this conclusion on the basis of his mis-interpretation of Rousseau's General Will, which he equated with 'sovereignty. This position is obviously untenable in view of the moral significance that Rousseau attached to the nation. The State of Nature and the Social Contract are formal ideas of Rousseau. But he arrives at the starting point of his thought: Man is a political animal. Thus, he restores "political thinking to the plane on which the Greeks had placed it."[52]

Although he is not an individualist, he is unable to release himself from the impact of individualist school of his own contemporary Encyclopaedists. Cole has argued that Rousseau is in the tradition of Locke, Hooker and the Pilgrim Fathers and that he took 'social tie' as an alternative phrase for social contract.[53] This contention does not seem to be tenable, because Rousseau never went out in search of a natural man. Inspite of the fact that he named his book 'Social Contract', he was in search of social ties. It is more appropriate to say that Rousseau used 'social contract' as a synonym of 'social ties' than *vice versa*.

Rousseau might have been influenced by many of his predecessor' and contemporaries, but that, in no way, minimizes his originality. While it is true that he is indebted to Plato, Hobbes, Locke and to many other thinkers, it should be noted that he borrowed from them whatever suited his temperament. Laski very aptly noted: "His work became a kind of autobiography externalized into a programmeso that . . while the nfluence of the other men on him are important, they are negligible beside the influence of Rousseau himself."[54] He belongs to no school of thought and he has prejudices against none. He borrows from all sources as long as they can give him something befitting the framework of his thinking and experience. He is a platonist because Plato has attached paramount importance to social ties, and has given for it a moral justification. He is a Christian because he staunchly believes in human brotherhood; he is a humanist and cosmopolitan. He appreciates the contribution of the Natural Law school in defining sovereignty and other related concepts. He belongs to the Encyclopaedist school because liberty is the central theme running through all his works. His is a school of thought to which none else belongs. In this sense, he is alone.[55]

Individual and the State

The relationship between the individual and the state is one of the chief concerns of political theory. Individual enjoys certain rights and owes certain duties to society by virtue of his membership of it and the State. Generally, the theorists have approached the issue from two sides. The individualist school has set out to enunciate the issue by defining the rights of individuals. The scheme of political obligation, which this school concedes, emanates from the rights guaranteed. The collectivistic school starts from the other end: it describes the system of duties to arrive at the corresponding rights, if at all.

All political philosophers fall under either of the two categories except for those who either stand on the cross-roads or do not accept such a dichotomy in principle. Rousseau is one of such exceptions. He does not only defy the dichotomous classification but has confounded his interpretors by enunciating principles said to belong to both the schools. He gives himself out as an extreme individualist at times and becomes an ardent champion of collectivism at others. No wonder that diametrically opposed political theories like anarchism and collectivism have both drawn inspiration from him.

There are at least two main ideas in Rousseau which closely approximate to anarchist views: one, man in the State of Nature and, two, the corrupting influence of the society. In the beginning, man was good. He was "a noble savage". The state of civil society completely altered him, so much so that all those qualities were no longer found in him at all. He became covetous and mean at the cost of his fellowmen. Natural Man has been used to living to fulfill his bare necessities. New society deprived him of his personal autarchy and brought him in conflict with his fellowmen. "He was born free and he is everywhere in chains."[56]

Prompted by this analysis of the State of Nature and the impact of social relations on it, some writers charge him of anarchism. Henri See says, for example, that Rousseau who is an individualist, reaches the height of anarchism in his second *Discours*. Although Rousseau modifies his position in *Contrat social*, See argues, he remains an individualist all the same. Rousseau is pre-occupied with and aims at assuring full development of individual and preserving his liberty. His social contract is a means to guaranteeing citizens the maximum liberty. "C'est en vertu de son individualisme que Rousseau a le premiere nettement degage la doctrine democratique de la souverainete populaire."[57] Faguet goes even a step ahead. He argues that Rousseau, in his early writings, begins with anarchist premises and provides them with anarchist substance and, much to his own surprise, arrives at anarchist conclusions. "C'est precisement devant ces conclusions anarchiques que Jean-Jacques Rousseau are cule, et c'est de cette reculde meme, que le *Contrat social* possede."[58]

This position does not seem to be tenable in view of the fact that Rousseau emphasises indispensibility of society for achieving moral ends. He describes the noble savage as innocent and good, but he does not imply that the State of Nature is his ideal state.   The State of Nature and the Social Contract were current concepts of contemporary philosophy. He found no other alternative but to utilize them in his own writings. What is important is that he puts the two concepts to the best use in his own analysis. It is, therefore, a narrow view of Rousseau to conclude that he was an anarchist: he was, in fact, far from it.

Was he an individualist, then? Rene Hubert says that Rousseau is every inch an individualist. Even from the study of *Contrat social*, which, according to him, is the key-stone of Rousseau's thinking, he does not hesitate to conclude that Rousseau is an ardent champion of the cause of individual.[59] In a remarkable analysis, Cassirer has shown that Rousseau "is a true son of enlightenment even when he attacks it and triumphs over it."[60] Rousseau is not satisfied with the concept of liberty held by *philosophes*. A true concept of liberty does not exclude submission, if the liberty is not restricted to intellectual sphere. He thinks that intellectual freedom serves no purpose unless it is coupled with moral freedom. This is how Cassirer proves "the inner spiritual unity" between Rousseau and his contemporaries despite an apparent doctrinal clash.[61]

Derathe is more specific in this regard. He considers Rousseau a step in the evolution of the Natural Law school of jurisprudence. He equates the General Will which is the central idea of Rousseau's philosophy, with sovereignty. Barbeyrac, according to him, paves the way for Rousseau's doctrine of inalienable sovereignty by extricating it from the inalienable right to property.[62] Thus, Austin is, Derathe would imply, in true Rousseauan traditions.

However, the most sophisticated interpretation of Rousseau from the point of view of individualism has been rendered by Alfred Cobban. He recognizes that Rousseau is an isolated figure, who neither adheres to a school of thought nor founds a new one to be followed.[63] It is true that Rousseau is different from earlier traditions of individualism because he has rejected the State of Nature[64] and has relegated the concept of social contract to secondary importance.[65] Rousseau's political philosophy starts with the individual and it ends with the individual, Cobban emphasizes.[66] Cobban gives full credit to the social dimension of Rousseau's concept of ethics and the individual. He mobilizes the process of the formation of nation-states to substantiate this argument.[67] Thus, Cobban finds many parallels in Rousseau and Burke. The full implication of this view-point has been worked out by Osborne.[68] Cobban reiterates that despite the nationalist framework, the central thesis of Rousseau remains in a general sense utilitarian and individualistic.[69] A commentator even opines that Rousseau was essentially a utilitarian.[70] Cobban, however, asserts that the concept of the General Will leads towards the rule of law.[71]

Many interpretors of Rousseau find in him shades of absolutism. The most classical formulator of this view-point is Vaughan. He thinks that if the second *Discours* and the first few pages of *Contrat social* are set aside, Rousseau's political philosophy gives an unmistakable impression of collectivism.[72] He pronounces that the book is "the porch of collectivism, as absolute as the mind of man has ever conceived."[73] From a passage in *Economie politique*[74] he jumps to the conclusion that Rousseau is the first outstanding exponent of organic theory of state.[75] Rousseau, he seems to argue, first isolates the individual in a political community and then throws him in the midst of an absolutist state. Duguit proclaims that Rousseau is the father of Jacobin dictatorship the Ceaserian despotism and the inspirer of absolutist doctrines of Kant and Hegel.[76] In this respect, Russell passes the most unkind strictures on Rousseau, when he denounces him as the ideological god-father of Hitler.[77]

Talmon moderates the harshness of the conclusions arrived at by such interpretators of Rousseau. He studies the phenomenon of totalitarian democracy in the context of mass society and discovers the genesis of this sort of absolutism from the General Will[78] which arises from "the totalitarian messianic temperament" of Rousseau.[79] The manner in which Sekou Toure and other African leaders resort to Rousseau's General Will as a justification of communaucracy, *ujamaa* and the *parti unique* is highly suggestive of Talmon's contention.[80]

These conflicting interpretations arise to a certain extent from a false notion which is an underlying assumption of most of the political philosophy. It is presumed that a philosopher can either champion the cause of individual's rights or denounce them. This implies that Rousseau is either an individualist or a collectivist. Rousseau, however does not accept it is a valid proposition. He believes in the essential duality of man and seeks a symbiosis of his individuality and sociality. In this sense, he can justifiably be considered a forerunner of modern sociology.[81] There are some interpretors who find in Rousseau a system builder. Bertrand de Jouvenel, for example, discovers in Rousseau a quest for "a true system of human heart."[82] Gray regards him a precursor of socialism on the basis of what Rousseau has written in the second *Discours*, specially the denunciation of property as the source of all social evils. Rousseau regards law as a device to protect possession from the havenots. He reveals the bifurcated nature of society by bringing out a contrast between the rich and the poor and, thus, invokes a doctrine of class war.[83] Gray, however, fails to read similar ideas in other political writings of Rousseau. On the other hand, Faguet recognizes a socialist flavour in the *Contrat social* although he refuses to accept Rousseau as a socialist on the ground that no means of establishing a socialist state has been prescribed in the book.[84]

Moreover, Gray singles out Rousseau and Marx for special condemnation.[85] This parallel is picked up by Laski who adduces to it a meaningful substance. He smells the Marxian concept of class-free society in Rousseau's General Will. "It is no accident," Laski says, " that the first sentence of the Social Contract should be the final exhortation of the Communist Manifesto."[86] Marx called upon workers to bring about a revolution because the proletariate have nothing to lose "but their chains".[87] Laski's contention is borne out by another parallel in the two texts. It was by mean of "an inconceiveable art" that Rousseau finds a means of reconciling freedom with subjection.[88] Marx, on the other hand, thinks that "an association in which the free development of each is a precondition of free development of all"[89] is historically inevitable.

A similar effort to reconcile the two strains in Rousseau is made by Hearnshaw who draws a parallel between the Biblical story of Paradise Lost and Regained and Rousseau's developmental logic from the State of Nature through the Social Contract to the General Will. Rousseau, according to Hearn-

shaw, depicts the State of Nature as an individuals's Garden of
Eden, in which the noble savage leads the life of a simple,
happy, sinless and careless existence. The fall of the noble
savage is indicated by the growth of inequality and the urge of
possession, as a result of which his primitive freedom is lost.
Rousseau seeks redemption by means of a Social Contract
which will restore liberty by combining equality with property,
mixing individualism with communal union and integrating
anarchic man in an organized society. Thus, Rousseau's General
Will is a rationalization of the Paradise Regained.[90] Faguet
takes only the next logical step to conclude that Rousseau is an
early Christian Socialist.[91]

These interpretors are impressed by Rousseau's intense search
for a formula which can bring about a reconciliation of the two
aspects of man. They forget that Rousseau was living in a
heterodox society in which blending of freedom and social regulation in a harmonious relationship was not a plausible proposition. His main difficulty, however, does not arise from the
incredibility of his ideals but from his search for an intrinsic
formula valid at all times and in all conditions. His dream of
homogeneity is highly commendable, even if he knows no means
to attain it. May be it is right that he is a utopian but he is
earnest about attaining his utopia. Green pays him the due tribute by developing a positive view of state on Rousseau's
promises. Rousseau's influence on Hegel's idealism should be
given credit to the extent,—neither more nor less,—Marcuse
traces the origin of social theory from it.[92]

The General Will: A Developmental View

Rousseau is unique. He belongs to no particular school of
thought, though he is indebted to all of them; and, yet, none of
the latter streams of thought has escaped his influence. He
neither propounds a theory of rights of individual, nor advances
a justification of an absolute political authority which suffocates
human freedom. Nor is he an anarchist, or a socialist. He is
simply a democrat and that also in an esoteric sense of the
term. He believes in the divine right of the people to live in
communities freely and distinguishes it, in a subtle way, from
the natural rights of the individual pleaded for by the contem-

porary Naturalists. His main objective is to seek recognition of the rights of the people to living in communities under egalitarian conditions so that no one is constrained in his free exercise of those rights.

Rousseau's contemporary thought bounds with political jargon of individualism including natural rights and individual liberty. He finds in them a systematic attempt to deny what Greek philosophers had taken for granted and, therefore, comes to its rescue. But, instead of asserting that man is a social animal, he pleads for in terms of current linguistic style. This is how he becomes a victim of a pattern of thinking which he seeks to destroy.

The supreme end of political philosophy, according to Rousseau, is to probe into the principles on which the foundation of a homogeneous state can be laid. It is his basic assumption that the political authority is socially necessary and every community is based on its recognition. "S'il n'y avait pas quelque point dans lequel tous les interests s'accordent," he argues, "nulle societe ne saurait exister."[93] Rousseau has a longing for only extending this area of agreement till a state is obtained where "each stands for all and all for each."[94] He entertained the possibility of citizens merging their interests in such a manner that complete unanimity is attained and the General Will emerges.[95] If political decisions are made by a freely constituted unanimity,[96] the dictates of the individual conscience and the sense of morality will coincide with the requirement of the social reason. Consequently, all the citizens will be able to act in unison[97] because law will cease to exercise any kind of restraint on their actions.[98] This short of liberty is, of course, invincible, while rights based on force can be overcome by a stronger force that be.[99] We cannot ignore that Rousseau also knows that the economic disparities constitute the chief obstacle to obtaining a true union of hearts and suggests that the state may reduce the gap between the rich and the poor by regulation so that such an ideal may appear to be feasible.[100]

But the Ideal State of Rousseau comes to grips with a mounting crisis as the consensus tends to decline gradually.[101]

Even if the political homogenity is disrupted by the highhandedness on the part of the rulers,[102] the consequences are the same: the social union is instantly evaporated,[103] the claim of the public authority to representing the public good is reduced to a meaningless pretension[104] and liberty is no longer possible.[105]

This analysis of the rise and fall of the General Will in political communities reveals to us Rousseau's latent faith in the idea of progress in human history. In the context of the middle of the eighteenth century, to conceive of a state based on the General Will presupposes not only a highly imaginative mind but a profound historical insight as well. Rousseau has both and, what is more important, he was conscious of his personal equipments. "Ce qui trompe les raisonneurs," he made a challenging observation, "c'est que, ne voyant que des Etats mal-constitues des leurs origines ils sont frappes de l'impossibilite d'y maintenir une semblable police."[106] Marx takes the next logical step when he says, "The philosophers have only *interpreted* the world differently; the point is to *change* it."[107] Rousseau and Marx have similar sense of purpose, but Rousseau lacks the means to reach his goal, whereas Marx evolved the mechanism of proletarian revolution to attain his.

The tragedy of Rousseau is that he lacks the tools of historical analysis. After the French Revolution had furnished some adequate material for historical analysis, Vico and Hegel evolved their historical theories and Thierry, Mignet and Guizot applied their mind on the existing data and utilized the existing tools and, thus prepared grounds for a scientific theory of history. In the absence of historical data, Rousseau makes shrewd guesses, as did Harrington and Winstanley, but is unable to evolve a political strategy by means of which he can translate his dream into a reality. This is the reason why he is probing in the past the elements of a society he designed for future. The ghost of homogeneous society embodying the General Will stalks through the pages of the *Contrat social*. It is the central concept of Rousseau's thought but whatever he says neither proves nor justifies it. In this sense, Rousseau deserves to be called utopian.

Rousseau's Influence

Rousseau is certainly utopian, but the state he envisages is not an Erehwon. His ideal state has given a sense of direction to numerous political movements. It inspired Jacobins of revolutionary France to establish a regime wielding popular sovereignty,[108] as it gave Napoleon Bonaparte a sense of historical mission.[109] The Paris Commune of 1871 too approximated to Rousseau's Ideal State to a great extent.[110] But if ever a political society exists that approximated to the ideals subscribed to by Rousseau, it is the pilot-state of Africa, Guinea, where, since independence, a conscious effort has been made to utilize Rousseau's concept of the General Will to motivate total mobilization of human energies and material resources and mass political participation in administration and decision-making.[111] Although a more relevant and concrete theory of *Asabiya*, propounded by Ibn Khaldun, was available to the West Africans particularly, as a part of their historical tradition[112], they fell back on Rousseau's General Will in an effort to resort to the socio-economic reconstruction of their newly independent countries.

In a general sense, Rousseau's influence is universal. The Western democracies are indebted to him for the notion of political consensus, which is the basis of any stable constitutional regime.[113] He provided justification for absolute authority in dictatorial regimes of the right variety as much as for single-party rule in the classless state. His notion of the General Will promised more than anything else, a broad platform for nationalists in Asia and Africa during the course of their freedom struggle as well as during the period of national reconstruction. His imprint is pretty distinct on collectivist and liberal theorists equally. Though a product of the eighteenth century Europe and avowed enemy of contemporary individualism, Rousseau transcends all boundaries of space and time in his influence.

REFERENCES

[1] C.E. Vaughan, *The Political Writings of Jean-Jacques Rousseau* (London, 1962), I, 111.

[2] F.J.C. Hearnshaw, "Rousseau" in his (ed.), *The Social and Political Ideas of Some Great Thinkers of the Age of Reason* (London, 1930) 183.

[3] Kingsley Martin, *The Rise of French Liberal Thought* (2nd ed., New York, 1954) 208-14.

4 Quoted in ibid.

5 Vaughan, n. 1, 21.

6 George H. Sabine, *A History of Political Theory* (London, 1952) 494.

7 *Le Contrat social*, Bk I, ch 6 (Cole's translation unless, otherwise stated): "trouver une forme d' association qui defende et protege de toute la force commun la personne et les biens de chaque anvcie et par laquelle chacun, s' unissant a tous, n'obeisse pourtantn qu'a lui-meme, et reste aussi, libre qu'auparavant".

8 "Par quel art inconcevable a-t-on pu trouver le moyen d'assujettir les hommes les rendre libres." *Economie politique*.

9 "A notre avis, la contradiction n'est donc dans *le Contrat social*. Mais elle se trouve entre *le Contrat social* et *la Profession de foi du Savoyard*. Le premier exalte la religion du citoyen, la seconde la religion de l'homme—la religion toute sentimentale, la plus individualiste possible." Cf. J.L. Lecerole (ed.) *Du Contrat social de Rousseau* (Paris, 1955) 39.

10 Hearnshaw, n. 2, 184.

11 "Ce coeur a la fois, si fier et si tendre, ce caractere effemine mais pourtant indomptable, qui, flottant entre la molesse et la vertu, m'a jusqu'au bout mis en contradiction avec moi-meme". *Les Confessions* Bk. I (English translation from Cohen's Pelican edition).

12 Sabine, n. 6, 486.

13 Emile Faguet, *Rousseau Penseur* (Paris, n.d.) 316: "There are two Rousseau: the sociologist Rousseau who was anti-social and anarchist and the political Rousseau who was ultra-social and ultra-archaic." (the author's translation).

14 "Tout ce qu'il y a de hardi dans *le Contrat Social* etoit auparavant dans *le Discours sur l'inegalite*: tout ce qu'il y a de hardi dans l'Emile etoit auparavant dans *le Julie*". *Les Confessions*, IX (Cohen's translation).

15 Sabine, n, 6, 494-5.

16 Hearnshaw, n. 2, 185.

17 Alfred Cobban, *Rousseau and the Modern State* (London, 1964) 19.

18 Vaughan, n. 1, 77-81.

19 Werner Jaeger, *Aristotle* (2nd ed., trans. Richard Robinson, New York, 1962)

20 Cobban, n. 17, 19.

21 G.D.H. Cole (trans.) *The Social Contract and Discourses of Jean-Jacques Rousseau* (London, 1955) v.

22 *le Contrat social*, Bk. II, ch. 4: "Ne vous pressez pas de m'accuser ici de contradiction. Je n'ai pu l'eviter dans les terms, vu la pauverte de la langue."

23 Quoted in Sabine, n. 6, 485.

24 *le Discours sur l'inegalite*, I: 'L'homme qui medite est un animal deprave."

25 *le Discours sur les arts et sciences*, II: "Ces vains et futiles declamateurs vont de tous cotes armes de leurs funestes paradoxes, sapants

les fondament de la fois et aneantissant la vertue. Ils sourient dedaigneusement a ces vieux mots de patrie et de religion, et consacrent leurs talents et leurs philosphie a detruire et avilir tout ce qu'il ya de sacre parmi les hommes.''

[26] Lecercle, n. 9, 38.

[27] Roman Rolland, *J.J. Rosseau: les Pages Immortelles* (Paris, n.d.) 11.

[28] J.S. Spink, *Jean-Jacques Rousseau et Geneve* (Paris, 1934) 30-49.

[29] Robert Derathe, *Jean-Jacques Rousseau et la Science Politique de Sen Temps* (Paris, 1950) 105.

[30] Rolland, n. 27, 21.

[31] *Lettre de la Montagne* in Vaughan, n. 1, II, 203-4. "Je peignais un objet existant et l'on voulait que cet objet changeat de face."; Judith N. Shklar, *Men and Citizens* (Cambridge, 1969) 3-34, makes a distinction between two models that Rousseau had before him—the Swiss village with agricultural simplicity, domestic education and moral virtue as opposed to the Spartan culture, characterized by a stern military discipline, political education and civic virtue.

[32] *Les Confessions*, III

[33] ". . .entrainee par le gout de richesse, le seduction du curiosite et l' attrait des choses nouvelles." (author's trans.) Bertrand de Jouvenel (ed.) *Du Contrat social* (Geneve, 1947) 35.

[34] Emile, V.

[35] *Contrat social* (first version) in Vaughan, n. 1, II, 487.

[36] Derathe, n. 29.

[37] Spink, n. 28, 31

[38] Lecercle (ed.), *Discours sur l'Inegalite* (Paris, 1954) 10.

[39] Ibid.

[40] Harold J. Laski, "Portrait of Jean-Jacques Rousseau", in *Essays on Disobedience* (London, 1931) 181.

[41] Ibid., 186-89.

[42] Spinks, n. 28.

[43] *Emile*, I.

[44] William Boyd, *The Educational Theory of Jean-Jacques Rousseau* (London, 1911) 217.

[45] Sabine's heading of the chapter on Rousseau—"The Rediscovery of the Community"—is highly suggestive. See Sabine, n. 6, 485.

[46] John Plamenatz, *Man and Society* (London, 1963) I,389.

[47] Hearnshaw, n. 2, 187f.

[48] J. Bronowski and Bruce Mazlish, *The Western Intellectual Tradition* (London, 1963) 322-30.

[49] Faguet, n. 13, 318. "La tradition protestante et Montesquieu, lu dans un espirit republicain, c'est tout *le Contrat social*." (Author's translation: "All that is *Social Contact* is the Protestant tradition and Montesquieu, written in republican spirit.").

[50] C.W. Hendel, *Jean-Jacques Rousseau: the Moralist* (London, 1934) II, 119-20.

[51] Derathe, n. 29, 51.

52 Alfred Cobban, "New Light on the Political Thought of Rousseau", *Political Science Quarterly*, Vol. 64 (2); K.F. Roche, *Rousseau: Stoic and Romantic* (London, 1974) talks of Rousseau's Stoic inspiration (10).

53 Cole, n. 21, xvi.

54 Laski, n. 40, 180.

55 Roger D. Masters, *The Political Philosophy of J.J. Rousseau* (Princeton, 1968) 53.

56 *Contrat social*, Bk. I, ch 1. "L'homme est ne libre et partout il est dans les fers."

57 "It is by virtue of his individualism that Rousseau has elucidated clearly the democratic doctrine of popular sovereignty." Henri See, *L'Evolution de la Pensee Politique en France au XVIIIeme Siecle* (Paris, 1925) 146 (author's trans.)

58 "It was precisely in face of the anarchist conclusions that Jean-Jacques Rousseau retreated and it is the same retreat which the *Contrat social* is possessed of." Faguet, n. 13, 312. (Author's trans.)

59 Rene Hubert, *Rousseau et Encyclopedie* (Paris, 1928) 127-34.

60 Ernst Cassirer, *The Philosophy of Enlightment* (trans. Fritz C.A. Koelin and J.P. Pettergrove, New Jersey, 1951) 273.

61 Ibid., 258-72.

62 Derathe, n. 29, 260.

63 Cobban, n. 17, 164f.

64 Ibid., 61-5.

65 Ibid., 73-4.

66 Ibid., 66-71.

67 Ibid., 99-125.

68 A.M. Osborne, *Rousseau and Burke* (London, 1940) 1-26.

69 Cobban, n. 17, 71.

70 J.H. Burn, "Du cote de Chez Vaughan: Rousseau Revisited", in *Political Studies*, vol. 12 (June 1964) 2.

71 Cobban, n. 17, 77.

72 Vaughan, n. 1, I, 38f.

73 Ibid., 39.

74 *Economie politique:* "Le corps politique, pris individuellement, peut etre considere comme un corps organise. Vivant et semblable a celui de l'homme."

75 Vaughan, n. 1, I, 57-8.

76 Quoted in Cobban, n. 17, 28.

77 Bertrand Russel, *A History of Western Philosophy* (London, 1945) 685.

78 J.L. Talmon, *The Origin of Totalitarian Democracy* (New York, 1960).

79 Ibid.

80 Gray Cowan, "Guinea", in G.M. Carter (ed.) *African One-Party States* (New York, 1962) 187; Madeira Keita, "Le Parti Unique en Afrique", in *Presence Africain*, XXX (Feb-Mar 1960).

81 Emile Durkheim, *Montesquieu and Rousseau: Fore-Runners of Sociology* (Ann Arbor, 1960) 135-8.

82 Bertrand de Jouvenel, "Jean-Jacques Rousseau", in *Encounter*, vol.

111 (Dec 1962) 42.

83 Alexander Gray, *The Socialist Tradition* (London, 1963) 85.

84 Faguet, n. 13, 307.

85 Gray, n. 83.

86 Laski, n. 40, 188.

87 Karl Marx and Fredric Engels, *The Communist Manifesto: Socialist Landmark* (ed. Laski, London, 1954) 160.

88 See above, n. 8.

89 Marx and Engels, n. 87, 146.

90 Hearnshaw, n. 2, 186-90.

91 Faguet, n. 13, 319.

92 Herbert Marcuse, *Reason and Revolution* (London, 1955).

93 "Were there no point of agreement between them all, no society could exist." *Contrat social*, Bk II, ch 1.

94 "Chacun envers tous et tous envers chacun d'eux." ibid., Bk II, ch 4.

95 Ibid., Bk IV, ch 2: "Plus le concert regne dans les assemblee, c'est-a-dire, plus les avis approchent de l'unanimite, plus aussi la volonte generale est dominante."

96 Ibid., Bk II, ch 4: "Ce qui generalise la volonte est moin des voix que l'interet commun qui les unit."

97 Ibid., Bk III, ch 1: "Tous ses membres puissent agir de concert."

98 Ibid., Bk II, ch 9: "Plus le lien social s'ettend, plus il se relache."

99 Ibid., Bk II, ch 4: " . . . de leur force que d'autre pouvoient surmonter, contre un droit que l'union sociale rend invincible."

100 Ibid., Bk II, ch 11: "Voulez vous donc donner a l'Etat de la consistance, rapporchez les degres extremes autant qu'il est possible ne souffrez ni des gens opulent ni des gueux."

101 Ibid., Bk IV, ch 1: "When the social bond begins to be relaxed and the State to grow weak, when particular interests begin to make themselves felt and the smaller societies to exercise an influence over the larger, the common interest changes and finds opponents; opinion is no longer unanimous; the general will ceases to be the will of all; contradictory views and debates arise; and the best advice is not taken without question."

102 Ibid., Bk III, ch 1: " . . . sitot qu'il (prince) veut tirer de lui-meme quelque acte absolu et independent, la liaison du tout commence a se relacher."

103 Ibid., Bk III, ch 1: "A l'instant, l'union social s'evanouirait et le corps politique serait dissons."

104 Ibid., Bk IV, ch 1: "Quand l'Etat. . .ne subsiste plus. . .que le plus vil interet se pare effrontment du nom sacre du bien public, alors la volonte generale divient muette."

105 Ibid., Bk IV, ch 2: "Quand ils cessent d'y etre, il n'y a de liberte."

106 Ibid., Bk IV, ch 1: "The theorists are led into error because, seeing only states that have been from the beginning wrongly constituted, they are struck by the impossibility of applying such a policy to themselves."

[107] See Karl Marx, "Thesis on Feuerbach", in C. Wright Mills, *The Marxists* (London, 1963) 71.

[108] See Lord Elton, *Revolutionary ideas in France, 1789-1871* (London, 1959) 39ff.

[109] J.H. Rose, *The Life of Napolean I* (New York, 1902) I, 39, See also John Plamenatz, *The Revolutionary Movements in France* (London, 1952) xi.

[110] Franz Jellinek, *The Paris Commune* (London, 1937).

[111] F. Gigon, *Guinee: Etat-pilote* (Paris, 1959) 37ff.

[112] '*Asabiya* (communal solidarity) was evolved by Ibn Khaldun as a concrete sociological concept within a theoretical framework of a political-historical sociology drawing its data from societies characterized by the contradictions between sedentry towns and nomadic tribes. Therefore, it is more relevant to African situation. It was certainly an integral part of the West African tradition as the processes of Arabization and Islamization has reached the region. Sekou Toure belonged to the composite culture produced by the twin proceses.

[113] John Chapman, *Rousseau: Totalitarian or Liberal?* (New York, 1956) 124ff.

MARXISM: THE ETERNAL DIMENSIONS

V P. Verma

After going through the recent developments in political theory, one cannot but come to the conclusion that political science has failed to correct itself from the bad effects of uncontrolled circularity. One may be surprised to encounter numeroust heories centred around the systems approach, but one must ask the question, what impels us to devise theory after theory, to know the purpose and significance of such theories. Natural scientists devise theories, because they wish to reduce their respective phenomena by a process of logic to something already known or evident; or when they fail to cope with the facts as per the existent theories; or perhaps, finally at the maturity stage of science, to strive for unification and simplication. Political scientists are not different from the natural scientists in this respect, but we can assert with confidence that political science is far from the final maturation stage. Obviously twentieth century political scientists, preoccupation with theory building is due to the fact that they have failed to cope with the challenge of Marxism with the existent theories. Behaviouralism, functionalism, structuralism and systems approach are all evidence of such awareness of inadequacy. What Karl Marx tried in his simplicity was to free the social sciences from the procrustean logic of Aristotle, the metaphysical duality of Plato, and the many related off-shoots of traditional Greek philosophy, which have been cultivated all through the ages in the Western thought. How one novel contribution, spelling a break with the ossified past, releases a flood of sympathetic and hostile formulations, is best witnessed in the phenomenon of Marxism during the last ninety years. It seems that political science has become a miracle creed for none of its developments can claim immunity from the Marxist view of social existence. This essay tries to unfold some of the fundamental aspects of Marxism which have potentialities to generate a continuum.

Framework of Dialectical Continuum

To some,[1] man is a Time-abstracting animal, but all such Time-abstraction involves some kind of symbol manipulation. The wonderful power of abstraction enables man to abstract subtle, profound, or apparent experience; but it is not necessary that such abstractions must correspond to the reality. Why abstractions fail to correspond to reality? The science of dialectics tells us that abstractions can be either particular reductionism or individual holism, but they never reach the realm of universals. As we are aware, Aristotlean logic had given currency to the idea that man can comprehend the objective world rationally. Hegel went a step ahead and propounded and illustrated in his works, that the pure thought without any empirical foundations is enough.[2] It seems that reductionistic and holistic conceptual systems have limitations, for they are the two sides of the same coin. In a circular process one may choose any arbitrary inertial reference point but invariably one lands in one half and misses the other half. Apparently there is asymmetery as well as expansion of uncertainty in all such frameworks resting exclusively on the abstractions. All twentieth century political theories suffer from such limitations. Marxism rests on dialectics, which not only discovers the evolutionary actuality of systems approach, but also can unfold revolutionary potentiality. On the plane of thought, Hegel had earlier illustrated such dialectical transverse motion by constructing a system which could take off from matter to life, transcend from institution of family to the institution of state, and soar from world history to conscious human freedom. What is objective is also subjective, and what is subjective is also objective; but what is important, is to find their asymptotic continuum. Those who fail to discover dialectical asymptotic continuum, for them nature is a blind necessity, however for Hegel, nature was a mere autonomous process of self-direemption.

To offer a crude analogy, Hegelian dialectics takes off from the inertial reference point of electro-magnetic field devoid of polarity, in other words, Idea is presented as non-dual absolute truth. On the other hand, Karl Marx starts from the inertial reference point of electron and magnetic fields, and assumes that polarity is at the root of all development. This rejection of Hegelian adiabetic ground is meaningless for on the actional plane, Karl Marx is correct. What is perhaps most significant at the actional plane, is the fact of entropy or thermal choas, which in any social system manifests itself in the form of class-struggle and class-exploitation. Philosophers have failed to define the course and end of human knowledge, which not only involves the progressive development of 'entire human race' in a evolutionary pattern, but also the sublation of overgrown forms, both social and natural. In dialectics, it is the totality of subjectivity, i.e. entire human race, which determines the evolutionary procession and entropic sublation of objectivity, and its record is called history. What Karl Marx calls as the 'entire human race', Hegel identifies the same totality of subjectivity as the process of 'Notion'.[3] There is a substantial agreement between Karl Marx and Hegel, for both rest their thought on the foundations of dialectics, without accepting particular empiricism and individual idealism. Their difference is in name only, for to discriminate between electro-magnetic and electron fields, one finds only a difference of degree and not a quantitative one.

After the discovery of quantum physics in the early twentieth century, it almost became a fashion in Western thought to attack Marxism as a determinist creed following classical Newtonian physics.[4] Marxism came to be equated with an atomistic reductionism, where matter was viewed exclusively as a kind of discrete *a priori* with no field possibilities or exclusion of indeterminism of elementary particles. No dialectics worth its name can afford partial treatment of the totality of subjectivity which is also the totality of objectivity. For example, Karl Marx interpreted the European subjectivity in all its socio-economic as well as cultural-political aspects as the emergence of the phenomenon from capitalism to imperialism during the nineteenth century, not as a national one but an international one. One way of denouncing Marxism is to equate it to economic determinism, which implies the worst kind of reductionist fallacy. Karl Marx himself described his logic as dialectical materialism, but dialectical materialism is not historical materialism, or historical materialism cannot be equated with economic determinism. On the plane of action, dialectics is the best key to unfold the course of the totality of subjectivity, which manifests itself as exclusive individuality and monopolist particularity. As in the case of an elementary particle, its individual motion and particular charge are dependent on the field, similarly there are different individual activities and class characters in different social systems in different ages, but the notion fails to cast as under the characteristics of subjective exclusiveness and monopoly. For this reason of subjectivity, there is perpetual class-struggle and class-exploitation. The emergence of subjectivity has invariant contents, for it may appear as territorial domination of the globe at one moment, and as the phenomenon of finance capital in the next, and in our age of post-industrial revolution, it is already asserting as pooling of advanced technology.

One may discover a number of formal categories to describe the phenomenon of totality of subjectivity and imperialism is just one of these categories, but what is important, is the dialectical attitude:

> The physicist either observes physical phenomena where they occur in their most typical form and most free from disturbing influence . . . Intrinsically, it is not a question of higher or lower degree of development of the social antagonisms that result from the natural laws of capitalist production. *It is a question of these laws themselves, of these tendencies working with iron necessity towards inevitable results.* The country that is more developed industrially only shows to the less developed, the image of its own future.[5]

The process of blind necessity, which Marx thought was *De te fabula narratur!* is but the Hegelian notion of autonomous process of self-direemption, and therefore, is not mechanistic. In the Space-Time continuum, apparently there are no fields, radiation, charge, chemical reactivity, magnetism, gravitation and like forces, but all is existent. Karl Marx was the first social scientist to point out the existent social classes, which the earlier philosophers missed altogether:

> I paint the capitalist and landlord in no sense *couleur de rose.* But here individuals are dealt with only in so far as they are personification of economic categories, embodiment of particular class relations and class interests. My stand-

point, from which the evolution of the economic formation of society is viewed as a process of natural history, can less than any other make the individual responsible for relations whose creature he socially remains, however much he may subjectively raise himself above them.[6]

Class consciousness is a better way of describing an individual in society, for if it was not so, why then science should classify the individual elementary particles on the basis of their charge, mass, spin, statistics, life time, decay scheme and so on, which serve as the sure guide to place them in infra and ultra part of the spectrum.

What is the significance of class consciousness which rejects the thesis of individual consciousness in social relations ? Here it is presumed that there is correspondence between individual mass (property) and the individual charge (consciousness) which is also supported by the fact of equivalence of mass (property) and energy (social potential capacity). In other words, the possession of property by an individual determines both his conscious as well as unconscious behaviour in society. It is true that individual mass of an elementary particle itself is undergoing change thereby transforming its charge (consciousness) and there are at least three elementary particles which are without mass. It is true that love (graviton), wisdom (photon), and detachment (neutrino) are powerful forces which often transcend class consciousness.

Karl Marx thought by turning Hegel right side up again, he discovered "the rational kernel within the mystical shell" but what he actually stumbled at was the mystical kernel within the rational shell. Hegel equated the rational with the actual and therefore, skipped the possibility of potentiality, and Marx committed the same mistake of partial projection: he took actual and rational as in variant and forgot their mutuability and relativist correspondence. No dialectics is possible without metaphysical contents and Einstein was right when he said: "I believe that every true theorist is a kind of tamed meta-physicist, no matter how pure a 'Positivist' he may fancy himself. The meta-physicist believes that the logically simple is, also the real."[7]

Karl Marx, therefore, wrongly assumed that this dialectic method was "not only different from the Hegelian, but is its direct opposite," for in a transverse motion neither matter nor consciousness are prior to each other, but one may presume so. Marx was annoyed with Hegel that he had mystified the dialectics by projecting the externality through the spectrum of Idea, but it is well-known, that no meaningful perception is possible without some conceptual framework. One has to admit a kind of simultaneity and correspondence between perception and conception, at least on the non-astral plane. Ordinarily human perception is two dimensional but man interprets the four dimensions through the conceptual framework of receptors. It is well known that in a picture there are only two dimensions and our retinal images are so, but one experiences the depth perception also? In fact, it is neither the matter nor the intellect which are mysterious, but what brings about the elements of spontaneity and naturalness in all such phenomenon, can be termed as mysterious.

Let us admit that metaphysics is a fact of life and we are all tamed metaphysicians when we speculate. Philosophers and scientists all feel the menacing presence of solipsism but none is prepared to accept its unavoidable influence. We may realise the significance of dialectical solipsism by turning to the ancient man, by tracing how he believed the origin of the cosmos. It appears rather strange that all civilizations have one common thing and that is the heritage of dialectical solipsism. One may denounce the ancient human mythology as primitive animism but the wonder of all wonders is the present science has not refuted the dialectical mode of thinking but continues to support it. It is meaningless to raise the controversy that the actual is real and the potential is illusory or vice versa; what is important is that the discovery of anti-matter establishes the fundamental dialectical thesis. Maurice Goldhaber of the Brookhaven National Laboratory has speculated on the possible existence of two separate worlds—one composed of matter and the other of anti-matter. Inspired by the primeval atom of Abbe Georges le Maitre, he suggests that the universe originated from a single particle called universon. This divided immediately into a pair of particles—the cosmon and the anti-cosmon. They flew apart with great kinetic energy (by some unspecified process, i.e. dialectics) and eventually decayed, one giving rise to the cosmos we know, the other the anti-cosmos beyond reach of our observation.

Perhaps the radio energy being emitted by our galaxies and cloud dusts is due to some anti-matter being injected into our cosmos.

Joseph Campbell[8] is right when he contends that both the Orient and Occident shared the 'Myth of the One that Became Two.' What is significant in this shared myth is the dialectical principle of sub-division which keeps the oscillating universe moving due to its perennial search for its other. What is sub-divided is perhaps the total subjectivity or Notion as we have contended earlier. Brihaderanyaka Upanishad gives us a dialectical analogy as to the origin of the universe: "The universe was nothing but the Self in the form of a man. It looked around and saw that there was nothing but itself, whereupon its first shout was, 'It is I!' whence the concept 'I' arose (And that is why, even now, when addressed, one answers first, 'It is I!' only then giving the other name that one bears). Then he was afraid. (That is why anyone alone is afraid.) But he considered: "Since there is no one here but myself, what is there to fear? Whereupon the fear departed. (For what should have been fear? It is only to a second that fear refers). However, he still lacked delight (therefore, we lack delight when alone) and desired a second. He was exactly as large as a man and woman embracing. This Self then divided itself in two parts; and with that, there were a master and a mistress. (Therefore this body, by itself, as the sage Yajnavalkya declares, is like half of a split pea. And that is why, indeed, this space is filled by a woman). The male embraced the female, and from that the human race arose. She, however, reflected: "How can he unite with me, who am produced from himself? Well then, let me hide! She became a cow, he a bull and united with her; and from that cattle arose. She became a mare, he a stallion. . .Thus he poured forth all pairing things, down to ants. Then he realized: "I, actually, am creation; for I have poured forth all this."[9] This pouring forth of One into many, whether it pertains to Cosmon or to Brahman, it has a dialectical significance. Similar endorsement of dialectical thinking can be found in the Book of Genesis as well as in the Chinese diagram of symbolic representation of the *tao* pouring forth the spiral of the *yang* and the *yin*.[10] The myth of *The Golden Bough* is another version of dialectical Becoming, where *Diana* and *Virbius*, *Artemis* and *Hippolytus*, are mere complementary forces of polarity. The Egyptian and

the Mesopotamian civilizations had their own dialectical traditions. Somehow all scientific discoveries, from evolution to
entropy, and from conservation to catastrophies, and like
others, simply confirm the existence of dialectical principle, and
we human beings who live in a Platonic cave, cannot escape
contradictions.

Philosophers[11] have ridiculed dialectics as the employment of
reason beyond experience and yet no philosophy is devoid of
dialectical mode of reasoning. Plato's Being and Becoming;
Aristotlean actual and potential; Lucretius' atom and void; Ac-
quinas' being and contingent; Spinoza's substance and accident;
Locke's primary and secondary qualities; Cartesan mind and
body; Baconean natural philosophy and metaphysics; Harvey's
structures and functional utility; Newtonian action and reaction; Kant's noumenal and phenomenal—are some of the outstanding examples of conscious and unconscious dialectical
reasoning. One wonders why some topics with dialectical import
have constituted the perpetual theme of philosophy, psychology,
ethics, political theory, theology and other allied disciplines?
Some of them are causality and freedom; finality and blind
necessity; chance and probability; virtue and vice; passion and
reason; desire and duty; structure and function; and like.

Karl Marx spent sleepless nights to understand Hegelian
dialectics. Marx was very much fascinated with dialectics which
traces man's evolution from matter in Hegelian system. Marx
straight away applied dialectics to the realm of politics. Hegelian
politics was centred around abstract right, and Karl Marx translated this abstract right as capital. He elucidated that capital
presupposes surplus value, and surplus value in turn rests on
capital and labour power rather on the abstract principle of one-
ness, i.e. family love. Uncle Hegel, your logic of nature seems
alright but your politics of abstractions leads to exploitation.
Hence the only answer was to abolish the abstract right of
property and to establish the socialist economy, viz. abolition of
landed property, rents for public purposes; income-tax progressive
and graduated; no right to inheritance; centralization of credit/
banks; centralisation of communication and transport; and
finally establishment of classless society. What is most significant,
is the fact, that both Hegel and Karl Marx rest their thought on
dialectics and believe: (1) that dialectics can unfold truth; (2) in

dialectical motion, contrary and defective truths are harmonized; (3) dialectics as an idea of evolution and entropy; (4) dialectics as a process of blind necessity; (5) dialectics as a process of natural history; (6) there is a kind of inevitability of dialectical necessity; (7) social use of value and not socially useless production; and (8) progress institutional.

The aim of dialectics follows from the primacy of the mind's concern with truth: whether it is viewed from the point of epistemology, logic, or axiology. Human thought is affected by the total experience, whether we call it subjectivity (total) or notion at a particular moment of history. Truth does not expose itself fully either through the exclusive pursuit of externality (viz. the conviction of empiricists) nor through exclusive contemplation of ideation, viz. the faith of idealists, nor through the so-called total perspective (viz. the thesis of phenomenalogists and synthesists), but through the simultaneous dialectical positing of atomistic, meta and synthetic views.

Extension of Marxism: Revival of Hegel

Dialectics is a concept of fields and no amount of Aristotlean categories can adequately describe it. Marxism finds itself bound and limited whenever sympathetic theories try to enclose it in dogmatic interpretations. On the contrary, Marxism can extend *ad infinitum* within the Hegelian background. Since Marxism stands on the solid dialectical foundations, it has nothing to loose from its critics, for their attack is mostly of the nature of self-reflection. Marxism has been appropriated by the Soviet, Chinese, Cuban, Vietnamese, East European and other cultures, but none of these traditions can claim the exclusive priesthood of Marxism. Perhaps the most appropriate concept to designate the totality of matter, which is the other name for mind, is the field concept which includes all states of form and still persists in vacuum also. It is needless to assert that Lukacs' *History and Class Consciousness* (1923) and the rediscovery of Marx's *Economic and Philosophical Manuscripts of 1844*, have revived Hegel, for Marx and Hegel are the two sides of the same coin. Perhaps dogmatic interpretation of Marxism exclusively based either on economic determinism or historical materialism has done more harm to Marxism than is often realised. The elucidation of Marxism ha not found support in the formulation of the theories of infrastructure but on the other hand, in the projection of literary superstructure. During the twentieth century, Marxism finds its extension in Lukacs' *Theory of the Novel* as well as in his *History and Class Consciousness*, in Ernst Bloch's *Hope the principle*, in Benjamin's *Origins of German Tragedy*, in Adorno's *Philosophy of the New Music*, and in *Negative Dialectics,* and in Sartre's *Critique of Dialectical Reason*. Some of the dogmatic followers who love Aristotlean logic of 'yes' and 'no' place Marxism directly opposite to liberalism, empiricism, and logical positivism. They try to have their own feudal circles and proclaim it as Marxist culture. Marxist attitude is dialectical, which is the same as that of a scientist, who appreciates liberal freedom but opposes its exclusive individualistic traits, approves measurability of empiricism but cannot accept its findings as final and as the whole truth; and adores simplicity and economy of logical positivism but cannot be party to reductionist fallacy.

Another way of dogmatising Marxism is to denounce all Anglo-American thinking as non-dialectical and to emphasise that only German and French traditions are capable of dialectical thought. Whenever dialectics is brought down from the universal to the particular and individual levels, it gets dogmatised and individualism triumphs as the champion of empty liberty. Why should Karl Marx insist: "The Communists are further reproached with desiring to abolish countries and nationality," and "What else does the history of ideas prove than that intellectual production changes its character in proportion as material production is changed," and further "Communism abolishes eternal truths, it abolishes all religion and all morality, instead of constituting them on a new basis, it therefore, acts in contradiction to all past historical experience."[12] In the case of communsitic thought which in fact is the dialectical thought, one can hardly separate the political from the economic, or the ideological from the cultural.

Sartre deserves praise for reiteration of the theory of mediation in his *Critique of Dialectical Reason,* which was a mere extension of Hegel's logic. All such attempts to break forth from the narrow bounds of Aristotlean logic and to unify the particularities and individualities, so as to bring them on the level of universals is dialectical and communistic. Ideology is a mere individual abstraction of the universals and science of dialectics acts as an eternal reservoir. No wonder all those who profess to be neo-Hegelian idealists, simple revisionists, existentialists, new leftists, and from extreme left deviationists to ultra-Bolshevists—all are Marxists. What a wonder, there exist all shades of Marxists in the world today, each answering to the specific needs and problems of its own socio-economic systems. Industrial revolution ushered in the mainstreams of industrial and peasant Marxisms and the post-industrial revolution[13] is bound to break forth the developed and developing categories of Marxism, but those who boast of Beyond Marxism, are living in fool's paradise. Dialectics knows how to unfold the relationships of the parts to whole, of the concrete and the abstract, and between the subject and the object, but followers of Aristotle can hardly get out of mechanistic inertial reference identifications.

Dialectical Coordinates

Karl Marx rightly identified all cultural phenomena as superstructure, and since Marxist logic rests on the socio-economic base it gradually came to be known as infra-structure. "In spectroscopy all greater wave-lengths beyond visible spectrum" are called infra-red structures and smaller wavelengths prior to the visible spectrum are labelled as ultra-violet structures. Mesons which are known to keep the uncleus of an atom intact belong to infra-red spectrum and electrons which decide the chemical behaviour of the atoms belong to the ultra-violet spectrum. Hegel was right when he contemplated the evolution of state, starting from the family as the basic unit of infra-structure and the corporate life as basic unit of ultra-structure. One may very well treat the social corporate life as the extension of cultural phenomena. Our social sciences, on the other hand, have coined functional adjuncts as structural ones, i. e. socio-economic functions are equated to infra-structure ? Perhaps social sciences can have a lasting gain if they accept structures of family and society as basic and allot them the appropriate categories of infra and ultra-structures. It seems there is a temptation on the part of over-enthusiastic theoreticians to treat super-structure as ontological and infra-structure as atomistic, the obvious consequencs of such speculations are mere imaginary or symbolic resolution of political contradictions.

One may contend, with certain reservations, that a sociology of literature and culture can trace their origins in the ancient romantic mythology,[14] as relations of production are linked with the invention of history. But all such theorization may not affect the unity of political visible spectra. To account for both evolutionary as well as revolutionary developments, one must fully understand the relativity of infra and ultra dimensions, i.e. four-fold continuum of socio-economic base and political cultural super-structure. This answers all those who advocate 'value free' approach in political science, which at best can be a kind of an optical illusion. Dialectical consciousness can certainly shatter the syntactic or static thoughts but it cannot escape the subject-predicate trap, if it fails to realise unity of mind and matter. A binary system of conceptualisation, where mind and matter are treated as two incommensurable realities, two independent codes, or systems of signs, two symmetrical terms, may be an operational convenience. But in fact, both mind and matter represent one and same entity, subject to same laws of evolution, entropy, and conservation, and undergo transformations, through the same states. Dialectics in this sense of non-dual Identity goes beyond the language of causality and often treats objectivity making use of analogy or homology. It often happens that it is near the truth but far from common fashionable marketable commodities. One must recall the discovery of electro-dynamic laws by Faraday, who was not at all accustomed to Newtonian system. Since he did not receive a regular college education, free from the traditional way of thinking, he felt that the introduction of the field as an independent element of reality might help to coordinate the experimental facts. The same is true about the dialectics.

Whatever is perceived or projected, is actual but not real, for what is perceived is particular and what is projected is individual. Human mind accustomed to binary mechanism oscillates between the atomistic reductionism (particular view) and the holistic extensionism (individual view). If we reverse the process we have a microscopic magnification and telescopic shrinkage of matter (mind). Cultural microscope gives the clear view of infra-structure, and similarly one can have a beautiful view of super-structure through a socio-economic telescope. It is not to be taken that culture is less complex than the socio-economic phenomena, but simple dialectical application can make it so. Engels was aware of such wonderful possibilities and while praising Balzac, he emphasized the need of investigating socio-economic infra-structure through the cultural ultra-spectrum: "complete history of French society from which, even in economic details (for instance, the re-arrangement of real and personal property after revolution) I have learned more than from all the professed historians, economists, and statisticians of the period together."[15] One may say with confidence that Soviet theoreticians try to dogmatise Marxism by asserting that all idealistic and metaphysical methods are hostile to Marxism. It seems that Maoist strategy of 'Cultural Revolution' has proved much more sensible than the mechanistic application of economic laws to socialism.

Marxism is certainly not a narrow spectrum of vision where everything is viewed from the exclusive window of economic determinism, which may be expedient enough but certainly ignores the idea of progress. Communism as such is not a doctrine of distributive justice or cheap economism, but an ideal of raising the mankind to a stature of universal equality. In a state of communistic super-conductivity there is complete unison, but others prefer a state of thermal chaos since it affords them many choices. For instance, Music, though a fact of super-structure, has always played a mighty harmonising role. At festivals and other community functions it often acts as a levelling force, and this is especially witnessed in the societies with primitive cultural bias. What should be the music like of the complex developed societies ? A society with socio-economic capitalist base cannot have a harmonising music, and T.W. Adorno is right when he observes that the Western music is polyphonic and unnatural. In a society where infra-structure is highly individualistic one has but to conclude safely that there must be a parallel pluralistic development of super-structure.[16] Why there is so much alienation and boredom ? To answer this question, one has simply to go back to primitive starting point from where this regressive dialectical process started leading to uneven and yet unnatural development. The Western music, which in fact is the specimen of Western super-structure, reflects the development of its infra-structure which is full of individualistic and particular contradictions. There are contradictions between state and individual, capitalists and workers, public sector and private sector, and almost every walk of life. The contradictions of super-structure are always the contradictions of the infra-structure as well. It often happens that contradictions get out of control, and the modern state with all its liberal pretensions assumes a totalitarian role. Thanks to tele-communication and computer synthesis, state machinery is powerful enough to organise people, things, and their motion into a single market-system. Thomas Mann's *Doctor Faustus* highlights such capitalist ambiguity. Thanks to one-sided projection of the capitalism, one has but to agree with Thomas Mann, that it has become "the most colossal absurdity of our epoch." What the Western scholarship adores as the liberal way of living is as much a fact of the absurdity of the capitalist socio-economic system. What is good about gross display of selfish motivations which is a kind of vulgar materialism?

Political Hermeneutics

This takes us to the realm of hermeneutics, and if we accept its perennial nature, then it refutes the claim of some scholars that dialectics was virtually a Hegel's intellectual invention. The primitive man thought that the objective external world is identical with that of spirit (*Hari*), and through the multiplicity of becoming this identity is realized. Hegel's *Phenomenology of Spirit* is just the reiteration of the immance of Identity which had confounded many Western scholars. What we call the projection of externality in the form of expanding universe, is the display of this Identity, all profoundly involved and penetrated by the immance. The *Phenomenology of Spirit* is a story of an evolutionary-entropic-conservation procession. It is an unfoldment of the successive stages through which consciousness enriches and solidifies itself. What is to be noted that how dialectics can transcend itself from the most individualistic and subjective shell to the condition of Absolute Spirit. One becomes many and includes within itself all the abundance and multiplicity of externality. There takes place the separation between the subject and object, which is only on a divisive actional plane, but in the ultimate analysis there is One non-dual Being. In our own country, this kind of logic has thousands years of tradition, but its most vocal proponent was Shankaracharya. According to Shankaracharya,[17] the actuality of existence was a mere illusion (*Maya*) and for the same reason for T.W. Adorno this kind of logic is "a thought of such boundless assertions renouncing the attempt to perpetuate itself in definitive and determinate form" which suggest a dilemma. "In the sense in which we now-a-days speak of anti-matter," and therefore, for him "the Hegelian texts are anti-texts."[18] Dialectical thought is not uncommon to Indian tradition. The famous Indian poet-saint Kabir tells us that the nature unfolds herself in a dialectical pattern. For him this dialectical drama of nature is a mighty wonder of all ages. She remains a wonder because she is neither a reproduction nor a creation. She has no foundation and therefore, whatever exists in her is merely a kind of relativity. She seems to be devoid of discrimination and her heavy roller of blind necessity levels all, sparing neither the sinner nor the virtuous. She is ever on the run of the cycle of life not to make the life eternal, but to dance a cruel dance of murder and transitoriness. She is expert in hide-and-seek game, for a while she displays her macro form and then switches on to micro one, but seldom she reveals her total naked form. She has the power over the learned and the fool and all worship and adore her. All disciplines, all research, all theories, are a tale of her fragmentary revelation. Philosophers and religious saints thought she walks and the rapid flux of her crooked becoming is the source of all sin. All of them concentrated on the notion of immutable Being against the background nature. Some thought that the Being is her creator and others took the Being as her preserver and destroyer. Some viewed the Being as the same as Becoming and treated nature as a kind of an autonomous machine having a kind of feedback system of creation, preservation and destruction. We have quoted the views of Kabir[19] in detail to bring home the fact that Hegel's otherness and Marx's alienation are nothing but the category of Indian *Maya*.

Should one take hermeneutics as political ? At least Hegel thought so and some of the Marxist writers like Benjamin, Marcuse, Schiller, Ernst Bloch, Georg Lukacs and Sartre think so. But theoreticians who follow the Moscow line hardly digest such metaphysical dialectics of transformation.[20] Those who deny political hermeneutics deny the existence of cultural environment and for them socio-economic mechanism is the sole reality. This kind of narrow approach to the world revolutionary movement can hardly be called dialectical. A consistent dialectical theory requires continuity of all elements of the theory, not only in history but also in cultural-political environment. There is hardly a linear evolution of cultural coordinates and history, but in fact there is a kind of co-variance of infra and super-structures. When disciplines are classified as infra and super-structure subjects, than they have their group properties. Dialectics and the theory of social evolution are not contradictory theories, for transition from one system to another irrespective of immediate socio-economic as well cultural-political coordinates, subscribed by both. The partial dialectics following the doctrine of economic determinism believes in a simplification that those who own means of production control the state machinery as well, which is somewhat mechanistic equivalence of inertia and gravitational mass. However the dialectical principle of equivalence is different; it is the equivalence of cultural-political environment and socio-economic base, a process of non-linear transformations of the four coordinates. The fundamental investigations of Gauss and Riemann had suggested and Lorentz transformations agree that in a case of group transformation all continuous transformation of the coordinates take place. In social sciences, dialectics also believes in the continuous flow of cultural, political, economic and social coordinates.

One of the basic problems contemplated by Newton was: why inertia resists acceleration ? Two centuries later, in social context, Karl Marx framed the same question: why capital resists change ? Within the framework of classical mechanics, the only answer which Newton could get was that inertia resists acceleration relative to space and, therefore, concluded *spatium est absolutum*. Since cultural-political framework acts as a kind of environment to socio-economic activities, the Newtonian assertion was akin to Hegelian thesis of Idea is absolute. Karl Marx, on the contrary, took not the spatial environment as absolute but the matter as absolute which later on came to be identified wrongly with the infra-structure. In hermeneutics, Idea and Matter, are one and the same thing but when Idea or matter take to operational flight, it has infra and super-structural wings.

Hermeneutic ideas have a peculiar force of not only taking the consciousness to transverse illumination but also they act as transforming agents of the infra and super-structures. Why it is so, perhaps when reality of life is presented in its most naked form, it has a revolutionary impact. Let us have a cursory glance of such ideas. Benjamin states "that the writer shrouds in silence: namely, that passion lose all its rights, under the laws of genuine human morality, when it seeks to make a pact with wealthy middle class security."[21] Schiller subscribes "As long as we were merely the children of Nature, we were both happy and complete; we became free, and lost both. Whence a double and most unequal longing for Nature, a longing for her *bliss*, a longing for her *completeness*. Only sensual man bemoans the loss of the first; only ethical man mourns that of second."[22] Herbert Marcuse contends "our culture must lead us back to Nature along the path of Reason and Freedom. They are therefore the representation of our lost childhood that which will eternally remain dearest to us."[23] Ernest Bloch wishes us to contemplate: "Just as the darkness of the lived instant represents one pole of conscious anticipation and of the anticipating disposition of the world as well, so also material astonishment, with that outright adequation which is its content, constitutes the other one; and each tugs powerfully at the other, the symbolic intentions of the Supreme and the Omega imply the darkness of the Alpha."[24] George Lukacs philosophises: it is the epic of a world abandoned by God," and the "negative mysticism of godless epochs."[25] Hegel was no fool to peg his tent amidst the sky, far from the earthly inertial well, all twentieth century space research and earthly observation follows Hegelian methodology of satellite communication.

Marxism projected as negative infinite

So far we have projected Marxism as Phenomenon of Identity, ever expanding and yet devoid of any limitations. Many superficial theories have been framed to discredit Marxism, mostly based on the logic of consistency, since its substance, the mystical kernel remains beyond the reach of such critics. There are a few who follow non-Aristotlean logic, who take Marxism as a kind of a semantic state: "I see communism as a semantic state conceived by Karl Marx, nurtured by Lenin, and sovietized in Russia. Who will deny that these semantic states, and similar ones, were real forces in shaping world history?"[26] One might agree that fascism is a kind of a semantic state, for there is conscious effort to make one leader a dictator, equate him with the entire nation, suppress the entire opposition, and to bring about one party rule, and finally to foster state economic controls, but to describe Marxism on the similar lines is a travesty of truth. What one comes across in recent political thought is a kind of conscious effort to theorise to project Marxism either as an ideology of mechanistic nature, or as a system which is neither feasible nor viable. Any ideology is an abstraction andas such has the contents of partial truth and any system is a continuum and as long as the coordinates remain the system remains.

David Easton in his preface to *A System Analysis of Political Life* views politics not as specimen of infra-structure rather than a phenomenon of super-structure; "I explore in detail what may be called the life processes of a political system, those kinds of functions through which it performs its characteristic work as a political system. I continue to view political life as a system surrounded by a variety of environments. Because it is an open system, it is constantly subject to possible stress from these environments." It is questionable whether David Easton stumbled at the living political system or not but what is the purpose of such one-sided projections: "Our problem will be the deceptively simple one: How does it come about that any type of system can persist at all, even under the pressures of frequent or constant crises?" What are the tools with which he expected to withold the mighty tide of change? The same old art of abstractions: "theory building is like a good photography" and one might ask him very well, from where the dimension of depth perception comes in a photo? Obviously the purpose and strategy for such theorizing is to prevent social change and David Easton is honest enough to confess his Platonic design: "In its ideal and most powerful form, a general theory achieves maximal value when it constitutes a deductive system of thought so that from a limited number of postulates, assumptions and axioms, a whole body of empirically valid generalizations might be deduced in descending order of specificity. It is for this reason that mathematical formulation of general theory is often cited as the optimum mode of expression."[27] Apparently this system is an exercise to create a machine with a kind of feedback system so as to give purpose and direction to limited probabilities within it. There is no room for Leibnian contingency or dialectical expansion of horizon, but a purpose to bring the range of theoretical inquiry within manageable bounds. It also implies marshalling all loose theories into sub-systems of an heirarchy. It endeavours to construct a functional framework of concepts for the analysis of presumed static political system. What is strange in all such theorising is that while Hegel and Karl Marx recognised the appropriate structures and therefore, constructed their system around the actuality of Spirit or matter, but Lasswell, Kaplan, David Easton and others of their empirical tribe have taken up the husk as the spirit, and intend thereby to invert the conceptual structures. David Easton admits that "What frequently passes for theory in social research consists largely of the investigation of alternative concepts, dispute about their utility, their clarity, and implications."[28] One might ask David Easton then, what is the difference between medievial scholastic and modern empirical approach, if both are not different designs to serve the same ends? What is menacing about all such regimental approaches is that it emphasises on particularities rather than the professed general system approach, "conceptual analysis rather than the formulation of generalizations." The strategy is the same as Nazi training of troops, the coordination of their muscles and mind through intensive physical drill. Let us regulate the senses and through them we shall regulate the receptors. The banner of discarding generalizations is raised, for no empirical verifications can establish them. The immediate task, therefore, is the discovery of right type of particularities, i.e. concepts which can produce a general theory. Since concepts themselves cannot build a system, we find ourselves face to face against neo-teleology. David Easton suggests: "To select some value as the organizing principle and to construct a body of concepts and propositions around it." This kind of projection of the unconscious to exploit the conscious is known to our theoreticians as the Normative Approach. To support its credibility, Easton cites the example of the capitalist value of maximizing profit, which has already paid considerable dividends, and why not use 'democracy' as a kernel of the Western system?

Democracy has become a semantic state in the West and it continues to serve as an ethical focus despite the fact that representation is not representiveness. Exploiting this republican myth, a normative theory using democracy as a focus is presented as a general theory of politics. What are the possible necessities which compel Easton and others to revive Platonic ethical myths in new forms? Marxist socio-economic structures in the communist countries are not holding any immediate threat to capitalism but Marxist cultural-political environment is proving extremely hostile, and therefore, the central problem is "How can any political system ever persist whether the world be one of stability or of change ?" Hegel to cement the bonds of state had stated "state is an ethical idea," and for that reason Hegel if often accused as the proponent of fascism. Can Western democracies escape the same charge? To prevent the Marxian onslaught of change, Easton is not preaching that "state is a march of God on earth" but projects the idea that all that is possibly worthwhile is the Western democracy, and all else is a design of the devil. The consequences are, one is forced to view everything from the narrow and arbitrary spectrum. We are given to understand that there is no possibility of political anthropology as a discipline. Let us maintain the analytic distinction between political and other forms of social behaviour, and the possibility of return to primitive communism shall be negated. One of the odd corollary of such system approach is "what is social is political" and therefore 'political behaviour' can be linked with other aspects of social relations. What is absurd about such an inertial system projecting only two coordinates is that it ignores the other important and unavoidable coordinates, i.e. cultural and economic, by doing so, it hopes to sustain the illusion of the persistence of vision that there is no change. Thanks to Western scholarship which presents Marxism as deity incarnate of Becoming, since there is equivalence of Being and Becoming, Marxism cannot be devoid of its eternal contents.

If Marxism is unscientific, then there is no necessity to

imitate scientific theories to counter its threat. Political science at its inception depended heavily on history, but soon history was discarded being taken as a Marxist bias. Now empirical research implied break with generalised history and constructions of functional models. The study of state machinery, i.e. government became the subject matter of political science. In functional approach one faces the flux of variables, and political science was, therefore, engulfed in an identity crisis. In the 1930s the Chicago School, under the leadership of Charles Merriam, inducted behaviourial research in political science. It was contemplated that scientific theories can be used to develop the institutions of governments and the science of psychology can play a key role in political research by serving as an index of human behaviour. All this was done taking the Western democracy as the finality. New techniques of legislative and electoral analysis were invented. The entire scientific methodology was reduced to one behavioural mechanism, which in itself was in an embryo state. Twentieth century science has invented sophisticated array of instruments to multiply the power of perception. For example telescope, microscope, stethoscope, X-rays, oscilloscope, Geiger counter, radar, radio, television, transistor, electron microscope, Tiros satellite and other instruments have brought home the fact that the actuality of objectivity is far from mechanistic one to one correspondence. When Aristotlean terminology was found inadequate classical science added such terms like factor, variable, attraction, repulsion, analysis, field of force, dynamics, progress, evolution, interaction, vector, environment and other related ones. Obviously acceptance of behaviourial approach in political science was with a view to serve the ultimate normative end of safeguarding the democracy. It is true that all such empirical abstractions serve the limited purpose of accurate measurement of political phenomenon within the narrow inertial framework sometimes, but can rarely accomplish the feat of scientific generalizations to stall the portending change. One can understand why the scientific thought led by Russell, Whitehead, Bridgman, Bentley, Bachelard, Karl Popper, Mach, Wiener, Shannon, von Berta-lanffy, and the Vienna Circle had surroundered themselves to Einsteinian relativity, but in political science mechanistic trends were reinforced. The half-baked psychometrics with which political science started its empirical revolution was soon converted into ethical semantic reactor of political behaviour. According to Heinz Eulau political analysis was "those perceptual, motivational, and attitudinal components which made for political identifications, demands and expectations, and his systems of political beliefs, values, and goals." Like his dogmatic counterparts, Lasswell thought, politics was but an exercise in cheap economism, where investigations remain within the narrow framework of who gets what, when and how. It seems dacoits, thiefs and smugglers have become politicians. At the academic level, behavioural jargons proved more abstruse than Hegelian thought and its avowed purpose of training citizens to understand government mechanism and to elicit their participation in democratic process, proved futile.

Despite its earlier failure, surprisingly enough behaviouralism was revived again in the fourth generation (1940-1960). One must ask, what is the secret of behaviouralism emerging victorous on every battle-field of political science? It is a well known fact that social sciences were trying to march abreast of natural sciences, and therefore, were gripped with the fascination of some kind of general and unified theory. Keeping in view this objective, ideas of developmentalism, social-system approach, structuralism and functionalism, and interactionism came into vogue. Karl Marx had suggested to transcend the blind economic forces of capitalism and to plan economy in a way to usher in socialism, but twentieth century social scientists went a step ahead and started manipulating political machinery to prevent change. The government as the nucleus of social system has become an unconscious end where conscious objective is to use an individual as mechanical automata fed on patterns of choice interdependence but without independence. Thanks to invention of behaviourial psychometirics, an individual in the Western democracies is left at the mercy of powerful centralised state machinery, operated through intelligence agencies. With increasing quantum of individual ignorance and stupefying complexity of modern problems, the state machinery, a tool in the hands of few is an exclusive arbitrator of everything. An individual is expected to be Aristotlean social animal but not Marxian political one. Behaviouralism being an atomstic and reductionistic approach has found its limitations, but in normal times, it is a handy tool of decision making for the state machinery. Political scientists are making efforts in this direction, and daily they are inventing new theories "to legitimize a political order, existing or potential."[29] The very fact of the perpetual search for theory building is a proof that the mighty challenge of Marxism remains.

Hegel and Karl Marx believe that the spirit (matter) following the pattern of evolution and revolution, perpetually cast as under the husk of dead political forms. But in the West democracy is a sancrosanct cow, which enjoys the reputation of a political system where stability persists. What kind of equivalence one finds in this inertial system which enables it to have such boastful claim of permanence. According to Robert A. Dahl, it has some functional as well as structural institutions which keep its equivalence intact and, therefore, promote continuum. If we follow the principle of inertial and mass equivalence, then we may infer that universal suffrage, two-party system, and frequent alterations in office from one party to the other as electoral majority, etc. are inertial institutions. On the other hand, mass institutes of participation in elections, opportunity to criticise, the conduct and policies of officials, and freedom to seek support for one's views, are mass institutions. According to Tocqueville, stability of the system is due to peculiar American culture, and Robert A. Dahl stretches further this hypothesis by concluding that there is a persistence of stability because of the existence of "the universal belief in a democratic creed." It is stated that in the United States, the great bulk of the citizens possess a fairly stable set of democratic beliefs at a high level of abstractions; and citizens have come to belief "that the American political system is consistent with democratic creed." What keeps the system going is a reversibility of choice: "widespread adherence to the democratic creed is produced and maintained by a variety of powerful social processes," and "despite wide agreement on a general democratic creed, however, citizens frequently disagree on specific applications, most of the members of the political stratum agree as to the democratic norms; professionals have acquired high political skill; and on all disagreements or rules and procedures legitimacy is sought."[30] How long this consensus on the democratic creed is likely to last ? Robert A. Dahl himself is aware of the transiency of such semantic stability: "Neither the prevailing consensus, the creed, nor even the political system itself are immutable products of democratic ideas, beliefs, and institutions inherited from the past. For better or worse, they are always open, in some measure, to alteration through those complex processes of symbiosis and change that constitutes the relations of leaders and citizens in a pluralistic democracy."[31] Nevertheless the West is possessed with the spirit of negative infinite. "Now a days, the *Republican* form of government is considered as the best constitution, to the jargon of democrats, it is vehemently supported by the aristocracy, and the rich elite alike, for it invariably saddles them in power; such a constitution, though the best, cannot be realized under all circumstances; and that, while men are what they are ... satisfied with less freedom."[32]

Our treatment of recent political theories is far from exhaustive for want of space and keeping in view the relevance of the topic, but examples can be multiplied to establish the thesis that Western scholarship is obsessed with Marxism as a philosophy of change, and the change is what they dread most. What is significant in these developments, is the fact that unlike the earlier philosophers, political scientists are not concerned with the description of the system, but believe in active manipulation of politics not only to prevent change at home but also bring a favourable change abroad to promote their system. International relations have acquired a special significance in the twentieth century. All such system theories are normative abstractions with view to bring about coordinate transformations within democratic inertial system and therefore rest on special relativity and may not last for long. Marxism, with Hegelian background, assumes the role of general relativity, it is not impossible to introduce arbitrary continuous transformations as the idea of class struggle and therefore, Marxism can annul the capitalist socio-economic relationships.

Conclusion

The question, what is eternal, is often contemplated as viewing the Time-dimension either as infinite or denying the process of becoming altogether. The empirical Western mind normally takes the eternity as infinite duration. Anything which appears as continuum of succession and duration, without limits and proceeds *ad infinitum* is eternal. For that matter the concept of universe itself can be taken as eternal. In other words, the process of Becoming itself is eternity. One has simply to discover that the Becoming is nothing but another name for dialectical unfoldment of universe, then Marxism automatically attains eternal dimensions.

Another way of contemplating the eternal is to deny the existence of Becoming altogether and treat Being as immutable, an approach of negative infinite. In other words, this refers to Hegelian phenomenology of Spirit, where Spirit remains Spirit, despite the fact it moves from nothing to nothing (the process of Becoming). What is non-dual is taken as eternal. But the affirmation of Being is also the affirmation of Becoming, if Being is eternal so is the process of Becoming. Human thinking is conditioned to circularity, and can at best view eternity either as continuum or as metaphysical immutability. In the empirical perspective of continuum one finds eternity reduced to an infinite succession of moments of duration. In other words, here we find actuality of Time spread out in the potentiality of Space, and what can possibly extend itself here is the background of Space. Newton also believed the same and took Space as absolute. On the other hand, in meta-perspective, one finds the potentiality of Time as immanent within the actuality of sub-divided Space, and therefore, eternity is supposed to stand still as a focus. Aquinas discriminates between the now of Time and now of eternity, somewhat akin to flowing Becoming and immutable Being. This kind of meta view of eternity is supported by Christian theology, Plato, Plotinus, Shankracharya, Sufis, Zen Buddhists and other spiritual traditions. Twentieth century science has discovered that space and time are not exclusive entities, thereby rejecting Newtonian contention of Space is absolute. There appears a strange and yet prototype of meta view of eternity in the form of Space-Time four dimensional continuum. In other words, in all our abstractions of space we are unconsciously aware of Time, and in all our abstractions of Time is conditioned on unconscious awareness of Space. This mechanism of reversibility is the cleverness of nature; and what is immediate and standing still is taken as eternal by the finite human perception. Space-Time four dimensional continuum is eternal in this sense.

According to Einstein, if we have a set of coordinates and continuous coordinate transformation takes place, we have a lasting system. This system, apparently follows the dialectical principle of equivalence. Karl Marx's contribution to the notion of infra-structure and Hegelian notion of super-structure, has a powerful potency to generate a symmetrical tensor field as well as non-symmetrical tensor field in social systems. Since politics is confined only to the sphere of Becoming, here we can term anything as eternal which possibly can acquire the character of continuum of duration and succession. Here transcendence of Spirit is a contingency, but socio-economic and cultural-political transformations, is an acturality. It is impossible to demolish dialectics which operates on a field pattern. The entire Western system of democracy can collapse if the dialectical contents of 'competiton' are taken away, for the same reason, socialist systems also need 'cultural revolutions'. The acceptance of evolution and denial of the possibility of revolution by Western scholars has given Marxism an eternal dimension. Marxism reinforced by metaphysical dialectics has both negative and positive demensions, and therefore, its denial as well as affirmation, both contribute towdars its eternity.

REFERENCES

[1] Korzbski in his work *Manhood and Humanity* (New York, 1921) has developed the notion that plants live by 'binding energy'; animals, in addition to being energy-binders are also space-binders; and man is the only being who is not only energy-and space-binder but also 'time-binder', This is certainly an improvement on the physical and behavioural homeokinesis view of Darwin, Mendal, Sechenov, Freud, Sherrington, Pavlov, Jackson, Wertheimer, Kohler, Papez, Hebb, McCulloch, G. Harris, Gesell and Piaget, for their concept of man is at best is that of 'a biological being chemically driven'.

[2] See Hegel's *Philosophy of Natnre*, where starting from inanimate matter Hegel dialectically arrives at life and finally at Spirit.

[3] Hegel in his *Science of Logic* describes Notion as "the *dialectical movement* of *substance* through causality and reciprocity in the immediate *genesis* of the Notion, the exposition of the process of its Becoming. But the significance of its *Becoming*, as of every becoming, is that is is the reflloction of the transient into its *ground* and that at first apparent *other* into which the former has passed constitutes its

truth.   Accordingly the Notion is the *truth* of substance; and since substance has *necessity* for its specific mode of relationship, freedom reveals itself as the *truth of necessity* and as *the mode* of *relationship proper to the Notion*".

4 Marxism has been equated to an ideology and in the writings of S.M. Lipset, E. Shils, C. I. Waxman, A. Sehlesinger, M. White, D. Bell, Raymond Aron, Talcott Parsons, J. K. Galbraith, W.W. Rostow, P.A. Sorokin, and others one finds a concerted at attack the concept of ideology.

5 Karl Marx's preface to the first edition of *Das Capital*.

6 Ibid.

7. Albert Einstein, "On the Generalized Theory of Gravitation", *Scientific American*, vol. 188, No. 4, April 1950, pp. 13-4. This dis-covery of Einstein certainly refutes the positivist attack on Marxism. But the positivists and logical positivists, from Kant to Karl Popper attack indeterminism knowing fully well that indeterminism is a fact of existence and cannot be dispensed with. Their basic contention derives from David Hume. Recently Russell and Wittengenstein have lent them support.

8 Joseph Campbell, *The Masks of God: Oriental Mythology* (London, 1962), p. 9.

9 Ibid., pp. 9-10.

10 According to Lieh Tzu : "There is a Creative Principle which is itself uncreated; there is Principle of Change which is itself unchanging. The uncreated is able to create life; the Unchanging is able to effect change.   That which is produced cannot but continue producing; that which is evolved cannot but continue evolving. The law of constant production and constant evolution at no time ceases to operate."

11 Descartes, Locke, Hobbes, Gassendi, Galileo, Newton, Kant, Mill and others reject dialectics as theory of potentiality and, therefore, take it out of touch with fact or experience. Bacon states: "So great quan-tity of matter and infinite agitation of wit" but it ends in "hair-split-ting" or "logic chopping". For Kant dialectics at best can be a general logic, which always remain a logic of illusion.

12 Karl Marx, *Communist Manifesto*, Ch. II.

13 The synthesis of computer and telecommunication has ushered in a new technological revolution in the twentieth century, which is known as post-industrial revolution. Some of its speculators are: Lewis Mumford, Siegfried Giedion, Jacques Ellul, Harold Adams Innis, Marshall McLuhan, Norbert Wiener, and R. Buckmaster Fuller.

14 In India *Ramayana* and *Mahabharta* are such outstanding examples.

15 Marx and Engels, *Uber Kunst und Literatur* (Berlin, 1953), p. 122.

16 William James attacked Hegelian subjectivity as a kind of pluralistic mystic, but ironically the Western system itself is a living example

of the Pluralistic escalation of Notion.

[17] In the *Vedanta Sutras of Badaryana* and *Crest Jewel of Wisdom*, Shankarcharya argues Brahama's creative activity as a mere sport, and, therefore, all doctrines of creation at best can be a description of the apparent world, and Nescience must persist.

[18] T. W. Adorno, *Drei Studien zu Hegel* (Frankfurt, 1957), p. 136.

[19] In this connection, see *The Bijak of Kabir* and especially the *Ramainis*, where Kabir describes the features of *Maya*.

[20] For example Lev Moskvichov's, *The End of Ideology Theory: Illusions and Reality* (Moscow, 1974), is a hopeless attempt to defend the Ideology theory.

[21] Walter Benjamin, *Schriften* (Frankfurt, 1955), p. 429.

[22] Schiller, *Philosophische Schriften* (Basel, 1946), p. 226.

[23] Herbert Marcuse, *Philosophissche Shriften*, p. 210.

[24] Ernst Bloch, *Das Prinzip Hoffnung*, pp. 353-54.

[25] George Lukacs, *Theorie des Romans*, pp. 87 and 90.

[26] J. Samuel Bois, *The Art of Awareness* (Durbuques, 1966), p. 25.

[27] David Easton, *A Systems Analysis of Political Life* (New York, 1965), p. 9.

[28] Ibid., p. 10.

[29] Robert A. Dahl, *Reading in Modern Political Analysis* (Englewood Cliffs, N. J., 1968), p. 61.

[30] Ibid., pp. 219-27.

[31] Ibid., p. 223.

[32] V.P. Verma, *Political Philosophy of Hegel* (New Delhi, 1974), p. 147.

POEMS OF KARL MARX

Subrata Mukherjee

Karl Marx is generally described as a philosopher, a social scientist and a revolutionary. This is more or less an apt description of a man who did not differentiate between theory and practice and for whom revolutionary politics was as important as theorising for the revolution.

As happens with most generalisations, the one about Marx ignores some minor aspects of Marx's activities, one of them being the poet Marx. In spite of the fact that for a time in his youthful days Marx took to poetry writing seriously, this is the most neglected aspect of Marx's works.

The poetic phase of Marx was short-lived and in later life he showed little interest in his own poems, though his general interest in poems continued throughout his life. In his Middle Ages, Marx contemplated a long poem, which however did not materialise.

Marx's interest in poems may be attributed to many factors. This is of interest because the young Marx was passionately devoted to poetry. His interest in poems received a good deal of encouragement from Ludwig von Westphalen, to whose daughter, Jenny, Marx was subsequently married. The young Marx's literary and artistic interests received enthusiastic response from him. About this exciting relationship between two men, one young and the other old, yet guided by similar interest, Berlin writes:

> He [Westphalen] belonged to the generation dominated by the great figures of Goethe, Schiller and Holderlin, and under their influence had wandered beyond the aesthetic frontiers so strictly established by the literary mandarins in Paris, and shared in the growing German passion for the rediscovered genius of Dante, Shakespeare, Homer and the Greek tragedians. He was attracted by the striking ability and eager

receptiveness of Heinrich Marx's son, encouraged him to read, lent him books, took him for walks in the neighbouring woods and talked to him about Eschylus, Cervantes, Shakespeare, quoting long passages to his enthusiastic listener. Karl, who reached maturity at a very early age, became a devoted reader of the new romantic literature: the taste he acquired during these impressionable years remained unaltered until his death. He was in later life fond of recalling his evenings with Westphalen, during what seemed to him to have been the happiest period of his life. He had been treated by a man much older than himself on terms of equality at a time when he was in particular need of sympathy and encouragement; when one tactless or insulting act might have left a lasting mark, he was received with rare courtesy and hospitality.[1]

Undoubtedly, the most important influence on the young Marx was Westphalen. However, Marx's father, Heinrich Marx, was also interested in poetry and encouraged Marx in writing poems. He was fond of Voltaire and Racine, and they reached Marx through him. He gave a lot of support to Marx in his endeavour, though he admitted that he did not know much about poetry and that even "in the sweet days of first love" he could not write a tolerable verse.[2] Added to these were the prevailing mood, as in the early nineteenth century, poetry was considered very important in Germany, especially in bourgeoisie homes. Heinrich Heine was Marx's contemporary (Marx and Heine were close friends for some time) and was a household name in Germany. Marx himself could recite long passages of Goethe's *Faust*. He was well read in the classics, contemporary German poets and Shakespeare. His liking for Shakespeare continued throughout his life.[3]

Surprisingly and contrary to his life-long dedication to politics afterwards, during this period, the poet Marx was not interested in politics. Marx, at this time, when many university students were being punished for political reasons, was a member of a poet's club (very likely the club had some political connotations, but it seems Marx was not aware of this and was a member only as a poet) and a tavern club. It seems that his first year in the Bonn University was very pleasant with his poetic activities. Marx's father was happy at the news of the poet's club and wrote to Marx at the beginning to 1836:

> Your little circle pleases me. . .better than the tavern. Young people who find pleasure in such a gathering are necessarily educated men and have a better sense of their worth as future good citizens.[4]

But when Marx wanted him to bear the cost of his first collection of poems, he advised Marx restraint. He wrote to Marx:

> A poet, a writer, must these days know that he has something sound to offer if he wants to appear in public. . .I will tell you frankly that I am delighted by your talents. . .but I would grieve to see you appear before the public as a common pietaster. . . . Only an outstanding man has the right to lay claim to the attention of a pampered world. . .[5]

When Marx moved from Bonn to Berlin, his interest in poems continued. At Berlin he felt more distant from Jenny and his poet friends of Bonn, and put most of his energies in writing poems. At Berlin he also attempted a fiction and a tragedy. The attitude and thinking of Marx, when he went to Berlin from Bonn, is described by Marx himself in a letter of a year later to his father. He writes:

> When I left you a new world had come into my existence, that of love, and at first indeed a hopeless love, drunken with longing. Even the journey to Berlin, which in other circumstances would have delighted me extremely, exciting me to the observation of nature and kindling the joy of life, left me cold, indeed put me into a remarkably bad humour, for the rocks which I saw were not more rugged, more insurgent than the emotions of my soul, the wide cities not livelier than my blood, the inn-tables not more overladen, more indigestible than the bundle of fantasies I carried nor finally, was art so beautiful as Jenny.
> Arrived in Berlin, I broke every existing connection, paid few and reluctant visits and tried to bury myself in science and art.
> My state of mind being what it was, lyrical poetry was my

first resort, at least it was the pleasentest and lay nearest.[6]

In Berlin, lyric poetry occupied the major portion of Marx's efforts and time. Unfortunately Marx's poems written in Bonn and in the autumn of 1836 in Berlin (all the poems written in Berlin were dedicated to Jenny) are lost. The poems that survive were written in early 1837. In this period Marx also attempted a fiction and a tragic play. Marx made unsuccessful attempts to publish these poems. In Marx's life-time only two of his poems were published in Berlin's *Athenaeum*, in January 1841.

As we have already mentioned, poems of Marx are the least known works of Marx. For a long time these were thought to be lost, as truly a host of them are. In 1929 sixty of his poems were discovered and published. But even after their discovery there was not much of interest in Marx's poems. There are several reasons for this neglect.

In his later life, Marx himself was not very enthusiastic about his poems. In fact, he was critical of them. Just after his interest in writing poems declined, Marx himself wrote about his poems:

In accordance with my position and whole previous development, purely idealistic. A remote beyond, such as my love, became my heaven, my art. Everything grew vague, and all that is vague lacks boundaries. Onslaught against the present, broad and shapeless expressions of unnatural feeling, constructed purely out of the blue, the complete opposition of what is and what ought to be, rhetorical reflections instead of poetic thoughts but perhaps also a certain warmth of sentiment and a struggle for movement characterise all the poems in the first three volumes I sent to Jenny. The whole horizon of a longing which sees no frontiers assumed many forms and frustrated my effort to write with poetic consciousness.[7]

Marx, in an assesment of his intellectual career in 1859. condemned his earlier works, except the following four:

(*a*) *The Poverty of Philosophy* (1847)
(*b*) *Manifesto of the Communist Party* (1848)

(*c*) *A Speech on Free Trade* (1848)
(*d*) *An Unfinished Series of Newspaper Articles Entitled Wage-Labour and Capital* (1849)

Not only he omitted his poems but also excluded from his list the well-known works like the *Economic and Philosophical Manuscripts* (1844), the *Holy Family* (1845) and *The Thesis on Feuerbach* (1845). Marx, however, did mention the manuscript of the *German Ideology* (1846) without naming it. But he also mentioned that he and Engels gladly abandoned it. Three years before his death, Marx was sounded on the eventual publication of his complete works. On this move, he reportedly said that "they will first have to be written".[8]

This neglect of Marx of his own works, including his poems, is to be explained by the nature of Marxian philosophy. Marxism is a guide to action and not merely to contemplation and Marx, true to his philosophy, was also a revolutionary. As Parsons remarks:

I suggest that the essential Marx was not the philosophical Marx, or the economic Marx, or the humanistic Marx, or the socialistic Marx, or even the prophetic Marx, though he was surely all of those, but the revolutionary Marx. The revolutionary Marx had his start in the young Marx and continued passionately until the day he died.[9]

Because of this Marx was interested only in the works which had a direct bearing and impact on the socialist movement of his time and consequently ignored the less important (i.e. less revolutionary) writings, including the poems. What Saint-Simon realised in the early 1820's (i.e. more industrialisation need not necessarily lead man towards the worse, but on the contrary in a changed polity, to the better) found its fuller expression in Marx, who laid down the outline for bringing the necessary change and worked for the change. As Berger puts it:

The publication of the Communist Manifesto in 1848 was the first full exposition of the new revolutionary attitude. Paris of the Commune of 1871 was the first battlefield, the Russian Revolution of 1917 was the first victory.[10]

The self-criticism of Marx and his revolutionary activities, without the mention of his lesser works like the poems made it obvious to Marxist scholars that they are insignificant and unimportant in the evaluation of Marxist thought.

The second important reason for their continued neglect is the opinion of Franz Mehring, who thought the poems to be unimportant. Mehring writes about them:

In general these youthful poems breathe a spirit of trivial romanticism, and very seldom does any true note ring through. In addition the technique of their verse is more clumsy and helpless than it had a right to be after Heine and Plateu had both sang. Thus the artistic talent which Marx possessed in great measure and which later expressed itself in his scientific works began to develop along peculiar by-paths. In the figurative power of his language Marx rose to the level of the greatest masters of German literature and he attached great value to the aesthetic harmony of his writings, unlike those poor spirits who regard a dry-as-dust style as the first condition of scholarly achievement; but still, the gift of verse was not amongst the talents placed in his cradle by the muses.[11]

The third important reason seems to be the timing of the discovery of the bulk of Marx's poems. The poems were rediscovered at the same time when the famous *Economic and Philosophical Manuscripts of 1844* was also discovered. As that book is much more important than Marx's poems, all the attention was diverted to the examination of the *Manuscripts* after its discovery, rather than to a critical and comprehensive analysis of Marx's poems.[12] This neglect of Marx's poems continuep even now.

Marx's poems, compared to his monumental later writings, are less significant. Some critics even go to the extent of commenting that they are read only because Marx wrote them. Demetz considers them to be artistically insignificant.[13] There is little doubt that most of his poems are romantic in character. But all these need not diminish the significance of his poems from an analytical point of view. These poems call for examination, not as poems only, but also as a part of Marx's literature, and also as, whether there are indications of Marxism in these poems or are they outside the mainstream of Marx's thought ?

McLellan argues that Marx's first contact with the university brought about a great change in his views from what he expressed at his Lycee, gymnasium, that is, his school leaving essay, in which Marx outlines ideas that was to shape his whole outlook subsequently. In that essay he wrote that "we cannot always take up the profession we feel ourselves suited for; our social relations have begun more or less to crystalise before we are able to determine them." McLellan put his main argument in the following words:

No longer was he inspired by the thought of the service of humanity and concerned to fit himself into a place where he might best be able to sacrifice himself for the noble ideal; his poems of 1837, on the contrary reveal a cult of the isolated genius and an introverted concern for the building of his own personality apart from the rest of humanity.[14]

This lack of continuity between the verses of 1837 and the works of early 1840s have been pointed out by Peter Demetz as well. Demetz separates from Marx's theory, Marx's personal admiration of Greek art and his devotion to Shakespeare, Goethe and Balzac. Demetz writes:

In Marx's and Engels' written remarks upon Shakespeare one will look in vain for the slightest trace of economic determinism; there is not the faintest hint of how future Marxist critics are supposed to treat Shakespeare. That does not mean of course, that Marx and Engels did not have their opinions about Shakespeare, all their lives they spoke of him with the same unchanging, ardent, completely non-political admiration. Basically, they both were rooted so deeply in the German Shakespearean tradition that it never occured to them for a moment to motivate their personal enthusiasm, shared with whole generations of German writers, with political or economic arguments.[15]

Demetz also points out the differences in literary tastes between Marx and Engels.[16] Marx liked the classics. On the other hand

Engels' literary inclinations were for nationalistic German poetry. "Engels' was prepared to submite his personal tests and judgement to the dictates of the times and to enjoy such literature as political theory required; Marx, however, remained true to his favourite authors and to Greek art against his own theory. In matters of literary taste Marx was by no means a Marxist."[17]

Demetz, however, makes a special mention of the epigrams directed against Hegel. According to him, in them, Marx with 'surprising accuracy' found the 'central dialectic of Hegelian philosophy."[18]

Bold in his celebrated anthology of socialist verses ignores Marx's poems.[19] It seems that he does not find any 'socialism' in his poems, though he maintains that Marxist philosophy has a unique attraction for artists, "who are notoriously unreconciled to the state of the world at any given time, and who urge on society the satisfying perfection of the greatest works of art."[20]

Johnston propounds a different view.[21] He finds a continuity in the style of Marx's writings. "His love of metaphor, his use of allusions, his construction of complex sentences, all bear witness to his early exercise as a composer of verse."[22]

Further Johnston considers that Marx, outside his romantic poems developed two major themes in 1836-37, 'which foreshadows his prose writings of the early 1840's.[23]
They are:

a) Marx satairises Hegel and Hegel's predecessors in a series of epigrams. His objection to German idealism in these epigrams are clear, and that "...as early as 1837 Marx has enunciated the theme that idealist philosophy is an abstraction, divorced from the real world and blind to its own separation from reality."

b) The second major theme of Marx's satirical verses are the Philistine doctors. He also criticises the inertia of the German public. In this category, as well as in the other, Marx's hostility to abstraction and theorising is clear. Moreover, in this lauer category, specially when Marx depicts an artist with emphasis on the isolation of a creative artist in society, there are indications of his famous theory of alienation, fully developed in the 1840's.[24]

There is a great deal of truth in Johnston's analysis and arguments. The epigrams of Marx have a definite political surface, are critical of vague speculations, depict the lonely conditions of man, all the subject matters fully developed afterwards. The objectivity which we find in the later works of Marx can equally be found in these epigrams. They are not non-Marxist or anti-Marxist, but are very much in the mainstream of Marx's thought. The continuity in Marx's thought may be explained by examining his poems as well. We find in his poems a resolve to do something purposeful and meaningful, the beginning of the revolutionary Marx:

> Never can I calmly realise,
> What steadfastly grips my soul;
> Never can I rest in comfort,
> Storms forever through me roll.

This resolution, in his poems, takes a definite shape and that is to revolt against all kinds of abstractions and idealisations, so fundamental to later Marxian thought. Marx's objection to German idealism is clearly expressed in the following epigram:

> Kant and Fichte like to whirl in the other,
> Searching for a distant land;
> While I only seek to understand completely,
> What I found in the street.

Here Marx clearly repudiates the idealist theory as abstract and spells out his own preference for the materialistic and the human world. He has no love lost for the 'distant land'. His search begins and ends 'in the street'.

The unrealistic and idealistic thought of Hegel and his followers is described in the following epigram:

> Pardon us creatures of epigram,
> If we sing disagreeable turns;
> We have schooled ourselves in Hegel,
> And from his aesthetics we have not yet been purged.

Again:

Because I discovered the highest,
And found the depths by pondering;
I am roughen, like a god, I hide in darkness, like him,
Long I searched and floated over the rocking sea of thoughts,
And when I found the word, I flung fast to what I had found.

Here, in this epigram, Marx's satire is clearly understandable. It is a clear indictment against those who ignore the realities and try to project something non-existant. The hollowness of such activities is again depicted in the following one:

Words I teach in a demonically confused to-do,
And everyone may then think what he chooses.
At least he will never more be restricted by limiting fetters,
For as out of a roaring flood pouring from a projecting rock;
The poet invents the words and thoughts of his beloved,
And perceives what he thinks and thinks what he feels;
Everyone can sip the refreshing nectar of wisdom,
After all, I am telling you everything because I have told you
                                                    nothing.

These epigrams dealing with idealism and Hegelianism clearly indicate Marx's later thought. In the 1840's Marx made a seething criticism of Hegel in particular and the idealist thought in general. His philosophical process began with a criticism of Hegel. In the *Manuscripts* Marx made a thorough examination of the Hegelian system. To take one example, in the *Manuscripts*, in the following passage he makes out the general nature of Hegelian thought and its deficiencies :

Hegel's *Encyclopaedia* begins with logic, with *pure speculative thought*, and ends with *absolute knowledge*. The self-conscious and self-conceiving philosophical or absolute mind, i.e. the superhuman, abstract mind. The whole of the *Encyclopaedia* is nothing but the *extended being* of the philosophical mind its self-objectification; and the philosophical mind is nothin, but the alienated world mind thinking within the bounds og its self-alienation, i.e., conceiving itself in an abstract mannerf *Logic* is the *money* of the mind, the speculative *thought-value*. of man and of nature their essence indifferent to any real determinate character and thus unreal; *thought* which is *alienated* and abstract and which ignores real nature and man.[25]

The epigrams also say the same thing. The disagreeable tunes are sung by those who are schooled in Hegel. The discoverer is an abstract man. He is not human but is like God. The theory of abstractions lead to narrations which do not explain anything. What Marx says in the *Manuscripts*, the echo of that may be found in the epigrams. The unreal and pure abstract thought of Hegel and other idealists like Kant and Fichte as Marx conceived of them, is clearly depicted in the epigrams. Marx's search is not for abstract ideas in distant lands, but for much more grassroot things, in the streets. The denunciation of Hegelianism is clearly manifest in the epigrams. They are very much parts of Marx's Marxism.

The origins of Marxian thought can be discovered in Marx's youth. The young Marx combined sharp intelligence with a "stubborn and domineering temper, a truculent love of independence, exceptional emotional restraint, and over all a colossal, ungovernale appetite.[26] This appetite was not merely quenched by writing romantic poems. These epigrams show the other interests of Marx, which was first reflected in his school leaving essay. This was not an unnatural development for Marx. During Marx's youth Trier experienced great unrest and was "rocked by social, political and economic tensions".[27] Westphalen was a 'fervent supporter' of the views of Saint-Simon and Marx was introduced to Saint-Simon by him.[28] In these circumstances, combined with his brilliance, it is very likely that Marx did not find any solace in abstract and idealistic thought and the epigrams were the first reflections of his rejection.

His criticism of the Philistine doctors depict his social consciousness. For example:

Damnable pack of Philistine doctors,
The world to you is a bag of bones.
If you have cooled the blood with my drogen,
And felt the pulse move, for the first time
You think, "Now I have done everything,
One can live in total comfort."
For you, the lord god was a clever fellow,

To be so well-versed in anatomy.
And every flower becomes a useful tool,
Only when distilled to herbal brew.

The depiction of the Philistine doctors precede his *Theses on Feuerbach* (1845) where he presents the role of the philosophers. Analogically the useless, Philistine doctors may well be compared with the philosophers who only interpret the world and have no intention of changing it. The social consciousness, humanism and compassion for the oppressed which mark the later writings of Marx, exist in these epigrams as well.

In the writings of Marx in early 1840's the conception of alienation occupies a very important place. This theme of alienation is not absent in Marx's poems. In his 'The Player' the theme of alienation emerges indirectly:

The player strikes up on the violin,
His blond hair falling down.
He wears a sword at his side,
And a wide, wrinkled gown.
" O player, why playest thou so wild?
Why the savage look in the eyes?
Why the leaping blood, the soaring waves?
Why tearest thou thy bow to shreds?
" I play for the sake of the thundering sea,
Crashing upon the walls of the cliffs,
That my eyes be blinded and my heart burst,
And my soul resound in the depths of Hell."
" O player, why tearest thou thy heart to shreds,
In mockery? This art was given thee,
By a shining God to elevate the mind
Into the swelling music of the starry dance."
"Look now, my blood-dark sword shall stab,
Unerringly within thy soul.
God neither knows nor honours art.
The hellish vapors rise and fill the brain.
" Till I go mad and my heart is utterly changed.
See this sword—the Prince of Darkness sold it to me.
For me he beats the time and gives the signs.
Ever more boldly I play the dance of death.

"I must play darkly, I must play lightly,
Until my heart, and my violin, burst."
The player strikes up on the violin,
His blond hair falling down,
He wears a sword at his side.
And a wide, wrinkled gown.

In "The Player", the artist is completely isolated. He is alone, alienated from society. This personal theme becomes more general in *Oulanem*, a poetic tragedy. This very concept becomes alienated labour in the *Manuscripts*. In the *Manuscripts*, Marx observes, answering the question, what constitutes alienation of labour, in the following paragraph :

First, the fact that labour is external to the worker, i.e., it does not belong to his essential being; but in his work, therefore, he does not affirm himself but denies himself, does not feel content but unhappy, does not develop freely his physical and mental energy but mortifies his body and ruins his mind. The worker, therefore, only feels himself outside his work, and in his work feels outside himself. He is at home when he is not working, and when he is working he is not at home. His labour is therefore not voluntary, but coerced, it is *forced labour*. It is, therefore, not the satisfaction of a need; it is merely a means to satisfy needs external to it. Its alien character emerges clearly in the fact that as soon as no physical or compulsion exists, labour is shunned like the plague. External labour, labour in which man alienates himself, is a labour of self-sacrifice, of mortification. Lastly, the external character of labour for the worker appears in the fact that it is not his own, but someone else's that it does not belong to him, that in it he belongs, not to himself, but to another. Just as in religion the spontaneous activity of the human imagination of the human brain and the human heart, operates independently of the individual—that is, operates on him as an alien, divine or diabolical activity—in the same way the worker's activity is not his spontaneous activity. It belongs to another; it is the loss of his self.[29]

In the case of alienation, the concept gets completely transformed in this passage from what it is in "The Player". In the Player alienation is an individual phenomenon, whereas in the *Manuscripts* it takes a definite social shape. But even in this case we should not forget that the concept was known to Marx during the days of verse writing. As such, even in this case, there is a continuity in the basic theme. The transformation takes place by a more positive analysis of social institutions.

Marx's poems do not lie outside the mainstream of Marx's thought. To say that they emerge before Marxism is as hollow as to distinguish between the 'young' and the 'old' Marx. The poems were written in the formative period of Marx's life and because of this suffer from some inadequacies from a Marxist point of view. For instance, they are very different from Mao's.[30] This may be explained by the fact that Mao's poems were written within the process of revolution; on the other hand, Marx's poems were written in his formative period, when, though his direction of thought was clear, he was yet to give a comprehensive shape to his ideas and take part actively in revolutionary politics.

In this, a comparison may be made between his poems and his doctoral dissertation.[31] In the doctoral dissertation, Marx expressed his dissatisfaction with the inherent passive, mechanistic materialism and admired the 'active side' which was understood and developed by idealism. Marx criticised Democritus because of thea bsence of 'Energizing Principle'. Epicurus, on the other hand, had dealt with the subjective and the active side. In the dissertation, there is no defence of materialism as Marx developed afterwards (for instance, in the *Theses on Feuerbach*), but his denunciation of the mechanistic materialism is clear. As such, the dissertation can be taken as the beginning of Marxist analysis of materialism.

Similarly, in the epigrams, we discover his protest against idealism and Hegel. But they do not take the definite shape we find in his later works. But the criticism of idealism, which led to subsequent developments, begins in these epigrams. Similar is the case with social consciousness and alienation, though they are less manifest.

Like the dissertation, the poems of Marx were the products of Marx's youth. But the ingredients of Marx's later thought are to be found in them. There is no Marx before Marxism and consequently the poems also form a part of Marx's Marxist literature. They are in the evolutionary process of Marxist thought. *Communism and Aughburg* (1842), *On the Jewish Question* (1843), *Economic and Philosophic Manuscripts* (1844), and the monumental later writings flow in the same channel dug by the young Marx.

REFERENCES

[1] Isaiah Berlin, *Karl Marx, His Life and Environment* (New York, 1959), pp. 32-3.

[2] Quoted in Joel Carmichael, *Karl Marx, The Passionate Logician* (London, 1967), p. 20. Marx's father was delighted at Marx's gesture in submitting his poems to him for scrutiny. He also thought that the career of his son as a poet would be a good one and would enable him to earn his livelihood. A career in law for which Marx was being trained at that time, he thought would take a much longer time, whereas poets earn fame early. Marx's father even proposed a topic to him for a long literary work so that Marx would "make a name for himself as fast as he could." The theme was an episode from Prussian history, with perhaps a background of the battle of Waterloo, which was to be "patriotic, full of feeling and worked out in a genuine German spirit." Westphalen did not think very highly of Marx's poems, but his daughter, Jenny (who was 21 at that time, Marx was 17), thought them to be excellent. Sophie, Marx's sister, told Marx that when Jenny used to read any new poem of Marx, she used to "burst into tears of joy and melancholy." It may be pointed out here that two other members of the Poets' Club were Karl Grun (1817-87) who afterwards as leader of the German Proudhonist fought many battles with his former friend, and Emanuel Geibel (1815-84), who later became the poet laureate of the Bavarian court.

[3] In the early 1860s, Marx revealed his favourite poets, Shakespeare, Aeschylus and Goethe. See "The Confessions of Karl Marx," *Review,* September 1966, p. 16.

[4] Peter Demetz, *Marx, Engels and the Poets* (Chicago, 1967), p. 49.

[5] Ibid., p.49.

[6] Quoted in H. P. Adams, *Karl Marx in his Earlier Writings* (New York, 1965), p. 19.

[7] Quoted in David McLellan, *Marx Before Marxism* (New York, 1970), p. 43.

[8] Martin Nicolaus, "The Unknown Marx", *The New Left Review,* March-April 1968, p. 41.

[9] Howard L. Parsons, "The Young Marx and the Young Generation", *Horizons, The Marxist Quarterly,* No. 26, p.18.

[10] John Berger, *Success and Failure of Picasso* (Baltimore, 1965), p. 125.

[11] Franz Mehring, *Karl Marx* (Ann Arbor, 1969), p. 2.

[12] Erich Fromm, for instance, considers the *Manuscripts* as the "most articulate expression" of Marx's philosophy. See his *Marx's Concept of Man* (New York, 1972).

[13] Demetz, n. 4, p. 50.

[14] McLellan, n,7, p. 45 and 46.

[15] Demetz, n. 4, p. 151.

[16] Ibid., p. 153.

[17] Ibid., pp. 126-27.

[18] Ibid., p. 51.

[19] Alan Bold (ed.), *The Penguin Book of Socialist Verse* (Baltimore, 1970). See Introduction.

[20] Ibid., pp. 34-5.

[21] William Johnston, "Karl Marx's Verse of 1836-1837," *Journal of the History of Ideas*, April-June 1967.

[22] Ibid., p. 260.

[23] Ibid., p. 261.

[24] Ibid., p. 263.

[25] Erich Fromm, *The Economic and Philosophical Manuscripts in Marx's Concept of Man* (New York, 1972), pp. 173-74.

[26] Berlin, n. 1, p. 11.

[27] Parsons, n. 9, p. 24.

[28] "Meeting with Marx", in M. Kovaevski, *Reminiscences of Marx and Engels* (Moscow), p. 288.

[29] Fromm, n. 12, p. 28.

[30] See *The Poems of Mao Tse Tung*, translated by W. Barnstone (New York, 1972).

[31] "The Difference Between the Democritean and Epicurean Philosophy of Nature" (Marx's Ph.D. Dissertation) in N.D. Livergood, *Activity in Marx's Philosophy* (The Hague, 1967).

HANNAH ARENDT'S CONTRIBUTION TO POLITICAL THEORY

L.S. Rathore

The most creative and unparalleled of contemporaneous contributions to normative political theory and political sociology in America has not come from native Americans but from transplanted Europeans, most conspicuously and notably from Hannah Arendt (1906-1975).[1] A prolific and plenteous writer, a copious and formative author, and a generative and life-giving thinker, Arendt by abandoning the orthodox modes of American political analysis, and by putting her faith in the uniqueness and responsibility of the individual human being, had conceived an opulent lore of evaluative traditions. She was concerned less with the general conditions of freedom in society than with the freedom of the person and with the possibility, for some few persons, of achieving a sense of individual self in present day mechanized society.[2] She was greatly moved, by a sense of loss, or by what Hegel had called 'our unhappy consciousness'. She was disdainful of the modern empirical approach that found its early representatives in thinkers such as Machiavelli, Hobbes, Locke, Hume and Mill, for they have, in her views, subverted an ancient edifice of durable growth. She took the position that we were now utterly free to construct our political future, and revealed her underlying sympathy and faith in the institutions nurtured and sustained by classical political philosophy. Her special quality "was a capacity for sustained and powerful thought applied to some of the crucial experiences of our century." In our cataleptic and disintegrating society, faced with the massive intrusion of criminal violence and volcanic outbursts of fear or terror to maintain domination, combined with the mad fury towards destruction and ruin, Arendt made a zestful appeal and invocation to return to the probity of the classical tradition. A woman of enormous erudition, she had published extensively on the major problems of contemporary political theory and sociology and established her reputation as a philosopher of the first rank. Her defence of the classical tradition was scintillatingly expressed and brilliantly elaborated in a number of her writings, which have began to fructify in recent years.

During a career of almost continuous intellectual engagement, Arendt produced two of the most illuminating and profound studies of the modern experience—*The Origins of Totalitarianism* (1951) and *Eichmann in Jerusalem* (1963)—in addition to several other seminal books on politics and culture. *The Origins of Totalitarianism* is a book that surpassed all her writing in its intellectual rigour, encompassing scope and historical profundity to a rare degree. It is an imaginative and scholarly attempt to look at the emergence of the totalitarian regimes as a social and historical phenomenon of our generation, where all intermediate or secondary institutions between the leader and the 'masses' are eliminated, and the ruler, unrestrained by legal or political checks, rules by terror. Totalitarianism is held in low estimation and Arendt despises and disregards it, mainly because it retards human imagination and restrains the autonomy of the individual soul. The discretionary fetters and controlled bridles put by the totalitarian systems are injurious to the healthy development of the individual and full-bloomed advancement of mankind. Based as it is on terror and forcible subordination and servitude, it cramps human initiative, enslaves freedom and hurls the individual towards the worst kind of dependence and thralldom. Arendt, therefore, scolds totalitarianism in all its forms. *The Eichmann in Jerusalem* contains penetrating analysis of revolutions, violence, terror and other impediments that encourage pseudo-scholarship and block human progress and freedom. In another book, *The Human Condition* (1958), Arendt deals with the impact of work on the total life of the individual.[3] The book contains arresting insights, offers an encompassing interpretation of the modern 'scene', and the author attempts to describe the basic intellectual and moral orientation of modren culture and shows why that orientation is wrong. Despite its obscurities, the book is filled with trenchant comment on the forgotten moral aspects of labour and work in contemporary society. In her leading essays, *Between Past and*

Future: Six Exercises in Political Thought (1961), Arendt has sought to elucidate the emptiness of our public life, our specific alienation from public undertakings, and seeks to come to terms with the democratic and industrial revolutions, and maintains that we must act as if we have to find our existence anew, and that, to order our life and find a place in our world, we must resolve to rely on our unsupported selves. For us neither a commonly accepted metaphysics nor the memory of a shared past can give the stamp of authenticity to our day-to-day behaviour. In her volume, *On Revolution* (1963), Arendt proceeds to call attention to the great promise of public life in terms that idealize it, notwithstanding her historical approach. Vindicating unmediated public action, she romanticizes the heroic revolutionary bands whose members, all self-selected, fight simultaneously for freedom and for themselves, thus, doing justice to man's noblest aspirations. They are, in the words of Arendt, the 'lost treasure' of revolutions. The book *On Violence* (1970) is replete with prescriptive norms and Arendt appears to remind us that the revival of a meaningful public order would, to a great extent, depend upon the re-animation of the nobleness enshrined in the classical tradition. In Hannah Arendt's writings, thus, there is a deep yearning and longing desire for a renewed moral upsurge. Her forceful writings present a call to the individual to break the rancid shackles of bondage, and unchain the putrid and reeky ossified structures that ensnare and entwine the individual. Arendt, therefore, fearlessly proceeds on to create a purified and laudable public order so that an individual could lead a life of dignity and honour.

Critique of Behaviouralism

Arendt was a puissant critique and powerful opponent of the behaviouralist approach in social sciences, which according to her, prepares the ground for totalitarianism. In America, she writes, floods of foundation money are channeled into the various research projects carried on by behavioural social scientists, a deluge of books on the subject has appeared, there is an all-out effort to solve the riddle of human behaviour, and even a brand new science, called 'behavioural sciences' have emerged.

But Arendt warns of the grave consequences of behaviouralism, for ultimately it would prove fatal to the moral development and human freedom. In its search for regularity and constancy in human behaviour, she argues, the behaviouralists contribute to the making of a uniform stereotyped 'man'. Making a frontal onslaught on Eastonian system approach, she characterises it as "an Archimedean approach" in which we try to look at earth from a point outside it, and deplores the fact "that we think and consider everything in terms of processes and are not concerned with single entities or individual occurrences. . ."[4] She believes Eichmann who was responsible for sending off train-loads of Jews to the place of their execution in the most punctilious and efficient manner to be a typical example of this kind of man that the system thinking of our time is likely to produce—a creature who knew how to 'behave' efficiently but had suppressed entirely the knowledge of how to 'act' responsibly.

The behaviouralists are cold-blooded enough to "think the unthinkable", and they even do not think. Instead of indulging in an old-fashioned, uncomputerizable activity, the behaviouralists reckon with the consequences of certain hypothetically assumed constellations without, however, being able to test their hypotheses against actual occurrences. The logical flaw in these hypothetical constructions of future events is always the same: what first appears as a hypothesis—with or without its implied alternatives, according to the level of sophistication—turns immediately, usually after a few paragraphs, into a 'fact', which then gives birth to a whole string of similar non-facts, with the result that the purely speculative character of the whole enterprise is forgotten. Needless to say, this is not science (Arendt quotes with approval Noam Chomsky and Richard N. Goodwin) but pseudo-science, "the desperate attempt of the social and behavioural sciences", in the words of Noam Chomsky, "to imitate the surface features of sciences that really have significant intellectual content." And the most obvious and "most profound objection to this kind of strategic theory is not its limited usefulness but its danger, for it can lead us to believe we have an understanding of events and control over their flow which we do not have", as Richard N. Goodwin pointed out in a review article that hadt he rare virtue of detecting the "unconscious humour" characteristic of many of these pompous pseudo-scientific theories.

Arendt asserts that events, by definition, are occurrences that interrupt routine processes and routine procedures, only in a world in which nothing of importance ever happens could the futurologists' dream come true. Predictions of the future, she says, are never anything but projections of present automatic processes and procedures, that is, of occurrences that are likely to come to pass if men do not act and if nothing unexpected happens; every action, for better or worse, and every accident necessarily destroys the whole pattern in whose frame the prediction moves and where it finds its evidence. (Proudhon's passing remark, "The fecundity of the unexpected far exceeds the statesman's prudence", is fortunately still true. It exceeds even more obviously the expert's calculations). Arendt writes that even to call such unexpected, unpredicted, and unpredictable happenings "random events" or "the last gasps of the past", condemning them to irrelevance or the famous "dustbin of history", is the oldest trick in the trade; the trick, no doubt, helps in clearing up the theory, but at the price of removing it further and further from reality. Arendt argues that the main danger is that these behavioural theories are not only plausible, because they take their evidence from actually discernible present trends, but that, because of their inner consistency, they have a hypnotic effect; they put to sleep our commonsense, which is nothing else but our mental organ for perceiving, understanding, and dealing with reality and factuality.[5] The behavioural group of thinkers have been vehemently attacked by Arendt for she attempts to rejuvenate and resurrect the normative political theory. Her writings for want of a better categorisation could be styled as neo-normativism, which has provided solace to many of the groping souls in the present-day industrialised society.

Totalitarianism and Freedom

Arendt is opposed to totalitarianism of all kinds, for it impedes the progress of mankind, somnolences initiative, and places dead weight and lumber on human freedom. The concentration and extermination camps reveal the futility and ludicrousness of totalitarian regimes. The extermination camps—

where everything was an incident beyond the control of the victims as well as the oppressors, where those who were oppressors today were to become victims tomorrow—created a monstrous equality without fraternity and without humanity, an equality in which dogs and cats could have easily partaken, and in which we see as in a mirror the horrid image of superfluousness.[6] The totalitarianisms create a world of the dying, in which men are taught that they are superfluous through a way of life in which punishment is meted out without connection with crime, in which exploitation is practised without profit, and where work is performed without product. This is the theme of her book *Origins of Totalitarianism* which is one of the most interesting works in political science to appear since the war.[7] It contains many insights, of which three in particular stand out.[8] First is the recognition that totalitarian lawlessness is lawlessness of a particular, and novel kind, since it is lawlessness masquerading as constitutionalism: the state machine emasculated and manipulated by the party, nevertheless remains in being and on show. Arendt is right to stress this difference. even if her emphasis on the role of the party is too great, Second, Arendt recognized that ideology in the totalitarian systems has little to do with ideas or benefits, but is an instrument for manipulating the population, and thus helping to consolidate the running elites' hold over it. And thirdly, she discerns the special function which terror performs for the totalitarian leader: this is not merely to frighten people into submission, but rather to isolate each individual, to leave him enclosed by a wall of loneliness, shut off from the support and comfort of his family, his friends and, of course, any kind of free association of his fellows. Arendt writes: "Terror is no longer used as a means to exterminate and frighten opponents, but as an instrument to rule masses of people who are perfectly obedient. As techniques of government, the totalitarian devices appear ingeniously effective. They assure not only an absolute power monopoly, but unparalleled certainty that all commands will always be carried out." Based upon 'murderous domination' totalitarianism presupposes "the existence of one authority, one way of life, one ideology in all countries and among all peoples of the world." Arendt, therefore, expresses abhorrence of totalitarian systems and forms, and makes a dexterous plea in favour of normative concepts of human progress and freedom.

The Human Condition

Arendt in her work, *The Human Condition*, attempts to describe the basic intellectual and moral orientation of modern culture and shows why that orientation is wrong. She argues that the keynote of modern culture is a fundamental skepticism about the powers of the human mind to discover the nature of reality. She assigns the disease to — for example, Galileo and Descartes—and locates the disease in the general areas, for example, 'rationalism', 'utilitarianism'. She gives expression to the increasingly popular 'existentialist' strain in contemporary political theory and argues that there is a kind of thought that has a deeper validity than the thought that fits the canons of science and traditional logic.

Arendt attempts to describe, and to philosophize upon, one main aspect of "the human condition"—the *vita activa* to which modern culture has ascribed the supreme value once reserved for the *vita contemplativa*. The *vita activa* consists of three fundamental human activities—'labour', 'work', and 'action'. 'Labour' is the activity by which men keep themselves and their species going, its products are short-lived and are immediately consumed in the interests of the life-process. She defines 'labour' as toil that is never finished, toil that has to be begun again the moment it is completed, like women's housework or the tilling of fields. Labour leaves no trace behind it when it is done; it is consumed like a loaf of bread or, in the case of the tilled field, requires renewed and incessant labour. 'Work', in contrast, aims at production of articles for use, and not simply for quick consumption. The products of work have a life beyond the biological process. Objects like a table of a house or a sculpture belong to the man-made world. It makes man feel at home in nature and affirm his stability and 'permanence'. It populates the world with durable things, and offers "mortals a dwelling place more permanent and stable than themselves".[9] The third and highest sphere of human behaviour Arendt calls 'action'. It is the individual's behaviour that makes stories and history; the world of words and deeds, where man reveals neither his skills nor his products but himself in his relations with other men; and so it is that part of the *vita activa* that gives moral significance to all the rest. Action would thus include the life of politics and thought the ordering of society and of ideas —corruptible, of course, but still capable of man's noblest efforts.

According to Arendt, the modern world has given 'work' the supreme place in the *vita activa,* and so it developed a utilitarian perspective in which everything is viewed as a means to something else, and even the structure of reality itself is conceived as a free construction of the human mind. When it is taken out of its proper place in the natural hierarchy of human activities, 'work' produces a view of the world in which nothing has any intrinsic value of its own, and represents an ideal that cannot sustain itself. Accordingly, 'labour' has come increasingly to take its place, and the ideals which are now coming to the fore are the ideals of 'labour'. So 'the good society' toward which we seem to be moving is a society of consumers, insatiably devouring more and more, and passively oscillating between the anodyne of routine and the shock of cheap sensations. This, in Arendt's view, is an account of "what we are doing".

Arendt's distinction between 'labour', 'work', and 'action', though it fades when it is pushed, nevertheless, suggests three possible levels of sensibility and aspiration, and three standards by which we can appraise what we are doing with ourselves in industrial society. It is nowhere clear, however, whether 'labour', 'work', and 'action' refer to three distinct classes or activities (as Arendt usually seems to suggest), or to three elements that can be found, at least potentially, in any activities. Arendt's moral arguments are marred, furthermore, by a tendency to state personal, and sometimes rather odd, preferences as though they were universal psychological truths. Despite deficiencies, *The Human Condition* reminds us of the forgotten moral dimensions of 'labour' and 'work' in contemporary society. She evolves an elaborate, pessimistic view of the modern world where automation tends to convert work back to labour and where the formulas of science block rather than aid human communication. But she believes that we can avoid the dangers of passivity and sterility if we "think what we are doing", and if we retain the political freedom which nurtures the life of free thought. Arendt, for all her impressive learning, comes out here as first and foremost an effective moralist, and the entire theory of modern culture is abundantly ethically loaded. She deplores the human condition in contemporary industrialized society and, directly or indirectly, suggests a full-fledged return to the classical tradition.

Creation of a New Foundation for Human Community[10]

Arendt elucidates the emptiness of public life, specific alienation of the individual from public undertakings, and more recently the erosion of the political foundations of the present day society. She says:

> Whether we like it or not, we have long ceased to live in a world in which the faith in the Judaeo-Christian myth of creation is secure enough to constitute a basis and source of authority for actual laws, and we certainly no longer believe, as the great men of the French Revolution did, in a universal cosmos of which man was a part and whose natural laws he had so imitate and conform to. . .
>
> Our new difficulty is that we start from a fundamental distrust of everything merely given, a distrust of all laws and prescriptions, moral or social, that are deduced from a given, comprehensive, universal whole.

She, therefore, argues that the political foundations of modern society have been shaken and even destroyed. Each of the revolutions of the modern age (excepting, she says, the American) should be understood as a gigantic attempt to re-build them, "to renew the broken thread of tradition, and to restore. . . what for so many centuries had endowed the affairs of men with some measure of dignity and greatness". Ours is a political realm "with neither authority nor the concomitant awareness that the source of authority transcends power"; ours is a realm "without the religious trust in a sacred beginning", a realm, what is more, "without the protection of traditional and therefore self-evident standards of behaviour." The origins of this condition, according to Arendt, are to be found in the dissolution of an impressive Roman amalgam—authority, religion, and tradition. This, then is the predicament of contemporary society.

Arendt, therefore, makes a fervid plea for the creation (not merely to discover) of a new youthful foundation for human community. For her the classical antiquity possesses the highest uprightness and integrity. She reminds us that we have today access to classical tradition only in the midst of revolution, when we get intimations of its true character. This means, she argues, we are today able to discover our authentic selves and define our public virtue only momentarily during the exhilarating moments of revolutionary action, whereas on the contrary our lives were continuously meaningful in times of classical antiquity: choices were genuine, deeds were glorious, freedom was action, events were memorable, speech was public, life—the highest form of human life—was lived in the Greek polis. Action and contemplation, work and leisure, were in an ideal state of harmony. Arendt, thus, not only laments the loss of ideal life, but solemnly pleads for the resurrection of the classical virtues for the creation of a purposeful public order.

Arendt states that it had been the genius of Roman politics, to maintain the balance by introducing authority, religion, and tradition. This trinity was later wrecked and subverted by Luther, Hobbes, and the secular humanists. Ultimately a modern faith in history replaced the metaphysics that had previously kept our existence from seeming futile. The historical process itself was summoned to dignify our deeds and trials. But having been delivered to an undifferentiated process of history, we have been deprived of distinctions. We have lost our balance. While Hegel inaugurated the reversal of the traditional hierarchy of values, demoting contemplation and giving pre-eminence to action, it was Marx, according to Arendt, who most specifically expressed the break in the tradition of political thought by recommending that man cease philosophizing and commence acting. Convinced that philosophical truth was known, that it fully existed in the common world of man and no longer had to be discovered by philosophers prepared to leave the cave, Marx could confidently counsel action. And as he substituted action for philosophy, he substituted labour for contemplation, postulating labour, and not reason, to be the distinguishing mark of man. He thereby threw man back on his own resources. And yet he expected man to use them so as to create a regime of leisure. It is Arendt's view that the bedeviling, repressive character of Marxism stems from Marx's accepting man as a labouring animal now and as a free being only in the future.

Arendt, unlike Marx, seeks to address herself to the immediate present, to our condition here and now. And this condition, she observes, is one which presents us, for the first time since classical antiquity, with a truly extraordinary option. Because absolutely nothing is left of our past (save in America where, as she has put it, the revolution to restore Roman foundations was a success) and because absolutely nothing blocks our future, we may now confront "the elementary problems of human living-together". Between an infinite past and an infinite future we stand tensely poised in the midst of a great void, possessing nothing save our world and our lives. Evoking the great catastrophes of the age (catastrophes she lifted out of history and idealized in her inquiry into totalitarianism), she is able to alert us to a singular, awesome opportunity: the opportunity to found our existance anew. Because the sources of authority have eroded, because the ultimate goals of political communities have been questioned, it has become necessary for us, as she says:

> . . .not only to find and devise new laws, but to find and devise their very measure, the yardstick of good and evil, the principle of their source. For man, in the sense of the nature of man, is no longer the measure, despite what the new humanists would have us believe. Politically, this means that before drawing up the constitution of a new body politic, we shall have to create—not merely discover a new foundation for human community as such . . . In historical terms, this would mean not the end of history, but its first consciously planned beginning, together with the better realization that nothing has been promised to us, no Messianic Age, no classless society, no paradise after death.

The public freedom we have gained is meaningless, however, unless we support it so that it will dignify and transcendent our personal existence. Our private life lacks point, Arendt reflects, unless we know that when we find ourselves in solitude we are not alone. We must act on the realization that unless our private existence carries within it the promise of its public vindication, we will be driven to despair and inconsolable dejection and pessimism. She thus reveals her underlying sympathy for the classical political philosophy, and without extending a clearly formulated invitation, she appears to assert that a revival of a meaningful public order would be a more promising possibility if such a revival is somehow oriented by the classical tradition, and not by the empirical approaches.

The Normative Legacy

Arendt leaves a normative legacy of major importance and durability. She is close to Rousseau in the stress she lays upon an ever-renewed consent as the basis of authority. She realises that although mankind is passing through 'dark time' still the individual can 'expect some illumination'[11] from the virtuous lives and prescriptive writings of some men and women. She has an admiration and enthusiasm of the ancient world and even Hellenism determines her definition of politics; thus she can write, for example, that "we understand the political in the sense of the polis". By an extensive body of systematic argument, Arendt supports the contention that politics provides the only guarantee of our sanity, that political activity alone confers meaning upon life, and that in it the highest form of happiness is to be found. This is in sharp contrast to the views of Michael Oakeshott, who writes, "politics, we know, is a second-rate form of human activity, neither an art nor a science, at once corrupting to the soul and fatiguing to the mind, the cativity either of those who cannot live without the illusion of affairs or those so fearful of being ruled by others that they will pay away their lives to prevent."[12]

It would be most appropriate to sum up the contribution of Arendt in the words of a distinguished philosopher, Hans Jonas, who has said of her: "She did not strive for originality, she just was original. Things looked different after she looked at them. Thinking was her passion, and thinking for her was a moral activity...whatever she had to say was important, often provocative, sometimes wrong, but never trival, never negligible, never to be forgotten."[13]

REFERENCES

1 Mason Drukman, *Community and Purpose in America: An Analysis of American Political Theory* (New York, 1971), p. 364.

2 Daniel Bell, *The End of Ideology* (New York, 1962), p. 21.

3 Of the extensive literature dealing with the impact of work on the total life of the individual, another book of significance is Erich Fromm, *The Sane Society* (New York, 1955).

4 Hannah Arendt, *Between Past and Future: Six Exercises in Political Thought* (New York, 1961), p. 61.

5 Hannah Arendt, *On Violence* (New York, 1970), p. 8.

6 Hannah Arendt, *The Origins of Totalitarianism* (New York, 1951), p. 430.

7 Noel O'Sullivan, "Hannah Arendt: Hellenic Nostalgia and Industrial Society", in *Contemporary Political Philosophers* (eds.) Anthony de Crespigny and Kenneth Minogue (London, 1975), p. 244.

8 Leonard Schapiro, *Totalitarianism* (London, 1972), p. 102.

9 Hannah Arendt, *The Human Condition* (New York, 1959), p. 152.

10 Abstracted from Henry S. Kariel, *In Search of Authority: Twentieth-Century Political Thought* (Toronto, 1964), pp. 246-49.

11 Hannah Arendt, *Men in Dark Times* (London, 1970), p. ix.

12 Michael Oakeshott, in his introduction to Thomas Hobbes, *Leviathan* (Oxford, 1960), p. xiv.

13 Quoted by Richard Kostelanetz, "Dissecting the 20th Century", *The American Review*, vol. 22, no.1, Autumn 1977, p. 66.

PART II
The Indian Perspective

RELIGION, POLITICS AND SOCIETY
A STUDY OF GURU GOBIND SINGH'S IDEAS

J.S. Bains

The Sikh religion, as conceived by its founder, Guru Nanak and preached by the later Gurus, is a thoroughly practical and useful code of conduct. It aims at the spiritual and moral regeneration of not only the individual but and also the society in which he lives. Besides its emphasis on the acceptance of One Almighty God as the mover of things, it cherishes the inculcation of ethical virtues in man and insists on his living a moral life, looks with disdain at those who equate religious living with a life of renunciation. Sikhism, in other words, caters to the spiritual needs of the *whole* of the man. That is why the Sikh view of life considers the activities of the individual and the society as amenable to spiritual influence and as capable of making a significant impact on the social, political, economic, and other aspects of man's life.[1]

Guru Gobind Singh, unlike his predecessor Gurus, lived a very active life. Ever since he was designated as the Guru at the tender age of nine, he came into continuous conflict with the existing social, religious, and political order and had even to take up sword against the Hindu as well as the Muslim rulers. In order to give a practical manifestation to his views on these matters, he organised the Khalsa which was to serve as a nucleus for the realization of an ideal society of his conception and to achieve the ideals which were to form the bases of that ideal society. The Guru was an extremely well-read person and his mastery of Sanskrit, Hindi and Persian literature was unique. He presided over a court of fifty-two poets, established literary centres of wide repute, and brought a classical and cosmopolitan awareness to bear upon his own splendid compositions. The above observations on the then existing social and political order provide us with a wealth of material which may be read with profit by social scientists.[2]

Authority and Legitimacy

In conformity with the teachings of Guru Nanak,[3] the Tenth Guru argued that authority in every sphere derives its validity ultimately from God and not from any earthly source. On this point he agreed with the early Christian thinkers who believed that the spiritual as well as the secular authority is derived from the same source. In the *Zafar Nama* the Guru had mentioned that the God is the true Emperor of earth and heaven and that he is the master of both the worlds.[4] A similar idea was in his mind when he uttered the following words:[5]

> By his [God's] *hukum* are all things formed,
> Not one is blessed, save by his *hukum*, and
> By his *hukum* alone nature doth run her course,
> All serve beneath his *hukum*, and none may act
>   without it.
> Under Thy *hukum*, O God, hath all been done,
> And naught is of itself alone.

He dilated upon this point with more clarity when he said:[6]

> The successors of both Baba Nanak and Baber
>   were created by God Himself.
> Recognize the former as a spiritual
> And the latter as a temporal King.

In the *Bachitar Natak* while relating the story of how the Bedis had lost their dominion he said:[7]

> Afterwards again quarrels increased among the Bedis,
> which no one could adjust.
> It was the will of God
> That sovereignty should pass from their family.

It is clear from the above that Guru Gobind Singh believed in the divine origin of authority. In all spheres it is the God who confers authority and for legitimacy of one's authority, one has to look to the former and not any one else. In this connection, it is of interest to note that the Guru had claimed a divine sanction for his own mission.[8] In the *Bachiter Natak*, he has narrated how God asked him to go on his special mission:[9]

> I have cherished thee as my son,
> And created thee to extend My religion.
> Go and spread My religion there,
> And restrain the world from senseless acts.

The Guru, however, emphasized that while exercising power as a mandate from God a person in authority must always act according to the dictates of God; for, then only can he be able to enjoy authority on a permanent basis. If he does not abide by God's mandate; if he annoys the weak; if he plunders the people; if he engages in activities prejudicial to general welfare; if he puts the fulfilment of material pleasures and desires as the prime motive of life; and if he digresses from religious and moral teachings and from the principles of justice, he incurs the wrath of God who may then deprive him of his position and bestow the same on someone else.[10] The Guru quoted the God as saying:[11]

> When I created this world
> I first made the demons, who became enemies and
>   oppressors.
> They became intoxicated with the strength of their arm s
> And ceased to worship Me, the Supreme Being.
> I became angry and at once destroyed them.
> In their places I established the Gods :
> They also busied themselves with receiving sacrifices
>   and worship,
> And called themselves supreme beings....
> They altogether forgot My orders,
> And became absorbed each in his own praise.
> When they did not recognize Me,
> Then I created men.
> They too fell under the influence of pride. . .

The Guru made it clear in unmistakable terms that a ruler must always be responsible to God for all his activities. This meant that the primary allegiance of a man is to religion.[12] In this connection, he questioned the prevalent view that Aurangzeb was a religious person.[13] While he praised the latter for many of the religious attributes of his personality and also his distinctive achievements, he found that Aurangzeb's policies were unjust and contrary to the principles of religion. In the *Zafar Nama* the Guru had said: "God will grant thee the fruit of the evil deed thou design.... I do not deem thou knowest God, since thou hast done act of oppression".[14] Pointing to Aurangzeb he said: [15]

Did I not know that thou O faithless man, were a worshipper of wealth and perjurer ? Thou keepest no faith and observest no religion. Thou knowest no God and believest not in Muhammad. He who hath regard for his religion never swerveth from his promise. Thou hast no idea of what an oath on the Quran is and canst have no belief in Divine Providence . . .

Condemning the religious bigtory and political intolerance of Aurangze as inconsistent with divine mandate, he said : [16]

Did thy God ask thee to tyrannise over others ? Fie on thy sovereignty and on thy regard for God and religion ! But, hear me: do not employ the sword to murder the innocent, for the God on high would for sure punish thee. Fear God, therefore, who is the Master of the earth and the heaven, and whose vengeance is terrible, who fears no one and is the protector of the poor.

The Guru emphasised that one must conform to God's will and mandate in order that one's claim to legitimacy may stay intact. He added:[17]

My protection is God than whom there is no better, nor higher. He who acteth honestly, him the God saveth to perform his service. How can an enemy touch his person of whom God on high is the friend and refuge ? Life is but for a brief few moments. Change is the law of life. Whoever cometh here, also quiteth the scene. So, whatever one's strength, one must annoy not the weak and thus destroy one's roots.

The threat to established authority would not arise so long as the person concerned exercised it for the betterment of his subjects and did not get entangled in worldly pleasures and selfish pursuits.[18] In the Aristotelian vein, the Guru referred to many factors which serve as a basis for dissension among the people. He gave prominent place to desire for wealth, land, and women as basis for dissension among people. Similarly he also mentioned that pride, worldly love, lust and wrath contribute to the process of accentuation of dissentions. In the *Zafar Nama* there is a reference to lust for sex, revenge, intrigues, gambling, drinking, violence, adultery, falsehood and sensuality as causes of discord among kings.[19] While talking about the Sodhi race to which the Guru belonged, he said:[20]

Afterwards dissension arose among them,
And no holy men could arrest its progress.
Heroes and invincible warriors went about caprisoned
Took arms and went to fight in the field of battle.
For wealth and land ancient is the struggle,
To compass which men willingly die.
Wordly love and pride have extended quarrels,
Lust and wrath have conquered the whole world.

The emphasis on God as the ordainer of life and as the bestower of power and authority should not give us the impression that Guru Gobind Singh accepted the sanctity of any existing authority on the plea that it must have been ordained by God. No doubt the principle of the divine right of authority could be used in support of the status quo. And the Guru had mentioned that at times God may even give a tyrant to the people as a punishment for their wicked actions.[21] But he was quite convinced that those rulers who oppress the poor and exercise authority contrary to religious and moral codes forfeit the confidence of God and have, therefore, no right to hold on to their position. He had no doubt in his mind that the God's will could be known by the people. "When one's own will is attuned to His Supreme Will, then one feels and moves as He wants one to feel and move."[22] People who have a pure and clean heart and are moved by the love of God are always in a position to distinguish between good and evil and can, therefore, deside to support or oppose the incumbent of an office at a particular time.[23]

The Guru had shown that a lead for an action supporting or opposing a office-holder could very conveniently be given by those who through their deeds and actions may have established their reputation as selfless, just, and true lovers of God. Such persons may spearhead a movement in order to overthrow the wicked rulers. The Guru had also mentioned that at times in response to the prayer of the suffering humanity, God entrusts such work to the bold and the noble souls.[24] In the *Dasam Granth* there is a description of *Chaubis Avtars* whose main contribution is portrayed as the role they played as uprooters and destroyers of unrighteousness.[25] In *Chandi Charittar* addressing God, the Guru says: "It is Thou who created Durga and destroyed the demons through her."[26] In reply to Aurangzeb's message in which the Emperor had claimed rightful authority from God,[27] the Guru questioned the continuance of such a mandate and said:[28]

There is only one Sovereign, God the All-Powerful to whose Will both your Majesty and I are subject. But you recognize this not and discriminate and persecute the Hindus, and instead of doing justice practice discrimination and bring harm to their person and religion. God has sent me with a missionto restore righteousness on the earth. How can I be at peace you so long as our ways are different?

The question of legitimacy could also be tackled from another angle. The Guru felt that the public opinion regarding the policies of a ruler could be helpful in determining whether the latter conformed to the divine mandate or not. If a ruler oppresses his subjects, he exercises his power contrary to the divine will. In other words, the Guru felt that rulers must always be responsible to the ruled just as the leaders must always personify the aspirations of the led. This proposition is based on the presumption that God's will can exhibit itself in the people's will or what may be called as the General Will. The Guru had mentioned that while the "Guru's sovereignty is full of twenty measures—that of the *Sangat*, as the mouth-piece of the people, is of overriding paramountcy, of twenty-one measures."[29] He had pointed out that God would always be present in the general body of the Khalsa and that wherever even five Sikhs were assembled, the God would be with them.[30] That is why the Guru gave a pride of place to the *Sangat* and the *Gurmata*.[31]

In this connection, it is interesting to note that the Guru put the *Sangat* or the Sikh brotherhood on a higher pedestal. He gave the Sikh all the credit for his achievements and urged his followers to approach the *Sangat* for the settlement of their disputes or for general guidance. To Kesho who had deprecated the Sikhs, the Guru had said:[32]

All my battles I have won against tyranny
I have fought with the devoted backing of these people;
Through them only have I been able to bestow gifts.
Through their help I have escaped from harm;
The love and generosity of these Sikhs
Have enriched my heart and home.
Through their grace I have attained all learning;
Through their help, in battle, I have slain all my enemies.
I was born to serve them, through them I reached eminence
What would I have been without their kind and ready help
There are millions of insignificant people like me.

Similarly he emphasised that serving the common man was the ideal service and that the lowest is equal with the highest, in race, in political rights as in religious hopes. The Guru said:[33]

True service is the service of these people:
I am not inclined to serve others of higher castes;
Charity will bear fruit, in this and the next world,
If given to such worthy people as these.
All other sacrifices and charities are profitless.
From top to toe, whatever I call my own,
All I possess or carry, I dedicate to these people !

The Guru had so much veneration for the Sikhs that he bowed before them and paid fine when they objected to his saluting the shrine of Dadu against which he had previously given them strict instructions.[34] The classic example of the high esteem in which he held the Sikhs was when after selecting the "five loved ones", he drank the holy water at their hands and thereby gave the Khalsa the pride of having selected their leader. "In his system", therefore, it may be said, that "there was no place even for the privileges of the chief or the leader. No leader, he believed, could be fit to lead unless he was selected or accepted by the followers".[35] This emphasis on the popular basis of sovereignty and the equation of the latter with the divine mandate may be considered as a distinct contribution to democratic theory.[36]

A unique contribution of Guru Gobind Singh in the realm of politics and society was the remarkable way in which he organised his followers into a militant group so that they could be able not merely to withstand but also to counter the oppressive policies of the government of the day. Guru Nanak and the later Gurus had operated purely at the social plane. Though their activities often invited the displeasure of the orthodox segments of the society, they very seldom came into a violent conflict with the established political authority. They preferred to use the method of the dialectic to expose the fallacies of the prevalent customs and traditions and won followers thereby. While such a method had its own charm and it bore dividends, incidents occurred which were exploited by the authorities to commit atrocites on the Sikh leaders and took advantage of the peaceful nature of the Sikh movement. The martyrdom of Guru Arjun Dev and Guru Teg Bahadur on the orders of Jahangir and Aurangzeb convinced the Tenth Guru that force must be met by force. A few years earlier, the Sixth Guru had taken steps in this direction and had used the sword against the secular authorities.[37] While Guru Gobind Singh favoured the use of peaceful means for the resolution of conflicts and had even advised the people to be loyal to their sovereigns,[38] he also advocated the use of extreme means in order to vindicate one's own case. This approach is quite evident from the following couplet which is a part of a letter which he had addressed to Aurangzeb:[39]

When all other means have proven ineffective

It is right then to take up the sword.

The Guru was of the opinion that peaceful approach should be used not as a cover for weakness or timidity but as a technique or means in order to bring home to the opponent the justness of one's position. Similarly he did not advocate the path of peace if it meant compromising with tyranny. In his reply to the Sikhs of the Majha who had implored the Guru to make peace with the Moghuls, he said:[40]

I am fighting for a cause, not for myself. I have sacrificed my sons, my father and my mother for this cause. And, now you come to ask me to withdraw from the fight to save my person ? This will never be. Whoever wants to live in ignoble peace, may compromise with tyrany. I would'nt till I have breath in me, nor will those who will choose to follow me.

A similar reply was given to the Masands.[41] The Guru was convinced that the peaceful approach could bear fruit only if the opponent also had some scruples and has same regard for religious and ethical values. If the opponent did not have any regard for such values, the only remedy would be to pay him back in his own coin.[42] The Guru arrived at this conclusion after observing the harsh and unjust treatment being meted out to the people and which he thought was contrary to all canons of morality and justice. In conformity with this view, he rejected the proposal of a follower of Dadu that "if any one throws a clod or a brick at thee, lift it on thy head". Instead he said: "If any one throws a clod or a brickbat on thee, angrily strike him with stone".[43] Similarly he interpreted the request of the Hill rajas to borrow an elephant as a pressure tactic and told his mother who had intervened on behalf of the rajas:[44]

The hillmen have now come to beg with the humility of goats, but when they have received what they have asked for, they will assume the bravery of tigers—Mother dear, if we betray fear of them, they will soon be ready to devour us. They will only respect us when we show them the sword. If thou show a stick to a barking dog, he will fear to continue his barking.

In the same vein, he told the Prime Minister of Raja Bhim Chand who had come to seek the Guru's help against the Moghuls:[45]

Pay no tribute to the Turks. If thou pay it today, there will be another demand on thee tomorrow. But if thou fight and cause the Turks to retreat, then shall no one molest thee.

Sword Supreme

Guru Gobind Singh advocated the use of force only as a last resort. He knew that the rulers were maltreating their subjects and the latter had suffered heavily at their hands. That is why he felt that the people should prepare themselves for effective opposition to such authorities. In order to achieve these goals, he asserted that the old ideals of humility and surrender practiced by Guru Arjun and Guru Teg Bahadur should be substituted by those of self-assertion and self-reliance. That is why in place of the *Charan Pahul* which was being accepted by the earlier Gurus he introduced the practice of *Amrit* stirred with the double-edged sword. This symbolic change was meant to introduce and inculcate the war-like qualities amongst his disciples.[46] Throughout his life, the Guru was engaged in active military operations both against the Hindu Rajas and against the Moghul rulers. On the basis of his experiences with these rulers, he felt convinced that force must be met with force. That is why he almost deified the sword. In the *Vachitar Natak* he has at many places even accorded the status of God to *Sword* and has invoked its blessings in order to suppress the tyrants. In one of the couplets the Guru has said: "Food for the poor and Sword for the tyrant: O God, let both go hand in hand."[47] The supreme importance in which he held the Sword is clear from the following description he made of the latter:[48]

Sword, that smiteth in a flash,
That scatters the armies of the wicked
In the great battlefield;
O thou symbol of the brave,
Thine arm is irresistible, thy brightness shineth forth
The blaze of the splendour dazzling like the sun.

Sword thou art the protector of the saints;
Thou art the scourge of the wicked;
Scatterer of sinners I take refuge in Thee.
Hail to the Creator, Saviour and Sustainer,
Hail to Thee: Sword Supreme.

Similarly he held the wielder of the Sword in high esteem:[49]

O bow to the Scimitar, the two-edged Sword, the
   falchion, and the dagger.
Thou O God hast ever one form; Thou art ever
   unchangeable.
I bow to the holder of the Mace
Who diffused light through the fourteen worlds.
I bow to the Arrow and the Musket.
I bow to the Sword, sportless, fearless and unbreakable,
I bow to the powerful Mace and Lance
To which nothing is equal.
I bow to Him who holdeth the Discus,
Who is not made of the elements and who is terrible.
I bow to Him with the strong teeth;
I bow to Him who is supremely powerful,
I bow to the Arrow and Cannon
Which destroy the enemy.
I bow to the Sword and the Rapier
Which destroy the evil.
I bow all weapons called Shaster (which may be held)
I bow to all weapons called Aster (which may be hurled or
   discharged).

That the Guru gave supreme importance to the Sword is
clear from the fact that he introduced the Sikh prayer with an
invocation to the Sword: "Having first remembered the Sword,
meditate on Guru Nanak." Similarly he brought home to the
Saiyid of Sarhind the task which can be performed by the
sword. The saiyid had asked the Guru about miracles. The
latter drew forth a gold coin and said that it was a miracle
because everything could be purchased with it. On Saiyid's further enquiry whether he could mention any other miracle, the
Guru drew forth his sword and said that it was also a miracle

because "it could cut off heads and confer thrones and empires upon those who wield it with dexterity."[50] Similarly when Goddess Durga had failed to appear, the Guru after exposing the claims of Kesho left for Anandpur. On the way, in reply to the people who inquired from him about the appearance of Durga, he is said to have raised his sword aloft to say that by God's grace and assistance, his sword would perform the deeds which the Brahmins attributed to Durga.[51]

The veneration in which the Guru held the sword should not give any one the impression that Guru Gobind Singh believed in the dictum that might is right. The interchangeable use of the words "Sword" and "God" is based on the assumption that the wielder of the Sword must be imbued with a divine mission. The Sword must be used for the furtherance of a righteous cause and for the suppression of the wicked. The Guru has said:[52]

> This is the true manifestation of the godess of Power, the shining steel with which evil is punished and virtue protected and rewarded. He who is willing to taste its baptism for a righteous cause invokes the blessings of God.

The Sword used for *dharma, truth,* and *justice,* signifies divine beneficence, but if it is used for oppressing the people and for the love of power, it loses all significance[53] and God in his wisdom punishes such people.[54] The Guru had sought the attainment of divine *shakti* so that he may be able to use the Sword for the furtherance of righteousness. In this connection he had sought the blessings of *Shakti:*[55]

> Grant me this boon O God, from Thy Greatness,
> May I never restrain from righteous acts;
> May I fight without fear all foes in life's battle,
> With confidence courage claiming the victory;
> May my highest ambition be singing Thy praises,
> And may Thy Glory be grained in my mind;
> When this mortal life reaches its limits,
> May I die fighting with limitless courage.

It is only in the above sense that the doctrine of the *sword supreme* was understood by the Guru. Its significance lies in the fact that a person who wields the sword for the good of humanity puts the divine mandate into practice. The Guru had said that he who "has a moral cause to fight for always has God on his side"[56] and that "blessed is he who even when he wars keeps God in his heart."[57]

In the above context it should be of interest to note that the Guru firmly believed in combining spiritual achievements with physical prowess. He was convinced that one without the other would lead to sheer hypocrisy and ruthless tyranny. That is why he advocated that the spiritual uplift must be combined with Kashatriya spirit of valour.[58] In order to achieve this goal, he popularized heroic literature from the glorious past. He wrote poetry for the purpose of inspiring bravery and eliminating cowardice as also for inciting the people to revolt against tyranny. He also employed a host of poets and pandits who translated stirring stories from the *Ramayana* and *Mahabharata* in order to infuse war-like spirit among his followers. He had also chosen the Pauranic story of Durga's valorous fight with the demons with a view to infusing martial ardour into his people.[59] The Guru realised "what a vital part literature could be made to play in rousing the dormant energies of a vanquished and a degraded people. The stories from the old Sanskrit literature that he popularised in Hindi served as an effective handmaid to his constructive work, and, at the same time created a demand for literacy and education among his followers".[60]

The Guru also made arrangements to produce drums, kettle drums, conch-shells and other similar things in order to produce martial music.[61] He also popularised the singing of *Maru-Rag* and encouraged the manufacture of muskets, swords and arrows and urged upon his followers who come to do obeisance to him to bring horses and also offensive and defensive weapons as their offerings. The Guru took delight in wearing arms and uniform. He also initiated the custom of baptism by drinking sweet water stirrred with a double-edged sword thus signifying bravery and skilful use of arms as the essential attributes of a Sikh. It was with the same end in mind that the Guru changed the name of his followers into *Singhs*, making them lions, and thus making them the embodiment of bravery.[62]

Such a programme was extended to children also. Like Plato, the Guru wanted the children to imbibe from their very infancy the love for God and physical fitness through martial exercises. He used to take Zorawar Singh in his lap while watching Ajit Singh fence. Similarly Jhujhar Singh used to be brought by his nurse to witness the performance.[63] It was in the fulfilment of the same idea that the Guru named the offsprings of Sikhs as *Bhujhangis*, that is snakes. The Guru was convinced that a people must develop their physical and mental faculties so that they may attain perfection and be in a position to play a positive role in the affairs of the community.[64] "The fusion of the devotional and the martial, of the spiritual and the heroic, was the most important feature of Guru Gobind Singh and of his career as a spiritual leader and harbinger of a revolutionary impulse."[65]

Equality and Fraternity

The Tenth Guru was not happy with the existence of a caste-ridden Hindu society in which the Brahmins and others who enjoyed a higher social position exploited those who belonged to lower categories. He knew that the division of the Hindu society in water-tight compartments bred inequality and served as a stumbling block in promoting social intercourse and in fostering the necessary integration among the various sections of the Indian society for bringing into existence a composite culture. This also applied to the Muslims, especially the Mullahs who regarded the non-Muslims as *kafirs*, fit to be eliminated and urged upon the rulers to discriminate against them. The Guru was of the view that the human being is essentially the same irrespective of whatever religion, race, colour, creed, etc. he may profess. Like the Stoics he held that human beings belong to the same species, have the divine spark, and are equal in the eyes of God. This emphasis on the brotherhood of man and fatherhood of God was clearly portrayed by him in the following verse:[66]

He is also in the temple as he is in the mosque;
He is in the Hindu worship as he is in the Muslim prayer;
Men are one though they appear different.

The Hindus and the Muslims are all one.
Each have the habits of a different environment.
But all men have the same eyes, the same body,
The same form compounded of the same four elements,
Earth, air, fire and water.
Thus the Abekh of the Hindus and the Allah of the Muslims
 are one,
The Koran and the Puran praise the same Lord.
They are all of one form,
The one Lord made them all.

The idea of the unity of the God-head[67] was helpful in tackling the problem of inequality which had been created by pseudo religious leaders of both the Hindus and the Muslims in order to perpetuate their privileged positions. It cut at the roots of the controversy which had sharply divided the various religious communities. Moreover, it was based on the revolutionary concept that in the eyes of God, all human beings are equal even if they may have a different social status. God had given the same senses and the same soul to every one. All individuals are essentially equal, though their customs and habits may differ. These differences are primarily the product of the differing environments in which the people lived. The Guru, therefore, believed that the whole human race was one and looked forward to the emergence of a universal culture as the basis of a global fraternity.[68]

The idea of brotherhood of man was also a very revolutionary concept, specially in the context of the period during which the Guru lived. It aroused the weaker and the exploited sections of the society from their lethargy and showed them the vision of a future world in which they would be treated on the basis of equality and in which opportunities would be available to develop their potentialities for playing an active role in their own affairs. The Guru brought home to the people the message that they must assert their own rights and must organise themselves to achieve their goals. Unless the people brought into existence a tightly-knit organisation, they would not be able to make their presence felt nor would they be able to develop themselves as good citizens.

Guru Gobind Singh believed that the individual should develop an all-round personality so that the society, of which he is an essential unit, may also have a unique stature. That is why he laid a good deal of emphasis on hard work and honest living. He was of the opinion that a householder who lived honestly,[69] earned his livelihood by the sweat of his brow,[70] gave charity,[71] and at the same time believed in the Almighty helped to raise secular life to a higher pedestal. The Guru said:[72]

> O Sikhs, borrow not, but, if you are compelled to borrow, faithfully restore the debt. Speak not falsely and associate not with the untruthful…Live by honest labour and deceive no one. Let not a Sikh be covetous…look not on a naked women. Let not your thoughts turn toward that sex…Deem another's property as filth Keep your bodies clean.

Similarly he had said in some other context:[73] "I am pleased with those who, though they may wear coarse garbs, eat what they lawfully earn." In *Shabad Hazare* he enjoined the inculcation of mental detachment, continence, divine knowledge, prayers, communion with God, contentment, peace, avoidance of lust, anger, pride, greed and obstinacy.[74]

The Guru wanted to have no truck with those who under the garb of saintliness exploited the people. This applied to the Brahmins, the Mullahs,[75] and the Masands.[76] Above all it applied to the political rulers. Like St. Thomas Aquinas, the Guru expected an ideal ruler to be an embodiment of virtue, having full faith in the Almighty God and to be a protector of the innocent, the weak, and the righteous.[77] Such a ruler must not lose faith in these virtues even in the midst of the greatest calamity.[78] The Guru made a scathing criticism of those who, in order to realise their selfish goals, misled the higher authorities. Those who flatter the men in authority and thereby maintain their positions are also the enemies of the people. Similarly the leaders should be the servants of the people and should not exploit them for their personal ends.[79] The Guru was a perfect example of a selfless leader, admirer of the ordinary and poor people, a believer in the ultimate worth of the human being, imbued with the divine zeal and even willing to make secrifices for the common good.[80] He wanted to see each Sikh in his own image. As pointed out by a competent scholar:"The greatness of

Guru Gobind Singh's experiment lay in the harmonious combination of floating ideas and practices in a coordinated system which had a definite objective in view, viz. the organisation of an integrated self-reliant and dedicated community pledged to destroy evil and sin and to extirpate tyrants. The moral strength required for the of this difficult objective was to be derived from the unadulterated worship of one God and of one God only"[81]

Conclusions

Guru Gobind Singh believed that all authority—secular as well as spiritual—flows from God who is omnipotent and the final determinant of all things. He was, however, against the doctrine of the divine right of authority as was claimed by the despotic rulers. In his view, if a ruler strayed away from the divine mandate, if he engages himself in the satisfaction of personal pleasures and indulges himself in selfishness, greed, favouritism and corruption, he loses the mandate of God and such a person deserves to be thrown out even if people may have to use force in such a process. Similarly if such a person indulges in acts of high handedness and thereby alienates the sympathies of the people, he becomes disqualified to hold on to his position. The Guru believed that the ruler must be responsible to the ruled because God's will manifests itself through the will of the people.

In order to bring into existence an ideal society, the Guru laid emphasis on the regeneration of both spiritual and physical aspects of the personality of an individual. Such a person is to combine in himself the attributes of a devotee of God, of a warrior ever ready to fight for the truth, of a house-holder earning his livelihood by honest and hard labour and of one who treated every one as his equal. The Guru was himself possessed of all these attributes and many others. He was the first Indian leader who not only advocated but practised the principles of equality, fraternity, and democracy and stood for basing all human activties—political, social, and economic on ethical and spiritual foundations.

REFERENCES

[1] Teja Singh, *Sikhism: Its Ideals and Institutions* (Calcutta, 1951); M. A. Macauliffe, Wilson & Others, *The Sikh Religion* (Calcutta, 1958); John C. Archer, *The Sikhs* (New Jersey, 1946); Pritam Singh Gill, *Trinity of Sikhism: Philosophy, Religion, State* (Jullundur, 1973).
For a historical background and for a discussion of the views of the Tenth Guru see Max Arthur Macauliffe, *The Sikh Religion* (Oxford, 1909), vol. V; Indubhushan Banerjee, *Evolution of the Khalsa* (Calcutta, 1947),vol. II; Gopal Singh, *Guru Gobind Singh* (New-Delhi, 1964); *The Tenth Master: Tributes on Tercentenary* (Chandigarh, 1967).

[2] Darshan Singh Maini, in *The Tenth Guru: Tributes on Tercentenary* (Chandigarh, 1967), p. 52.

[3] J.S. Bains, "Political Ideas of Guru Nanak", *The Indian Journal of Political Science*, 1962, pp. 390-418.

[4] Quoted in Macauliffe, n. 1, vol. 5, p. 204.

[5] Quoted in Archer, n. 1, p. 210.

[6] Macauliffe, n. 1, p. 305.
Also Sawaiya 8: "O eternal and everlasting God! It is thou who caused the Vedas and the Katebas [Semitic books] to come into existence. It is thou who hath given the Gods, the demons and the good earthly spirits their proper places and assigned proper functions to them in the past and in the present". *The Sikh Review*, January 1963, p. 42.

[7] Macauliffe, n. 1, p. 284. Also:
Countless heroes very valiant without hesitation
    face the edge of the sword.
Subdue countries, crush rebels, and the pride of
    furious elephants.
Break powerful forts and even without fighting
    conquer in every direction—
But their efforts avail not; the Lord is the Commander
    of them all—the suppliants are many while there
    is but one Giver.
Ibid., p. 265.

[8] Indubhushan Banerjee, *Evolution of the Khalsa*, vol. II, p. 93; also Archer, n. 1. p. 225.

[9] Macauliffe, n. 1, pp. 296-99.

[10] Ibid, p. 204.

[11] Ibid., pp. 296-97.

[12] "There are two forces which claim allegiance of man's soul on earth, the truth and morality as Religion (House of Baba) and the State (House of Baber) as embodiment of secular power. The primary allegiance of man is to religion (Truth and Morality) and those who fail in this allegiance suffer under the subjugation of the State as they have no courage and hope which is formed through unswerving allegiance to religion. The Church must correct and influence the State without aiming to destroy it. The two must exist side by side but the primary alle-

giance is towards Religion, Truth and Morality." Kapur Singh, *Para-sharprasna* (Jullundur, 1961), p. 325.

13 Macauliffe, n. 4, p. 205.

14 Ibid,, p. 206: "Even thoughthou art strong, annoy not the weak. Lay not the axe to thy kingdom. When God is a friend what can an enemy do though he multiply himself a hundred times. If an enemy practices enmity a thousand times, he cannot as long as God is a friend, injure even a hair of one's head."

15 Ibid., p. 205.

16 Quoted in Gopal Singh, n. 1, p.

17 Ibid., pp. 57-58.

18 Banerjee, n. 8, p. 156.
    Also Guru's rebuke to Raja Ajmer Chand, n. 44, pp. 100-1.

19 See Dharam Pal Ashta, *The Poetry of the Dasam Granth* (New Delhi, 1959), pp. 138-41.

20 Macauliffe, n. 4, p. 299. Also:
    No body can compute the time
        when enmity, dissension and pride were diffused.
    In this world their basis is greed,
    By the desire for which every one killeth himself.
    Ibid., p. 292.

21 Kapur Singh, n. 12. The quotation of Kapur Singh is quite relevant in this particular context.

22 Teja Singh, n. 1, p. 13.
    Also Kapur Singh, n. 12, pp. 38-39.

23 *The Sikh Review*, January 1963, p. 16:
    The Panth, the Khalsa, I formed and helped to grow
    For the eternal Father had ordained it so.
    Hear Ye all my Sikhs the Father's behest for the future !
    From today the Granth, the Divine Word is the Master !
    The Guru Granth Sahib is the embodiment in visible
        form of all the Gurus,
    With heart, pure and clean, with the faith unbounded and serene,
    Let the Khalsa seek the Master in his Word;
    For the Word, the Granth, is the Guru, the Master from today.

24 The Guru's mission is stated in the *Bachitar Natak* as follows:
        The divine Guru sent me for religion's sake;
        On this account I have come into this world—
        Extend the faith everywhere;
        Seize and destroy the evil and the sinful.
        I assumed birth for the purpose
            of spreading the faith; saving the saints
        And extirpating all tyrants.
    Maculiffe, n. 1, pp. 299-301. The Guru here speaks as an instrument of God.

25 Ashta, n. 19, pp. 57-74.

26 A.C. Banerjee, "Creation of the Khalsa", *Journal of Sikh Studies*,

Vol. I (1974), p. 39. The word "sheenha" is used to indicate the mythi-
cal lion which Chandi rides during the battle with *sankha, astra* and
shastra in her hands. The demon *Madhukaitbha* is also mentioned.

[27] "Your religion and mine believe in the unity of God. Why should
there be any misunderstanding between us ? There is no choice for you
nor for any one else but to acknowledge my sovereignty which I have
obtained from Allah, the Almighty. If you have any grievance, come
and see me and I shall treat you as a holy man, but do not challenge
my authority, else I shall have to march personally against you."
Gopal Singh, n. 1, p. 45.

[28] Ibid., p. 46.

[29] Quoted in Kapur Singh, n. 12, p. 325.

[30] J.S. Grewal, "An Early Interpretation of Guru Gobind Singh's Mission", *The Tenth Master*, n. 1: ". . .Indeed Saina Pat [one of Guru
Gobind Singh's bards] makes it rather explicit that the true Guru and
the Sangat are one and the same. With his vague identification of the
Guru with God on one hand and a clear identification of the Sangat
with the Guru on the other, Saina Pat attributes almost a divine character to the collective body of the Sangat which becomes sacrosanct
and authoritative for its individual members." See p. 117.

[31] "All the available Sikhs sitting in the presence of the Holy Granth,
could take any political decision by unanimity and the acceptance of
the decision was obligatory for all. It was called *Gurmata*. It was the
Collective Will or General Will of the whole community....". Pritam
Singh Gill, n. 1, p. 281.

[32] Quoted in *The Sikh Review*, January 1963, p. 16.

[33] *Sacred Writings of the Sikhs* (London, 1960), p. 272.

[34] Macauliffe, n. 1, p. 228.

[35] Gokul Chand Narang, *Transformation of Sikhism* (New Delhi, 1956),
p. 81; also Banerjee, n. 1, pp. 118-20.

[36] Trilochan Singh, *Guru Gobind Singh* (Delhi, n.d.): "Guru Gobind
Singh wrote this song of the people 150 years before Marx was born
and 60 years before the world even heard of Rousseau and Voltaire."
See p. 21.

Also Kapur Singh, n. 12, p. 324. The learned author has explained the
relevant concepts as were understood by the Guru as follows: (1) The
Sangat means the local folk assembly of direct representation. (2) The
Panth is the whole commonwealth represented by the People's Assembly of indirect representation. (3) The *Khalsa* postulated the *sui gene-
ris*, inalienable sovereignty of the people. (4) The *condominium* of *Guru
Granth Sahib* and *Panth* implies that the exercise of power is always
subject to bonafides and good conscience. (5) The *Panjpiyarees* is the
doctrine of collegial leadership in the direction of state policies. (6) The
Gurmata is the symbol and form of the supreme authority of the Collective Will of the people duly formulated; and (7) the *Sarbatt Khalsa*
is the doctrine of completely equalitarian free Democracy."
Ibid., pp. 328-29.

Also, Pritam Singh Gill, n. 1, I, pp. 266-67.

37 Narang, n. 35, pp. 60-65.

38 To the soldiers of Budha Shah, the Guru said: "Be loyal to your sove-reign, leave life and death in the hands of God, Desert not your posts, abandon not your duty, and you shall be happy in this world and the next. If you die in the battle, you shall obtain glory to which not even monarchs can aspire. Shame not your sires and your race. He who for-saketh his master in battle shall be dishonoured here and condemned hereafter. The vultures, knowing him to be disloyal, will not touch but spurn his flesh. He shall not go to heaven hereafter, nor obtain glory here; abundant disgrace shall light upon his head. Be assured of this that human birth shall be profitable to him who loseth his life with face to the foe. For all the drops of blood that fall from his body, so many years shall he enjoy the company of his God." Sukha Singh's *Gur Bilas and Suraj Prakash*, quoted in Macauliffe, n. 1, pp. 31-32.

39 *Zafarnama*, quoted in Archer, n. 1, p. 203; also Gopal Singh, n. 1, p. 56.

40 Quoted in Gopal Singh, n. 1, pp. 58-59.

41 The Masands wanted peace at all costs. The Guru said: "How shall I conceal myself from those hillmen? I have received the immortal God's order to disclose myself, and you tell me to remain in concealment. I must obey God's order, not your. I have prepared the drum because my army would have no prestige without it. Even if Bhim Chand, Raja of Kahlur, and the other hill rajas grow angry, are we who sit here like women? We too shall meet sword with sword. If they keep the peace, so shall we. . .." Quoted in Macauliffe, n. 1, p. 6.

42 For conversation with General Sayyad Khan on similar lines, see Gopal Singh, n. 1, pp. 44-45.

43 Quoted in Macauliffe, n. 1, p. 228.

44 Macauliffe, n. 1, p. 140.

45 Ibid., p. 52.

46 Banerjee, n. 1, pp. 112-14.

47 Sawayyas 18, quoted in Gopal Singh, n. 1, p. 120.

48 *Sacred Writings of the Sikhs*, n. 33, p. 120.
Commenting on this point Narang says: "The Guru cherished the sword as an object of worship and some of his finest verses are those he employed to invoke its aid. His followers were required to stick to the worship of this great deliverer of mankind and those who were devout in the worship of the sword were promised exemption from every other kind of religious rites and ceremonies. The devotees of the sword were to be *Kriti-nasha, Kul-nasha, Dharma-nasha* and *Karma-nasha*, and their devotion to the sword was to be regarded as an act of the highest merit which would bring them power and prosperity in this life and bliss and beatitude in the next." Narang, n. 35, pp. 86-87.

49 Quoted in Macauliffe, n. 1, pp. 286-87.

50 Ibid., p. 232.

1 Ibid., p. 65.

[52] Quoted in Gopal Singh, n. 1, p. 22.

[53] Ashta, n. 19, pp. 183-86; Narang, n. 35, pp. 86-87; Mohan Singh, *Preet Lari* (January 1967), p. 15; Harnam Singh "Kirpan, the Sword of Righteousness", *The Sikh Review*, April 1963, pp. 33-36.

For the various meanings of the word *Sword*, see Kapur Singh, n. 12, pp. 138-41:

(1) It means a weapon which cuts at the very roots of the *avidya*, nescience that separates the transcient, puny, individual self from the abiding, immortal, Universal self. It is symbolic of the Transcental knowledge, the *Brahma jnan*, which destroys the illusion of the temporalia, the world of Time and Space, and leads to the Life everlasting. It is symbolic of the Guru Himself who is the Destroyer of Ignorance.

(2) The second meaning of this symbol is that the Sikh way of life is wholly governed by ethical principles, and it constitutes an intelligent, aggressive and useful citizenship of the world and not a slavish, conformist and self-centred social existence.

(3) It is, by tradition and association, a typical weapon of offense and defence and hence a fundamental right to wear, of the free man, a sovereign individual. The measure of freedom to possess and wear arms by an individual is the precise measure of his freedom and sovereignty. Since a member of the Khalsa Brotherhood is pledged not to accept any alien restrictions on his civic freedom, he is enjoined to insist on, and struggle for, his unrestricted right to wear and possess arms of offense and defence."

[54] Macauliffe, n. 1, p. 204.

[55] Epilogue to *Chandi Chariter*, in *Sacred Writings of the Sikhs*, p. 274.

[56] Quoted in Gopal Singh, n. 1, p. 44.

[57] Ibid., p. 38.

[58] "I am the son of a brave man, dot of a Brahmin;
How can I perform austerities:
How can I turn my attention to Thee, O God, and
forsake domestic affairs?
Now be pleased to grant me the boon I crave with
clasped hands,
That when the end of my life cometh, I may die
fighting in a mighty battle."
Quoted in Banerjee, n. 1, p. 117; also Ashta, n. 19, p. 57.

[59] In his *Chandi Charitra* (Hindi) *Chandi-ki-War* (Punjabi) poems he has described how Durga vanquished the demons. The production of this kind of literature was one of the means adopted by the Guru for the uplift of the spirit of man. Harbans Singh, *Guru Govind Singh* (1966), p. 41.

[60] Banerjee, n. 1, p.158.

[61] Macauliffe, n. 1, p. 6. The drums in those days used to be considered as a symbol of sovereignty.

[62] Kapur Singh gives different meanings to the word *Singh*:
"A Singh is one who has reached the goal, who has realised the Self,

and whose Self, therefore, is no more, whose ego and little personality are shed off and destroyed, and who thus has no proper particular name and so is designated by the generic term, Singh, so long
as he is active in the social and political context of the Sikh way of
life. "
Kapur Singh, n. 12, pp. 281-82.
Also: "A member of the Khalsa—a Singh—is one who is in\ constant
communion with the living God, without a thought of the other; who
is an embodiment of pure love and faith; and in whom there is
naught but one God; with Divine Light fully ablaze in his heart he is
awakened to discrimination between the Real and the unreal."
Ibid., p.282.

63 Macauliffe, n. 1, pp. 83, 93, and 120.

64 Ibid., p. 65
Also Teja Singh, n.1, p. 20; Banerjee, n. 1, p. 119.

65 Harbans Singh, n. 59, pp. 47-48.

66 Akal Ustat, in *Selected Writings of the Sikhs*, p. 269.

67 The Guru said: "Karta (the Creator) and Karim (the Beneficent) are
the same, Razak (the provider) and Rahim (the Merciful) are the same;
Let no one even by mistake suppose that there is a difference.
Worship the one God who is the one divine Guru for all; know that
His Form is one, and that He is the one light diffused in all." Macau-
liffe, n. 1, p. 275.

68 Kapur Singh, n. 12, I, pp. 39-40.
The example of Bhai Kanihya, who gave water in the battle-field
irrespective of friend or foe, very clearly establishes the above interpretation. See Gopal Singh, n. 1, p. 49.

69 "A hermit is best when alone; pure is his body and pure his mind;
but when there is a householder with a large family, his house is still
purer, and so are his body, mind and understading". Macauliffe,
n. 1, pp. 231-32.

70 The bulk of the people who came to the Guru belonged to the working
class and the Guru was happier in their midst than anywhere else.
Sitting among his Sikhs he once asked for a glass of water to be given
to him. The son of a wealthy merchant who had come to pay homage
to the Guru went and brought a tumbler which he presented to him
decorously. The Guru admired the promptness of the youngman, but
said that his hands were too delicate and had not yet learnt to engage
in work. He must not, he said, drink water off such soft hands.
Harbans Singh, n. 59, p. 87.

71 Macauliffe, n. 1, pp. 105, and 111-12.

72 Ibid., p. 117.

73 Ibid., pp. 111-12.

74 Mohan Singh, *Preet Lari* (January 1967), p. 18. The learned author
has argued that the real Sikhs of the Guru were like Plato's guardians.
For a similar view see, Banerjee, n. 1, p. 156.

⁷⁵ *Sacred Writings of the Sikhs*, p. 268.

⁷⁶ About the Masands the Guru said:

If any one go to the Masands, they will tell him to bring all his property at once and give it to them.

If any one serves the Masands, they will say, Fetch and give us all thine offerings.

Go at once and make a present to us of whatever property is in the house.

Think on us night and day, and mention not others even by mistake !

They put oil in their eyes to make people believe that they are shedding tears.

If they see any of their own worshippers wealthy, they serve up sacred food and feed him with it.

If they see him without wealth, they give him nothing, though he beg for it; they will not even show them their faces

These beasts plunder men, and never sing the praises of the Supreme Being.

Quoted in Banerjee, n. 1, p. 110.

⁷⁷ J. S. Bains, *Studies in Political Science* (Bombay, 1961).

⁷⁸ Shabad Hazare, *The Spokesman* (Guru Gobind Singh Number 1952) p. 12.

⁸⁹ *Sacred Writings of the Sikhs*, pp. 270-71.

⁸⁰ Kapur Singh, n. 12, pp.281-82; Mohan Singh, n. 74, pp. 17-18.

TAGORE AND THE CONSCIOUSNESS OF NATIONALITY

Isaiah Berlin

Although there are many elements, and factors, and signs, and criteria of nationhood, yet one of the most powerful, perhaps the most of all of these, is surely language. It may be counteracted by combinations of other factors—historical, social and geographical, but it is very strong. The more developed, mature and self-conscious a man becomes, the more he thinks and even feels in words, the less in sensuous images. Tagore, who was a great master of words, seems to me to have spoken about language and its connection with social and political life with acute insight, and what he said has great interest for us today.

I do not wish to praise or attack nationalism. Nationalism is responsible for magnificent achievements and appalling crimes; it is certainly not the only destructive factor abroad today—ideology, religious or political—and the pursuit of power by individuals and interests that are not national, have been, and are still, just as revolutionary, brutal and violent. Nevertheless, nationalism seems to me to be the strongest force in the world today. In Europe, where it first grew to overwhelming strength —one of the many forces released by the great French Revolution—it started—as we all know in alliance with other forces: democracy, liberalism, socialism. But wherever they fell out among themselves, nationalism invariably won, and enslaved its rivals and reduced them to relative impotence. German romanticism, French socialism, English liberalism, European democracy, were compromised and distorted by it. They proved powerless against the torrent of nationalist pride and greed which culminated in the conflict of 1914. Those who discounted its strength, whether Norman Angell or Lenin or the ideologists of dynastic empires or of world capitalist combines, and especially those who thought that they could harness it to their own particular purposes, failed to predict events and their adherents were punished accordingly. Communism, for instance, is certainly a great force today, but except in alliance with national sentiment, it does not advance. This seems to me to be the case in China, in the parts of Asia once governed by France or Holland, in Africa, in Cuba. When Marxism comes into conflict with national sentiment—we can all think of examples in very recent history—it suffers as an outlook and a movement, whatever the alliance with nationalism may add to its material power and success.

One may wish to condemn nationalism outright as an irrational and enslaving force as, for example, both Marxists and Catholics, enlightened internationalists and guilt-stricken ex-imperialists, and, naturally enough, its many victims of all classes and races and religions, have condemned it. But it seems to be even more important to understand its roots. Nationalism springs, as often as not, from a wounded or outraged sense of human dignity, the desire for recognition. This desire is surely one of the greatest forces that move human history. It may take hideous forms, but is not in itself either unnatural or repulsive as a feeling.

It seems to me that the craving for recognition has grown to be more powerful than any other force abroad today. This protean entity takes many overlapping and interacting forms: individual and collective, moral, social and political; nevertheless, it preserves its identity in all its incarnations. Small states demand to be recognised as sovereign entities with their own past and present and future, and struggle for equality with the great states and claim the right to survive, grow, be free, be allowed to say their word. The poor wish to be recognised as full human beings—as equals—by the rich, Jews by Christians, the dark skinned by the fair, women by men, the weak by the strong. Within modern centralized states minorities work and fight for power and status: this is felt acutely, perhaps most acutely in affluent societies. There, class consciousness is one of the most influential forms into which the demand for recognition pours itself.

In my own country, for example, it is perhaps the deepest root of our social discontents. The quiet economic revolution that has occurred both in Britain and in many parts of Europe, has cured many economic ills, raised the standard of living, increased the opportunities for economic advancement and political power over an area and to heights not known before. In the less unjust order of our time, it is no longer economic insecurity or political impotence that oppress the imaginations of many young people in the West today, but a sense of the ambivalence of their social status—doubts about where they belong, and where they wish or deserve to belong. In short, they suffer from a sense of insufficient recognition. Such people may be prosperous, take an interest in their work, realize that the Welfare State protects their basic interests, yet they do not feel recognised. Recognised by whom? By the "top people", by the ruling class.

In a society governed by an oligarchy—say by a hereditary aristocracy this can take the form of a straight political struggle for power by one social class against another.

In England, and in a good many other Western countries, the situation is a good deal more complex: there the unrecognised or under-recognised are conscious of the existence of a group of persons in their society who, without necessarily being in political control, nevertheless set the tone: socially or culturally or intellectually. These persons may belong to conflicting political parties; what they have in common is the self-confidence born of an assured position as arbiters of the general way in which life should be lived, of the way in which one should think, write, speak, look, educate, engage in argument, treat other human beings and in general conduct public and private life. Even when they rebel against some given political or social institution or orthodoxy, they do so in the right tone of voice, they speak by right and not on sufferance, as members of a natural elite. No doubt those who stand outside it, tend to exaggerate the power or the close-knit texture of the elite; yet, in unequal societies, men commonly know who stands in the way of their advancement. The elite exists. In England it is still to some degree hereditary and tied to the public schools, to the old universities, to the humanities, and it possesses a sense of solidarity which those who wish to be accepted by it envy and admire. They may, as is usual in such cases, affect to despise it, and describe it as useless, decadent, reactionary, a doomed class, condemned to disappearance before the forces of history, but at the same time they envy it and seek its approval even while they feel the very notion of status to be an unworthy category by which to classify human beings, and feel angry with their own inescapable, and resentful, consciousness of their own social positions. The excluded are not necessarily poor or politically powerless.

Sir Charles Snow's concept of two cultures seems to me fallacious; but what lends it plausibility is the fact that a good many natural scientists in Anglo-Saxon countries feel kept out of a world which they imagine to be living more enviable lives than their own. Even though it is recognised and asserted at all levels that it is they, the scientists, who, objectively, are more important, influential, original, far more crucial to the future of their societies than the humanist elite and the bureaucrats brought up in it, this gives them little comfort; for they know who truly dominates the scene. This paradoxical situation seems to occur whenever one process that vitally affects the development of a society falls out of step with some other equally central process or cluster of processes. Injustice, oppression, misery do not seem, at any rate in recent history, to be sufficient to create conditions for revolt or drastic change. Men will suffer for centuries in societies whose structure is made stable by the accumulation and retention of all necessary power in the hands of some one class. Ferment begins only when this order breaks down for some reason—the Marxist hypothesis of the influence of technological invention is illuminating—and a "contradiction" arises, that is, the development of one factor— say the possession of political authority or control by a ruling group, is no longer united to some other equally needed attribute, say economic power or capacity for administration. Then the equilibrium of the system is disturbed, and conflicts are set up, with corresponding opportunities of altering the distribution of power for those who seek to upset the *status quo*.

In our world the crisis is caused by the fact that individual talent and success, economic power and ability, and sometimes even political influence, have fallen too far out of step with the all important factor of the craving for social status. Lack of adequate status, humiliation of the parents and the sense of injury and indignation of the children, drives men to social and political extremism. It may take social or aesthetic and not political forms: it is the main force behind such phenomena as "angry young men", "beatniks", the addicts of Hip in America, and, to a perceptible degree, what Antony Crossland has called the Aldermaston Movement, which, inspired as it clearly is, by sincere political and social idealism, is also driven by a class discontent and acute status consciousness on the part of its members. This is not a novel phenomenon in the Western world. It is by now a truism that among the causes of the French Revolution, is the wide disproportion between the economic power of the French middle class in the eighteenth century, and its lack of social and political recognition. The revolutionaries of the nineteenth and twentieth centuries were as often as not sons of capable and self-made men who had been socially excluded or rejected, or found themselves in an embarrassing or false position in the social hierarchy of their time. This was conspicuously true of Russia too. Among the sources of strength of the Russian revolutionary movement was the combination of moral and political indignation directed against a corrupt and oppressive regime, with a quest for status by men whose resources and education entitled them to play a part that they were rigidly denied by the State. The great entrepreneurs of the rapidly growing trade and industry of the Russian empire—men of exeptional ability, imagination, ambition— could grow rich and economically powerful, but were by and large kept out of positions of honour and responsibility by the Court and the still aristocratically based regime. Pride and moral sentiment can, and do, outweigh material self-interest: the sons brought up on liberal sentiments imported from the West tended to sympathise with, and often threw themselves with passion into, the revolutionary movement which was openly directed against not merely the political, but also the economic order for which their capitalist fathers had fought so successfully. This happened in Central Europe and in the Balkans— young men with sufficient resources to obtain a far better education, especially abroad, than the majority of their country' men were turned by the humiliating inferiority of the families- social status towards extreme opinions and courses. I suspect this must have happened too to the sons of the rich bourgeoisie kept down by the Pashas of Turkey and Egypt and Syria and Iraq.

The dissatisfaction is, as a rule, directed against an identifiable elite—pillars of the establishment—the Pashas, as it were—

or it may break out against the very dissentients themselves, the Franklin Roosevelts, the Stafford Crippses, the Bertrand Russells; and many a revolutionary Girondin or radical of aristrocratic origin in France or Russia or America, men who, despite their radical views, are resentfully felt to belong to the ruling class and inherit its manners and its tastes. But the roots lie deeper—in the loneliness, sense of isolation, in the destruction of that solidarity which homogeneous close-knit societies give to their members. Ruskin and Morris, and before them Fourier and Marx and Proudhon, have long ago taught us to see that an increasing degree of industrialisation and mechanization leads to the disintegration of society, to degradation of the deepest human values—affection, loyalty, fraternity, a sense of common purpose, and all in the name of progress identified with order, efficiency, discipline, production. We are all too familiar with the results: the steady dehumanization of men and their conversion into proletariats—masses—'human material' machine and cannon fodder. This in time breeds its own antidote: the awakening in the most self-conscious and most sensitive among the victims or even among the accomplices of this process, if they have any strength of will, the awakening in them of revolutionary indignation fed by an immense desire to restore what they visualize as the broken social unity and harmony and equality (whether it ever existed or not); and with it, of the kind of uncalculating love and respect between men on which all true human relationships rest.

This demand to be treated as human and as equal is at the base both of the social and the national revolutions of our time: it represents the modern form of the cry for recognition—violent, dangerous, but valuable and just. Recognition is demanded by individuals, by groups, by classes, by nations, by states, by vast conglomerations of mankind united by a common feeling of grievance against those who, they rightly or wrongly suppose, have wounded or humiliated them, have denied them the minimum demanded by human dignity, have caused, or tried to cause, them to fall in their own estimation in a manner that they cannot tolerate. The nationalism of the last two hundred years is shot through with this feeling.

Nationalism is the direct product of wounds inflicted on a sense of common nationhood or common class or common race or outlook. Most commonly it takes one of two forms: either awareness of shortcomings, a conviction of backwardness or inadequacy, and an anxiety to learn from the superior class or nation, so as to emulate and reach equality, to obtain recognition by peaceful means or to extort it by violent ones. This is the ambition of new men and new states—"to catch up with and overtake"; to acquire whatever the modern age requires—industrial might, political unification, technological and cultural knowledge, until "they" can no longer afford to look down their long noses at "us". Alternatively, it sometimes takes the form of resentful isolationism—a desire to leave the unequal contest and concentrate on one's own virtues, which one discovers to be vastly superior to the vaunted qualities of the admired or fashionable rival. This is a natural form for wounded pride to take, whether in the case of individuals or nations. The rationalization of this feeling is painfully familiar.

Our own past, our own heritage contain far finer and richer things than the gimcrack goods of the foreigner—to run after the foreigner is in any case undignified, and treason to our own past; we can recover our spiritual and material health only by returning to the ancient springs which once upon a time, perhaps in some dim, scarcely discernible, past, had made us powerful, admired and envied. The students of Russian history are acquainted with the celebrated debate between Westerners and Slavophils in that country in the nineteenth century, a paradigm case. The former pleaded for science, secularism, the march of reason, enlightenment, freedom, all the fruits of civilization of which the richest flowering was to be found in the West. The latter denounced the West for its chilly inhumanity, its dry, narrow, legalistic, calculating philistinism, its oscillation between blind authoritarianism and anarchy, its social injustice, and above all, the lack of love in the relations of human beings amongst themselves; they called for a return to the "organic", "integral" society of the uncontaminated Russian past, when there was no bureaucracy, no deep gulf among the classes created by Peter the Great's break with tradition; they invoked the deep sense of fraternity that had once united the Slav tribes, when men were parts of one another, and did not clamour for rights; for a right is nothing but a frontier and a wall between human beings, something that excludes and extrudes, something that men bound by natural human feeling, like the members of a family, do not need in order to live together in peace and dignity and pursuit of the common good. The obvious point I wish to stress is that the Westerners and Slavophils represented two sides of the same coin—the demand for recognition. Nor did it die in 1917.

The same pattern of thought and feeling runs through in the German romantics—the writers and thinkers who bound their spell on their fellow citizens and created the idea of the nation as a great collective entity that expressed the *Volksseele*, and substituted intuitive "synthetic" insight and poetical sensibility for scientific analysis, calculation, Cartesian nationalism and individualism, for the "arithmetical democracy", the dead mechanical life, of the decaying West—that is, the French by whom they had been crushed and decimated in the seventeenth century, and humiliated culturally in the eighteenth.

Even in independent, proud and prosperous England, this mood grows powerful and articulate in the idealization of tradition and disparagement of rationalism by Burke and Coleridge, or the neo-mediaevalism of those who wished to return to pre-industrial Merrie England and to the old religion, or to renew it in the shape of a Tory democracy, or a Christian socialism which would restore the broken unity of social and spiritual life. It is to be found almost everywhere in Europe. This is still a form of the quest for recognition—of what we truly are and can be, of our mission and value in history—recognition if not by other nations, then, at any rate by our own kith and kin. There is always something of a sour grapes attitude about such attempts to withdraw into oneself for inner strength: if "they" will not recognise "us", "we" do not need "them", more than that, we despise them, we think they are doomed, they are the "rotting West", indeed the very things they think vices in us, our primitiveness, our childishness, our lack of the virtues they prize—sophistication, or political sense, or a modern outlook—are not deficiencies but spiritual and moral virtues which they are too blind even to conceive.

Something not dissimilar seems to me to lie at the back of the resentful attitude of those new nations which have exchanged the yoke of foreign rule for the despotism of an individual or a class or group in their own society, and admire the triumphant display of naked power, at its most arbitrary and oppressive, even where social and economic needs do not call for authoritarian control. Liberals rightly deplore and denounce such developments. Yet it is necessary to try to understand them. To understand is not necessarily to forgive: but neither may one point a finger of scorn before one has understood the fact that citizens of ex-colonial territories may prefer harsh treatment by their own kinsmen to even the most enlightened rule by outsiders. This is not a strange or a disreputable feeling. The consciousness that although all oppression is hateful, yet to be ordered about by a man of my own community or nation or class or culture or religion, humiliates me less than if it is done by strangers—no matter how considerate and disinterested—no matter how far removed from all bullying or exploitation or patronage—that sentiment is surely intelligible enough.

Yet the desire for self-government, for recognition, for social and moral equality, is often not capable of being satisfied by the attaining of political independence. For it may happen that the foreign culture has made a deep impress upon my own, and even when in some respects it has made inroads upon it, distorted it, and partially enslaved my own civilization, yet once I have tasted it, I cannot expel it from my system without great damage, cannot reject or blind myself to what is true or good or delightful or noble, merely because it comes from the wrong quarter. Once I have glimpsed such things I cannot forget them; and if, out of pride or desire for independence, I try to purge all memory of it from my system, this can only be done at a high and damaging cost to myself, by a great self-narrowing, by forcing obsolete armour upon my limbs, a deliberate reimposition of provincial standards, with the certain dangers of intolerance, stunting of growth, aggressive xenophobia, deliberate suppression of what only yesterday I knew to be the truth, charges justly urged against chauvinism and isolationism. That is a problem for all new establishments seeking to set up in freedom from their old masters, yet not to forget altogether those lessons which the masters taught them. The masters, as Karl Marx correctly maintained in the case of England and India, may not have had altruistic motives: they may have taught not in the interests of the pupil but in their own. Nevertheless, if Marx is right, they did drive their Indian subjects, it may be at times with brutality, through the unavoidable stages of material and intellectual development in far less time and with far greater effect than these populations could have done for themselves.

It seemed to me as I read Tagore, particularly about the tasks of education and unification in India, that the problems that faced him were not, as I have tried to say, altogether unlike those that troubled critics and reformers in nineteenth century Russia and Germany, and in other countries too—the United States in the twentieth century, and, I feel sure, Latin America too. For all these were cultures that, as a result of long years of foreign domination found themselves whatever their stage of development in an ambivalent position. For, on the one hand, foreign model exposes a society to the danger of breeding apes and parrots, and killing native gifts, or at any rate distorting their proper path of development in the service of alien gods. On the other hand, the poison, if it is a poison, will have sunk too deep. The Germans could not be expected to forget the Greek and Latin classics, Roman law, the writers of the French *grand siecle*, which were the very foundation of their education. The Russian experience is even more instructive. Peter the Great inflicted on his people a deep traumatic shock. He knocked down walls, blew open doors and windows, founded the beginnings of an educated class, a class that from its very birth, because of its un-Russian habits and outlook, its use of a foreign language—French—was divided from the main body of the people which continued to live in mediaeval poverty, ignorance, simplicity, and looked on the educated as semi-aliens. The wound went very deep. The problem of how it was to be healed preoccupied every public spirited, educated man in Russia for two centuries. The clearer sighted among them realized that the efforts of cultural invasion by French or Germans could not be solved by ignoring it, or by expelling the invaders—setting the clock back—for Russia lived in the world, and to barricade all entrances and exits, to build a Chinese wall, would not , long keep out political and economic forces pressing in upon it from outside and responding to similar forces inevitably stirring within it. Some bold reactionaries preached precisely this: if you stop secular education, arrest so-called progress, and freeze Russia as it now is, the fatal Western bacilli may perish: or at least work more slowly. But this method, the attitude of the Stoic sage—every crack stopped up against the external world—has never yet succeeded. Nor is an ancient culture sufficient to keep a modern people going; the new must be grafted on the old; that is the only alternative to petrifaction or the miserable aping of some ill understood foreign original. A nation cannot be treated as an exotic plant for long if it is to grow: it can grow only in the open air, in the public world that is common to all; one cannot be forced to feed exclusively on what is gone and dead in a carefully preserved artificial light, and achieve anything but a stunted growth.

A not dissimilar problem seemed to me, from what I have read in Tagore, to have faced India towards the end of the last century; and he never showed his wisdom more clearly than in choosing the difficult middle path, drifting neither to the Scylla of radical modernism, nor to the Charybdis of proud and gloomy traditionalism. I know that some have thought Tagore to have yielded too much to the West. I confess I did not find this so in those of his works that could be read in English. He seemed to me have kept to the centre. Not to give way at a critical point to the temptation of exaggeration—some dramatically extremist doctrine that rivets the eyes of one's own countrymen and the world, and brings followers and undying fame and a sense of glory and personal fulfilment—not to yield to this, but to seek to find the truth in the face of scorn and threats from both sides—Left and Right, Westernizers and Traditionalists—that seems to me the rarest form of heroism.

On one side England, on the other the marvellous Indian past. Tagore was very well aware that English literature was a menace as well as a boon. In an essay entitled "The Vicissitudes of Education", he said that those who forget India and identify themselves with the English that they learn at school are like "savage chiefs . . . when they put on European clothes and decorate themselves with cheap European beads." This occurs where, as Tolstoy said very sharply and brilliantly in his educational tracts, education has no relation to the life of the pupils themselves, but only to some other life, remote, beyond the seas. The inner neuroses which such conflicts must have created were not confined to India.

Tagore says that when this situation occurs, the discrepancy between education and life becomes acute, and then they "mock and revile each other like two characters in a farce"; and for this reason he called for a revival of the Bengali language--a natural medium at any rate some of this countrymen, not a borrowed suit of clothes however grand, however comfortable. Yet at the same time he realised that it was neither possible nor desirable to do, what some evidently wished to do, to shut the door on English, to cleans oneself of the Western disease, to return to the past, to the simplicity of an age without machines and reject the evil gifts the West—industrialisation and all the degradation and destruction of natural human values that it brought. He knew that the relation of India with England, for all its benefits, was nevertheless a morbid one: the English had come first as traders, then as masters, and despite exceptional men who served India in a pure spirit and wore themselves out in her service (and he pays noble tribute to such men), the relation of master and subject distorted the nature of both, and neither found it easy to recognize the other as a human being, to like or to dislike him as he pleased, as an equal, a *semblable*. Indeed it was this phenomenon that was marvellously described in his phenomenology by Hegel; and a hundred years later, in a very different fashion, by E.M. Forster. Nevertheless, Tagore understood the British character and British achievement, and he admired it. He judged England and Europe without passion; his appraisal seems to me clam, acute and just. What the British had brought must not be cancelled or thrown away. Nevertheless, one cannot create in a medium that embodies, and is the vehicle of, an alien experience; such a language must cramp the stranger and have the effect of a straitjacket upon his thought and imagination, and force it to develop in unnatural directions, sometimes (as in the case of a Conrad or an Apollinaire) into brilliant virtuosity at other times in painfully grotesque ways.

The first requirement for freedom, independence, awareness of oneself as an equal citizen of the world, is to be able to speak in one's own voice; better nonsense in one's own voice, than wise things distilled from the experience of others. "What the British have set up may be grand, but they do not belong to us. . .it will never do to seek to use somebody else's eyes because we have lost our own," said Tagore in his Presidential address to Congress in 1908. English is the window open to the great world; to shut it would be—I take this to be Tagore's feeling, a crime against India. But a window is not a door: to walk in through windows is absurd. "The British are behaving as if we do not exist. . .as if we were huge ciphers"—even Morely is guilty of this. How are Indians to direct themselves instead of being dependent on the placings of others? Only by acquiring strength. I quote from Tagore again: "The only gift is the gift of strength, all other offerings are vain."

Like Thucydides in the Melian dialogue, like Machiavelli, like all the great realists, he grasped that ignorance and utopian escapism, fed by sentimental evasion of the truth, can sometimes be as ruinous as cynicism and brutality; to illustrate this he tells the story of the kid and the Lord. The kid, constantly set upon by beasts stronger than itself, said in despair to the Lord "Lord, how, is it that all creatures seek to devour me?" The Lord replied "What can I do my child? When I look at you, I myself am so tempted also." Tagore draws from this marvellous and devastating fable the moral that one must be strong, for without strength there will be no equality, no justice. The equality of all states, great and small is a pious of idealistic chant. Justice to the weak, given human beings as they are, is rare because it is difficult; and to change human beings so that they will not be as they are, is utopian. One must seek to improve mankind by available means, not by demanding of them unattainable virtue which only the saints can emulate. Men seek recognition; rightly. They will not obtain it until they are strong. They must obtain strength by cooperation and organisation and expect no gratitude. There are other paths to power; but Tagore rejects them: Nietzschean amoralism, violence are self-defeating, for these breed counter-violence. On this he agreed with Mahatma Gandhi and Tolstoy; but he did not accept Tolstoy's angry simplifications, his self-isolating, anarchist attitude nor the Mahatma's essentially non-political, non-secular ends.

Organisation for Tagore means, even when he is thinking in purely cultural terms, the acquisition of Western techniques; moreover it needs the building of bridges between the educated and the masses, for unless this is done there will be elitism, oligarchy, oppression, and in the end, as always, that great and angry cry from the masses for recognition, which precedes the disruption of the social texture and the revolutionary upheavals, which may be unavoidable and right where things have gone too far, but bring justice at appalling cost. No. Strength must be sought rigorously, even ruthlessly, but by peaceful means. "The English hurt our self-respect. They do so because we are paupers: when we are strong, they will be brothers. Till then, they will despise us and not fraternise." Only unto him who hath shall be given. Begging will achieve nothing except further loss of the sense of our own worth. So long as India is weak she will be bullied and ignored and humiliated. This is the note—we have heard it more than once in this century: it heralds the dawn of the awakening social self-consciousness of a class or a nation or a continent. Only those who respect themselves will be respected by others. Therefore we must emancipate ourselves, for nobody else will help us. Indeed, if they help us too much, we shall, to that extent, remain unfree. The English say that they have given us justice. This may be so, but what we ask for, what all men ask for, above everything else, is humanity, and to get mere justice is "like asking for bread and receiving a stone. The stone may be rare and precious but it doesn't appease hunger." It will not be appeased until we awaken and set our own house in order.

Internationalism is a noble ideal, but it can be achieved only when the links in the chain—that is, every nation—are strong enough to bear the required tension. It is one of Tagore's greatest merits, and a sign of that direct vision and understanding of the real world with which poets are too seldom credited, that he understood this. He understood it at a time when there was much shallow internationalism in the air. Races, communities, nations, were constantly urged to abolish their frontiers, destroy their distinctive attributes, cease from mutual strife, and combine into one great universal society. This was well enough as an ultimate ideal: it would fit a world where peoples were of approximately equal strength and status; but so long as vast inequalities existed, these sermons addressed to the weak, who are still seeking recognition, or even elementary justice for the means of survival, had they been listened to, would merely (like the doctrines of free trade and disarmament) have achieved for them the unity which the kid achieved with the tiger when it was swallowed by it.

Unity must be unity of equals, or at least of the not too unequal. Freedom for the pike is death to the carp. Those who are scattered, weak, humiliated, oppressed, must first be collected, strengthened, liberated, given opportunity to grow and develop at least to some degree by their own natural resources, on their own soil, in their own languages, with unborrowed memories, and wholly not in perpetual debt, cultural or economic, to some outside benefactor. This is the eternally valid element in nationalism, the true and only case for self-determination—the forging of the national links without which there is no great chain of all mankind.

On either side of this stand the two powerful and attractive fallacies: on one side, the hungry wolves, in the clothing of sincere internationalists, preaching to the sheep the evils of petty and destructive small power chauvinism; on the other, the sick longing on the part of the sheep to be swallowed by the wolves, to give up the unequal struggle, to merge themselves in what they fondly imagine to be a wider unity, and lose their identify and their past and their human claims—the desire to declare themselves bankrupt, and be struck off the roll, and lay down the burden of freedom and responsibility.

Tagore stood fast on the narrow causeway, and did not betray his vision of the difficult truth. He condemned romantic over-attach ment to the past, what he called "the tethering of India to the past like a sacrificial goat", and he accused such men who seemed to him reactionary of not knowing what true political freedom was, pointing out that it is from English thinkers and English books that the very notion of political liberty was derived. But against cosmopolitanism he maintained that the English stood on their own feet, he maintained, and so must Indians. In 1917, he once more denounced the danger of "leaving it all to the master", be he Brahmin or Englishman. He said, in effect, that India must get rid of the English, but must cling to the tr uths by which the English have lived. India may be stabbed in the back by her own people in the course of this—by terrorists or by appeasers. This, he thought, would not be effective enough. Indians are numerous enough, he maintained, the land is big enough, to enable them to afford to press for their goals by peaceful pressure; and if they go on and on, all the millions of them, they will win in the end. And so it turned out to be.

It is, easier to exaggerate, to lean to an extreme. Perhaps only those who exaggerate are remembered in the history either of action or of thought. Plato and even Aristotle, the writers of the Gospels, Machiavelli, Hobbes, Rousseau, Kant, Hegel, Marx, all exaggerated. It is easier to preach passionately to a country that it should adopt some vast, revolutionary ideology, and centralise and simplify and subordinate everything to a single goal or a single man or a single party. It is not difficult to call for a return to the past, to tell men to turn their backs on foreign devils, to live solely on one's own resources, proud, independent, unconcerned. India has heard such voices. Tagore understood this, paid tribute to it, and revised it. He seems to me, during his long and marvellously fruitful life, absorbed in more creative concerns than social or political activity, to have aimed to make only what was beautiful, and to say only what was true. This entailed self-discipline, and exceptional, patience and integrity. In setting down his social and cultural and above all educational ideas, he tried to tell the complex truth without over-simplification, and to that extent was perhaps listened to the less. There is a remarkable saying by the American philosopher, C.I. Lewis, which I have always treasured. He said: "There is no *a priori* reason for thinking that, when we discover the truth, it will prove interesting." Neverthelesss, it is surely better for words to be true than interesting. I can understand well that a country, and especially a great country with a rich past and perhaps an even richer future, can justly feel proud of one of the rarest of all gifts of nature, a poet of genius, who even in moments of acute crisis, when he spoke to and for his countrymen, and they craved not for mere reason, but for signs and miracles, did not yield; but unswervingly told them only what he saw, only the truth.

NATIONALISM, MARXISM AND GANDHI

Bibekbrata Sarkar

The Indian national movement against colonial rule was not a unidirectional stream of mass effort governed by simple desire to win political freedom. It was a complex, multi-dimensional flow in which a number of competing, sometimes complementary, ideologies and techniques of struggle fought or accomodated each other for more than four decades. The liberal-constitutionalists, the Congress 'extremists', the militant nationalists, the Gandhians and the leftists made interesting contributions to the development of national struggle that was rich with interweaving patterns of political interaction. The interacting streams of thought and action also reveal a variety of lessons in political engineering. The context of politics in subjugated India—characteristically Indian yet typically colonial in important ways—offered large scope for experimentation in the theory and practice of mass mobilisation, organisation, propaganda and struggle.

At the turn of the century the Indian people lived in a society that was only loosely unified to serve colonial interests. But within the framework of colonial rule Indian social life remained fragmented. Some of the non-economic factors that contributed to the perpetuation of a poor and fragmented social existence were the caste system, multiplicity of languages, marked sub-cultural variations, religious differences, widespread illiteracy and poor communications. An ingenious welding of indigenous and colonial exploitation systems forced the vast majority of the Indian people to live in grinding poverty with practically no hopes of a better life. These, in turn, produced a sense of diffidence and utter helplessness that made people regard the foreign power and the existing socio-economic system as all-powerful, unresponsive and undislodgeable. Under the circumstances, the task of uniting the people of India to fight for a cause, however worthy, not only required dedicated application but also demanded courage, understanding, patience as well as techniques of mass mobilisation and struggle that would absorb or cut across the divisive forces within the Indian society itself. Two approaches to the problem--the nationalist-political and the socialist-economic—were tried in India in a variety of ways.

The freedom struggle in twentieth century India started properly with the rise of militant nationalist groups and the mass-based anti-partition agitations in Bengal at the turn of the century. The Indian National Congress was founded in 1885, but its leadership did not believe in struggle or in associating people with politics. As a result, their contributions to the struggle for freedom were largely peripheral. These include: bringing together on one platform the Western-educated elite of India, developing voluntary associations and Indian public life, demand for social and educational reforms, and encouragement of rational enquiry. The long-term value of such activities lay in creating an infrastructure of politics. But their approach to problems, characteristic of their liberal convictions, created an indirect and exclusive brand of politics that never had the outlook or the potentialities to be strong and effective. That is why the politics of early Indian liberals did not have a direct impact on the Indian political scene.

Politics of popular participation began in 1903 with the agitational activities protesting the proposed partition of Bengal, and the localised movements in Maharashtra under Tilak's guidance. The far-reaching significance of these movements is not always adequately recognised. Peaceful yet vigorous agitational techniques such as boycott, swadeshi, picketing, public meetings, demonstrations as well as the call for national education were all characteristic features of the anti-partition movement. All these later became part and parcel of the non-cooperation programme under Gandhian leadership. The anti-partition agitations were not simply ceremonial outbursts confined to a few places but a generally well-participated, organised movement spreading into towns and villages of Bengal. In East Bengal people of both communities took part in such peaceful political protest. In Maharashtra Tilak utilised mass gatherings at popular festivals to politically awaken them by reinterpreting religious symbols and anecdotes in terms of contemporary Indian politics and corresponding rights and duties of the people. The idea of non-cooperation and no-tax campaign, both of which Gandhi used, also found place in his exhortations. Some of the prominent leaders of these movements no doubt came from practically the same strata of English educated middle classes as the liberal leadership of the Congress. But unlike the liberal leaders they regarded the British connection as destructive and dehumanising, wanted freedom immediately and as a matter of right rather than as a series of progressive concessions granted by an understanding colonial authority. Clearly, their political posture was based on assumptions radically different from those of the liberal Congress leadership. It was marked by a proud attachment to the Indian civilization, directness of approach, an active programme, clear appreciation of the need to involve the people, an understanding of the basic techniques of mass action and the difficult art of projecting political issues to a people steeped in traditional mores and held back from action by fear and ignorance. There is no doubt that these agitational struggles with which a number of Congress extremists were associated showed political characteristics which were utilised later by the Gandhian leadership to build up and sustain nationalist movements of all-Indian dimensions.

Why then did these earlier efforts fail to grow into effective all-India movements? Certainly not because the issues involved were often regional or local. The same was true of Gandhi's movements on a number of occasions. Nor because the leadership lacked qualities of courage, understanding and political innovativeness. The real reasons were that the leadership got practically no opportunity to organise themselves or prove the worth of their techniques and approach as the prominent among them were either politically harassed by the government or quickly put in prison. Secondly, being in minority they could not utilise the advantages of an all-India platform such as the Congress—an advantage that Gandhi had. Thirdly, there was no major national event that could stir up the people emotionally or economically such as the Rowlatt Act, the Jallianwalla Bagh tragedy or the widespread economic distress and unemployment as followed the First World War. These constituted a potentially explosive backdrop to the non-cooperation movement under Gandhi's leadership. The differences of opinion between the new nationalist school led by Tilak, Aurobindo, Bepin Pal and Lajpat Rai and the established liberal school led by Gokhale quite expectedly split the Congress in 1907. The split helped none of the rival groups. It remained more as a record of the formal emergence of a forceful, dynamic school of nationalism than as an organisational or political gain for anyone. An organisational victory would have been of significant benefit to the new school. Possibly then we would have witnessed in India a type of nationalist movement quite different from the one led by the Indian National Congress later.

The liberal political stock went down considerably with the split as they could not come out with any new ideas to justify their actions against the new nationalists or to improve their own image. Bitter criticism of the new school without being accompanied by an active, alternative political strategy left the liberal politicians in a state of confused retreat. The new school of nationalism languished for want of leaders and an all-India platform. But an active programme of political worth was a crying need of the hour. A substantial section of the educated middle classes, especially the youth, in some of the provinces of India showing advanced politicisation felt increasingly restless for want of a meaningful programme of action. The political vacuum so created was partly responsible for the spurt in the formation of militant nationalist secret societies in Bengal, Punjab, Uttar Pradesh and some other places. The expressed aim of such societies was to overthrow British rule in India by striking terror among the administrators through individual assassinations or commando-type actions. The British response was ruthless counter-terror on a wide scale involving terrorisation of ordinary people. This left the general population in utter scare and deprived the young militant nationalists of much needed indirect support. By 1915 then the three strands of nationalism found the paths of advance almost blocked. The liberal school was discredited; the mass-oriented nationalism of Congress 'extremists' had not blossomed out into a full-fledged alternative; and the militant nationalists were in partial disarray because of severe governmental repression, lack of funds and above all the failure to get the support and cooperation of the people. So, it was becoming increasingly clear that without the sustained involvement and support of the masses no struggle was going to succeed in colonial India. And yet to elicit a diverse peoples' response was a difficult task. More so, because a special feature of British rule in India was that colonial exploitation was carried on through administrative policies of creating and utilising every kind of division among the people to keep them disunited and suspicious of each other. When functioning in close conjunction with the indigenous system of exploitation such a policy leads to slow, and indirect pauperisation, loss of morale and emaciation of a whole people without necessarily creating an atmosphere or psychology of public protest. A policy of sustained provocation punctuated with occasional atrocities, on the other hand, prepares people better to respond to a call for struggle. It is then not very surprising that the militant nationalists did not get the requisite mass support. Alternatively, humiliating as well as violent governmental repression in connection with the agitations against the Rowlatt Bill climaxed by the massacre of innocent people at Jallianwalla Bagh in 1919 in the context of a prolonged economic crisis created just that degree of desperation among the people which made them respond to the call of non-cooperation in 1920 under Gandhi's leadership.

The militant nationalists did not succeed in achieving their objective. They, however, influenced the development of Indian nationalism in unobtrusive but significant fashion. They showed that British rule in India depended essentially on an administrative set-up that thrived on fear and subservience on the part of a demoralised people and that with courage and conviction the foundations of misrule could be shaken. This was also the central theme of Gandhi's eloquent appeal to the people. Through their exemplary heroism the militant nationalists aroused patriotic feelings among the people and strengthened the emotional base of nationalist resistance. The continued harassment of the government by the militant nationalists until the mid thirties produced interesting political results. The government's concern and feelings of desperation, evident from the long note on terrorism published in 1933 as part of the Joint Parliamentary Commission's Report, created a readiness on its part to grant concessions to the less unsettling, comparatively peaceful variety of nationalism. The political tolerance shown by the British government to the Congress-led nationalist movement was in no small measure due to the government's eagerness to discourage militant nationalists and Marxists. The course of the Indian national movement would not have been what it was had the British government taken a less accommodative attitude as many other colonial authorities did.

From the preceding strands of nationalism Gandhi drew a series of practical conclusions marked by considerable political wisdom. It can be argued that Gandhi's political methods and the characteristically novel image of leadership that he projected on the political scene were really shaped by his moral convictions, upbringing and experiences of conducting small-scale struggles against authorities in South Africa and India. But these could equally relevantly be shaped also by a combination of his moral convictions and a sensitive understanding of the character, strength and weakness of the movements that immediately preceded his entry into national politics. The failure of the liberals showed him the futility of a too restricted elitist politics and a total, uncritical dependence on a foreign government. The force and novelty of the mass-oriented new nationalism, its techniques and the popular response it evoked made it clear to him how effective with the Indian masses could be a political language that is replete with symbols and free from jargon. The firebrand patriotism of the militant young men and women and the scare created among the people through ruthless, vindictive governmental repression could not have failed to impress upon him the realisation that to secure continued co-operation of the Indian people it would be necessary to create a pattern of politics that would be active yet peaceful, gradualistic but promising and, in a certain manner, accommodative enough not to provoke governmental hostility that could throw the people into scare and disarray. Gandhi's success in keeping a reasonably high degree of personal hold over the masses gave him another significant advantage. To an appreciable extent he could become a bridge between the poor, custom-ridden villager and the educated, urban folk. This particular functional dimension of his style added to his continued value as a leader and afforded him nearly complete freedom to mould the Congress-led broad spectrum freedom movement.

But this was not enough. The problem of India was to find the form and content of a struggle that would strengthen itself through the continued participation of the people and liberate Indian society from the shackles of colonial rule as well as those of its own. Gandhi's ideas and the manner in which he guided the Congress-led freedom movement sought to provide one answer to that problem. There were, however, many who never believed in the efficacy of his ideas and solutions. This included also a substantial number of those who accepted Gandhi's leadership and his formula of a nationalist struggle that seeks to bring all social classes within its fold. Naturally then, even after Gandhi's overall control over the Congress was well established the search for alternative models was on. The most challenging of these alternatives were the Marxist ones. The assumptions and the techniques of struggle of the Marxists stood in nearly direct opposition to those of Gandhi even as the two movements grew in India under the same general conditions. Gandhians aimed at securing the cooperation of as many classes of the colonial society as possible as a matter of ideological preference rather than as a shifting strategy of struggle. The Marxists wanted a struggle of the oppressed classes against oppressor classes, both foreign and native. In each case mass participation was essential for the success of the struggle. In colonial and semi-colonial countries this means developing an approach and a strategy that would make possible the involvement of large numbers of virtually uneducated, non-politicised peasants, nominally politicised, semi-urban, small working classes concentrated in a few cities and towns, and sections of the middle classes. And so, competition and mutual distrust between the Gandhians and the Marxists were built into the anti-colonial movement. As a matter of fact, the interaction of the two camps made up a lot of what we call Indian politics during the pre-independence days. In the process of this interaction, however, interesting changes came about in the character of the anti colonial struggle.

One of the important results of this interaction is seen in the political differentiations generated within the freedom movement by the juxtaposition of ideological appeals and pragmatic considerations. The left wing of the Congress represented at the leadership level by Jawaharlal Nehru and Subhas Bose, and the Congress Socialist Party are best examples of such differentiation. The Congress Socialists started their career in 1934 as a Marxist party different in important ways from the Communist Party of India which was formally founded on the Indian soil in 1925. The Socialists regarded the Congress-led nationalist move-

ment as a mass movement and wanted to stay within the
Congress to play the role of radicalising the masses by means of
Marxist propaganda and class organisations so that the struggle
for political freedom could transform itself into a socialist movement for the true economic emancipation of the masses from
the indigenous exploitation system as well. The communists who
owed allegiance to the Third International and followed the
political strategy laid down by that organisation, never quite
regarded the Congress as representative of the people, wanted to
stay outside it and work to wean away the masses from the influence of the Congress through Marxist propaganda and organisation. Their entry into Congress was meant to be a shifting
strategy of struggle. Nehru and Subhas while not calling themselves Marxists were nevertheless influenced by Marxian ideas.
The impact of the ideas of these two popular leaders, the Congress socialists and the communists could be seen in the manner
in which the political projections of the Congress changed over
the years. The extent of the change is best perceived by comparing the public image of the Congress in the late twenties and
thirties with that of the early twenties when the non-cooperation
movement was launched under Gandhi's overall leadership. In
words used by many Congressmen, in dimensions explored,
especially the economic and the international, and radical ideas
put before new audiences, the Congress left-wing and the socialists revolutionised the political image of the Congress and
presented the prospect of a two-phased revolution—the political
and the economic—in which the first would be both a preparation for and passport to the second revolution. They talked of
class antagonism, and of divesting the vested interests, if necessary, by force. This was a far cry from the self-sufficient village
economy, trusteeship and class amity that Gandhi believed in.
To be sure, the Gandhian leadership never approved of these
developments, and repeatedly censured the speeches and activities of the leftists; but the political differentiations in the form of
parties, groups or clusters of individuals remained within the
Congress, and the change in the Congress image had been
brought about.

Another significant and correlated development, also attri-
butable to the interaction of Gandhian ideas and Marxism, was
the radicalisation of the official Congress programme from time

to time, notably in 1929, 1931, 1936 and 1937. During the mid-thirties serious differences of opinion and bitterness developed between the Gandhian leadership and the leftists around a number of issues. The major ones among them were talk of socialism and class war from Congress platforms, the right of Congressmen to be members of class organisations, collective affiliation of trade unions and peasants' organisations to the Congress, talk about existence of class exploitation in India and making promises concerning the social and economic structure of a free India. The Congress decision to fight the elections and form ministries in the provinces in 1937 also became a hotly debated question. On most of these issues the leftists did not succeed in extracting concessions from the Gandhian leadership. But the pressure of the combined Left was growing stronger every year, and Gandhi saw before other leaders of Gandhian persuasion did that some accommodation of leftist demands had to be made to prevent the possibility of the Congress programme, vague and tied to the day-to-day activities, being widely regarded as merely a cover for perpetuation of existing social and economic injustices. This was seen as a positive factor that would erode Congress' popularity among the younger sections and the more awakened masses. To a considerable extent this awakening was the result of left propaganda and activities among the workers, peasants, the youth and the general masses.

The changes in the Congress Programme between 1929-1937 amounted to a number of strikingly bold admissions and commitments, such as the misery and poverty of the Indian people was due not only to colonial exploitation but also to the "economic structure of the society", "revolutionary changes in the present economic and social structure" was essential; "political freedom must include real economic freedom of starving millions"; "control by the state of key industries and ownership of mineral resources"; "labour to be freed from serfdom and conditions bordering on serfdom"; "freedom of organisation of agricultural labourers and peasants"; "radical change in the antiquated and repressive land tenure and revenue systems". Besides, a full-scale agrarian programme was adopted at Faizpore in December 1936. The anti-colonial stand of the Congress had indeed come a long way from the vague ideas of *swaraj* advanced in the early twenties. The Congress image

changed from one of studied silence about the indigenous exploitation system to one of concerned commitment. And with
that the character of the anti-colonial struggle under Congress
leadership also changed from that of concern for political freedom to a search for the true foundations of freedom. There is
no doubt that this change, whether representative of the majority opinion in the Congress or not, helped the Congress to keep
its hold over large sections of the youth and general masses.

Finally, the interaction of Gandhian and Marxian ideological thought currents also brought into existence certain movements that ran parallel to the Congress-led freedom movement,
bringing into sharper focus the special socio-economic problems
of large sections of the Indian people, namely, the peasantry
and the industrial working class. The Gandhian leadership
persistently refused either to take interest in the class organisations of peasants and worker or to grant them collective affiliation to the Congress. On the other hand, the leftists too refused
to give up class organisation. As a result, the trade union and
the kisan movements continued to run parallel to the Congress
movement inspite of there being a clear possibility that the anti-
colonial struggle would have been strengthened and perhaps
deepened had the movements run together. Here was then an
example of the resistance offered by Gandhian leadership.

Clearly then, the freedom struggle in India was not a simple
straight, onward movement which started with the non-
cooperation movement by the Congress under Gandhi's leadership and in which other streams of thought and action did not
play any significant role. It is indeed more to the point to
regard this gigantic movement as a highly interesting interacting pattern of competing and complementary roles of men and
ideas.

NEW LEFT IN INDIA
THEORY OF SOCIAL AND POLITICAL CHANGE

D. C. Grover

This essay propounds the hypothesis of New Left in India to determine its viability as a theory of social and political change. A look on the old Left[1] in this country reveals state of political passivity in which it finds itself today. To recall Lenin, who, on the failure of the European working class to respond to the Bolshevik Revolution, dubbed them as operating on the Left of the capitalist system. "Bourgeoisie encircle the proletariat on every side with a petty-bourgeoisie atmosphere, which impregnates and corrupts the proletariat andc auses constant relapses among the proletariat into petty-bourgeis spinelessness, disintegration, individualism and alternative moods of exaltation and dejection."[2] Same is true about the old Left in India, which is co-operating in the operation of bourgeois system in Kerala[3], West Bengal[4], and in the Centre.[5] The CPI since the Amritsar Congress of 1958, has striven to ensure that "Parliament becomes an instrument of people's will for offecting fundamental changes in the economic, social and state structure.'[6] Likewise, CPI-M has made a "serious estimation of the possibilities of using the parliamentary institutions to bring governments of transitional character into existence."[7] This derevolutionisation of the old Left has caused a vacuum, looking for social and political change outside the system. The New Left is emerging in response to compulsions for revolutionary transformation. Hence, this hypothesis.

New Left: Its Ingredients

What are the ingredients of the New Left to distinguish it from the old. For that one is to look to the Young Marx and his earlier writings. Marx's earlier works[8] present him as a humanist, interested in the problem of man's alienation in terms of the idea of creative freedom. Marx asserts that man has become alienated both from his environment and from his own self. This concept of alienation means that man has been removed from his natural environment so that his relationship to the environment, is no longer as immediate or intimate as it used to be. "The very moment civilization begins, production begins to be founded on the antagonism of orders, estates, classes, and finally on the antagonism of accumulated labour and actual labour."[9] Man becomes stunted and becomes something less than a human being. "What is left with the individual after all these changes have occurred is a mere rump, a lowest common denominator attained by lopping off all those qualities on which is based his claim to recognition as man."[10] The tragedy of alienation lies in the abstracted individual because he has lost touch with all human specificity. Man has been reduced to "perform undifferentiated work on humanly indistinguishable objects among people deprived of their human variety and compassion."[11] Young Marx seems to believe that all political and human relations can take natural spontaneous forms. Marx's whole view of the world is the understanding of the essence and tasks of man as such.

Man's alienation is the focus of the New Left. But this it finds not only in the capitalist system, but in communism as practised by Soviet Union and other communist countries. In his critique of Soviet Marxism, Herbert Marcuse condemns it as a "repressive, puritan morality rationalized on the basis of scarcity and external threats," lacking in the "free manifestation of potentialities."[12] It is in a way different in shaping the consciousness of individual, leading to the growth of one-dimensional man.[13] The dividing line between the two systems in gaining control of human mind and consciousness, has evaporated. Whereas this is done in naked form in Soviet system, it operates in subtle ways in capitaist countries. In the words of Herbert Marcuse:

> With the concentration of economic and political power and the integration of opposites in a society which uses technology as an instrument of domination, effective dissent is blocked where it could freely emerge: in the formulation of opinion, in information and communication, in speech and assembly. Under the rule of monopolistic media—themselves the mere

instruments of economic and political power—a mentality is created for which right and wrong, true and false are predefined wherever they affect the vital interests of society. This is, prior to all expression and communication, a matter of semantics: blocking of effective dissent, of the recognition of that which is not of the Establishment which begins in the language that is publicized and administered. The meaning of words is rigidly stabilized. Radical persuasion, persuasion to the opposite is all but precluded. The avenues of entrance are closed to the meaning of words and ideas other than the established one—established by publicity of the powers that be, and verified in their practices. Other words can be spoken and heard, other ideas can be expressed but at the massive scale of conservative majority (outside such enclaves as the intelligentsia),they are immediately "evaluated" (i.e. automatically understood) in terms of this public language— a language which determines"a priori" the direction in which the thought process moves. Thus the process of reflection ends where it started: in the given conditions and relations.[14]

One may infer that if the methods of democratic governments have been less extreme, less brutal than those of most totalitarian communist regimes, this probably reflects the usual stability of established democratic capitalist system, more so than any real appreciation of the value of dissent and dialogue about political fundamentals. This analysis of the New Left turns capitalist system into totalitarian democracy at par with totalitarian communism in alienating man.

The ideal of New Left is a new kind of society and a new kind of man in a non-repressive and "truly free civilization."[15] This model of social and political change finds expression in Jayaprakash Narayan, the spokesman of New Left in India. The exclusion of Naxalities from the category of New Left needs a word of explanation. It cannot be denied that this group of communist revolutionaries seeks change outside the bourgeois system. But their reliance on violence and armed guerilla warfare "offers very little that is either original or likely to be permanent."[16] This presents the Naxalites as "adventurists", and "ultra-left"[17] force in Indian politics. The New Left recognises Naxalism as a social phenomena, a product of discontent felt by certain sections of people. No matter on which issue violence breaks out, all these acts have got the unifying feature of demonstrating the utter inadequacies of the existing social system. Gandhi had warned about the outbreak of "violent and bloody revolution"[18] if the gulf between haves and have-nots was not eliminated in time. Jayaprakash in his response of New Left attempts to uncover the strands of social and economic conflict which has resulted in Naxalism taking root in India. "Is there any wonder that discontent, frustration, anger and want should turn the minds of some towards violence as the only possible saviour?"[19] To the Naxalities, the revolt comes to signify the harbinger of a new revolutionary era which would witness the elimination of all vestiges of the exploitative society. In the words of a Naxalite: "How do you expect a sensitive person to remain non-violent in a situation where people live and die on the streets, where laws are made only to be broken, where government exists only as a police force, where not to conform is a sin?"[20] Jayaprakash finds logic in the argument that Naxalite violence is basically a socio-economic problem and only superficially a law and order problem.

But the New Left rejects violence as it does not necessarily lead to social revolution. Power comes invariably to be usurped by a handful of the most ruthless among erstwhile revolution-aries. This is inevitable "when power comes out of the barrel of a gun and the gun is not in the hands of the common people."[21] Jayaprakash feels that the Naxalite violence is "an urgent call to demonstrate through positive action how the challenge of violence could be used to speed up the process of non-violent social change and reconstruction."[22] The alternative strategy is not to fight it with the violence of the state but to combat it with the "gun of the people," that is by trying to "create a voluntary force of constructive and service-minded persons in the Gramdan villages, particularly chosen from amongst the youth."[23] These non-violent volunteers may be called upon to perform the double task. One will be to put up non-violent defence against the eruption of violence, but more important will be the job to ensure the implementation of agrarian laws, aiming at equitable distribution of land among the landless. This job is to be done by the Gramdan volunteers as satyagrah is against politicians, administrators and money-lenders, who "have persistently defied and defeated for the past many years, and all others who aided and abetted these wrongs."[24] This is not to underestimate the role of the state nor a satyagrahi is uninterested in its effective and proper working. But it is clear that even with best of men in command, the state by itself cannot deliver the goods. The goal of the New Left is to create the power of the people along with the power of the state.

It is in this perspective that the communist revolutionaries as represented by the Naxalities cannot be treated as New Left. The New Left in India is too flexible to leave any scope for a violent and "totalitarian revolution."[25] Any movement, based on guerilla warfare is bound to fail if it does not carry the support of the masses. "The Vietnamese people's war of liberation was victorious because it . . . succeeded in leading the whole people to participate enthusiastically in the resistance, and to consent to make every sacrifice for its victory."[26] In the words of Che Guevara: "Guerrila warfare is a war of the masses, a war of the people. The guerilla band is an armed nucleus, the fighting vanguard of the people,"[27] and this kind of warfare without "the support of the population is the prelude to inevitable disaster."[28] The Naxalities did not wait for the mass support before beginning their war of class annihilation. This led to mass alienation that made it easier for the government to crush the violent movement, confined to terrorist acts of individual killing. But the rise and fall of Naxalism impressed the New Left in India that social and political change in the country could not be brought about without involving masses and the youth force, spread over a long period of confrontation with the establishment.

Youth Power

The focus of the New Left in India and in Europe is on the power of the youth. Expressing the same kind of frustration, the modern youth is "alienated with a vengeance and organised in his alienation," he is driven from "conformity to non-conformity."[29] The New Left attracts youth for its attack on bourgeois system of education, which "turns out people without any real culture, and incapable of thinking for themselves, but to fit into the economic system of highly industrialised society

. . . to be sacrificed on the altar of bourgeois appetites."[30] The univerities are attacked for they release "the indivisible, omnipresent dictatorship of forces which tend to integrate and assimilate all elements into the system."[31] This lends a new dimension to the struggle for the reconquest of individual autonomy, which, according to the New Left, can be attained by working among the forgotten, the poor, and the outcaste of society.

The emergence of youth power is tantamount to the recognition of youth as a new revolutionary class, destined to bring about social and political change. The working class no longer enjoys the glamour of being the only and exclusive instrument of revolutionary transformation. Jayaprakash Narayan finds fault with the Indian Marxists for their betraying the revolution. They "were so much taken in by the Stalinist and Leninist models that they became increasingly alienated from the Indian masses and often became stooges of external powers. Mao understood the problem of China against Stalin's Russia and totally sinified Marxism. But Maoism cannot be the solution for India's problems. Unfortunately, the crop of Indian Marxists has turned out to be no different from other Marxists."[32] As spokesman of the New Left in India, Jayaprakash Narayan addresses himself to the power of frustrated youth, and appeals to them to launch a *Youth For Democracy*:

The most serious danger comes from vitiation of the democratic process. The seminal role of elections in the democratic process and their significance for the people can hardly be over-emphasised. But since independence, elections have been growing more and more irrelevant to the people and to the democratic process. The reason is that money, falsehood, corruption and physical force have combined to erode steadily the very meaning and substance of elections...corruption of the electoral machinery, commonly manifested in intimidation and buying up of presiding officers, has been growing apace alongside of corruption in other fields.[33]

Inspiring the youth for action, Jayaprakash Narayan asks:

Will our youth continue to look idly at this strangulation of the democratic process at its very birth? Surely there cannot be a more important issue which should move the youth to action . . . What form their action should take is for the youth themselves to decide. My only recommendation would be that in keeping with the spirit and substance of democracy, it must be simultaneously peaceful and non-partisan.[34]

At this stage, it is relevant to note that JP's focus on youth power runs parallel to that of Herbert Marcuse, the spokesman of New Left in the West. In the words of Herbert Marcuse:

Students have raised a spectre—a spectre which haunts not only the bourgeoisie but all exploitative bureaucracies, the spectre of revolution which subordinates the development of productive forces and higher standards of living to the requirements of creating solidarity for human species, for abolishing poverty and misery beyond all national frontiers and sphere of interests, for attainment of peace. They have taken the idea of revolution out of continuum of repression and place it into authentic dimension, that of liberation [35]

What is evident from Marcuse's and Jayaprakash's observation is the discovery of youth, particularly students as a class of new revolutionaries. The obverse side of this evaluation is the reflection that in the majority of cases, the role of the working class has not contributed materially to the effectiveness of the individual as revolutionary material. For the same purpose students, on the other hand, have shown exceptionally effective qualities allied to their distinctive role. The student group contains a relatively high percentage of politically aware people. They are easily aroused to extremes, of which other groups are seldom capable, because of their youth, *esprit de corps*, and traditions of group independence from the general restraints of society. Their tendency towards excitable responses to political events is enhanced not only by the pressures of student life and their uncertainty as to their own future place in the country, but also by the proximity of large universities to the national and state capitals.

The students' upsurge in Gujarat in 1974 strengthened the conviction of the New Left in India that "struggle approach was the right one."[36] Jayaprakash does not share Vinoba's viewpoint that "systematic change in the political order could be brought about without a struggle, even a peaceful struggle."[37] On the other hand, "peaceful people's struggle for revolutionary changes would be more acceptable in Gandhi's India than elsewhere, and would not appear in the eyes of the revolutionary activists as chimera."[38] The youth, including the students, must naturally be in the vanguard of this mass non-violent struggle.

What lends weight to the hypothesis of New Left in India is the appraisal of the students and the youth as an answer to search for social catalyst. A protest against bad food in a college had snowballed into a statewide campaign against political corruption that had brought down the state government, and brought about the dissolution of the state legislature. It had shownwhat a mass movement ushered and organised by students, could achieve without getting involved in party politics. As in Gujarat,[39] the movement was started in Bihar,[40] relating to educational reforms and sufferings of the entire population. Jayaprakash agreed to guide them on two conditions: one was that they should be peaceful, and secondly, non-partisan. "The only way to achieve permanent social change is through non-violence." Violence would not work for tactical as well as for moral reasons. Jayaprakash asked students to give up studies and a year of education so that they could dedicate themselves to the movement for social and political change. "It is their movement; they started it and they must see it through. They have little to lose if colleges are closed. In fact, they will benefit."[41] The Allahabad High Court judgment in June 1975, invalidating the election of Mrs. Indira Gandhi on grounds of corrupt practices, and disqualifying her for next six years from having an elective office,[42] gave strength to youth participation in movement for total revolution. Jayaprakash Narayan expected the Prime Minister to resign with a view to "establishing a sound moral and political convention."[43] But Mrs. Gandhi refused to oblige. Interpreting the need for direct action on such an occasion, Jayaprakash recalled that democracy "did not only mean a government established by people's vote; it also meant that the people had the power to oust their rulers when found unworthy to rule."[44] In Mrs. Gandhi's refusal to resign, Jayaprakash Narayan found that "democracy" had "ceased to exist in India."[45] Non-violent resistance movement, backed by the youth power, had become essential for the restoration of democratic system.

The fall of Mrs. Gandhi's Government in the General Elections, held for Lok Sabha in March 1977 may be ascribed to youth power, generated by the New Left. Its impact is visible in the Election Manifesto of the Janata Party, which affirms "the right of peaceful and democratic dissent," conceding that "the ultimate guarantee of democracy and the final safeguard against exploitation and abuse of power is satyagraha or peaceful, non-violent resistance."[46] Jayaprakash Narayan ascribes the retarded momentum of the movement for social and political change to frustration among the people caused by failure of its adherents to "exercise a wholesome influence" on the Janata Government after "their election to the Lok Sabha and state legislatures."[47] Warning that as a consequence of the expectations of the people remaining unfulfilled, the authoritarian forces are raising their ugly heads, Jayaprakash urges that the only way to counter this menace is to revive the mass movement "spearheaded by the students and youths and bend the Government to fulfil its assurances."[48] As the Janata Government is following the path of the previous Congress Government, and "not doing anything to change the old system," it is necessary for the youth power to organise alongwith the people and start the second phase of the total revolution.[49] It is Jayaprakash's firm conviction that real social and political change would "only take place when the youth put in all their strength into it."[50] The New Left in India relies upon the youth power to come into confrontation with any establishment if it hinders the path to revolutionary transformation.

A number of theories have been employed to explain youth politics. One theory in particular receiving considerable attention is the generational conflict theory, explaining student activist behaviour. This theory presents two models; the functionalist model and the generational unit model. The functionalist view[51] suggests that lack of integration creates strain between the generation, forcing youth into a state of suspended alienation, which may lead to rebellion or withdrawal from society. Youth as age group, typically under thirty years of age, are primarily future-oriented and concerned with new ways to adapt to the life ahead of them. "Age serves a basis for defining the cultural and social characteristics of human beings, for thef ormation of some of their mutual relations and common activities, and for the differentiation and allocation of social roles."[52] The functionalist model of generational conflict predicts that youth as an age group find it increasingly difficult to achieve full psychological, social, economic, and political integration into society, and this lack of societal integration results in skepticism and detatchment which encourages youth to revolt in an attempt to take their rightful place in the social and political order.

The generational unit model[53] argues that it is the emerging consciousness of socially shared conditions that encourages youth to create new styles and mobilise politically. History is too one-sided and monistic adequately to explain the totality of social and political change. Certain cultural, social and intellectual trends provide the underlying currents that evolve into basic attitudes and behaviour within generations. Inherent in this fresh contact is a radical revitalisation process, which forces youth to make novel interpretations and adjustments to the cultural heritage. During late adolescence, the youth begins to live in the present, and becomes "dramatically aware of a process of destabilisation and take sides on it."[54] Youth must be drawn into vortex of social change for "participation in the common destiny."[55] The generation unit model has the flexibility to explain left and right-wing behaviour within the same generation, and thus is able to differentiate between radically divergent student political style.

Testing these theories in relation to New Left in India is largely a matter of determining whether recent youth unrest is primarily the result of structural alienation, or the product of emerging historical forces that stress the importance of consciousness and criticism of social conditions. The New Left in India aims to remove structural alienation among the youth, and, at the same time, it reflects the growing consciousness among them for a new and better social and political system.

Glimpses of contemporary revolution

The New Left in India presents a model of contemporary revolution, which is similar to Herbert Marcuse's vision of libertarian socialism, based on the concept of "subversive majority."[56] In the case of a revolution, its nature, and the way in which it must be handled, differs substantially according to whether the movement under consideration is contemporary revolution or a completed revolution. One gets glimpses of contemporary revolution in the mould of New Left in Jayaprakash's movement for total revolution. The term "Total Revolution" does not indicate any accomplishment, but is to be understood in terms of continuing revolution.

The operation of internal Emergency lends weight to Jayaprakash's contention that it is not safe to restrict the functioning of democracy to "elections, legislation, planning and administrative execution," and "there must be people's direct action," which would "almost certainly comprise, among other forms, civil disobedience, peaceful resistance, non-cooperation—in short, satygraha in its widest sense."[57] Despite the rule of Janata Party at the Centre and in several states, Jayaprakash Narayan does not think that "it will be possible to bring about any revolutionary change without the pressure and thrust of the movement."[58] This leads one to examine the ultimate objective of total revolution and its major aspects. Aiming at comprehensive change, and change in every sphere of life and organisation, Jayaprakash's total revolution is a combination of seven revolutions—social, economic, political, cultural, ideological or intellectual, educational and spiritual.[59] Everything is subject to change in this world; it is constantly changing and becoming new. What, then, does revolution or revolutionary change imply? For Jayaprakash, the process of revolution or revolutionary change is rapid, far reaching and radical too, and sometimes it leads to qualitative change in the object of change. But, "the revolution being peaceful, it was not to happen suddenly and swiftly.'[60] The whole truth is that the system as well the individual must undergo the process of change simultaneously.

Total revolution comes about by a double process that seeks to change the structure—political, economic, and social—while changing the individual intellectually, culturally, morally or spiritually. Jayaprakash's revolution, dealing with a total transformation of society, may be described as a double revolution. A truly successful revolution is one which transfers power not to a group, but to the people at large. As the revolution of the New Left, Jayaprakash's total revolution transfers total power to the common man. In the existing structure, the centres of political power are controlled by a group, and people have no option but to surrender to the will of those wielding authority above. Jayaprakash has likened this structure to an "inverted pyramid that stands on its head," and he therefore, assigns to political revolution the task to "set this picture right and stand the pyramid on its base."[61] The same is true of economic pyramid. Therefore, the task of economic revolution is to turn this pyramid upside down and stand on its base. Both these tasks must be fulfilled simultaneously.

The concept of total revolution gives a new dimension to Jayaprakash's communitarian democracy, doing away with "centralised control and party government."[62] JP comes close to Robert A. Nisbet, the New Left theortician who said that "the greatest single influence upon social organisation in the modern West has been the developing concentration of function and power of sovereign political state," but, to regard the state "as simply a legal relationship is profoundly delusive. The real significance of the modern state is inescapable from its successive penetrations of man's economic, religious, kinship and local allegiances and its revolutionary dislocations of established centres of function and authority."[63] Jayaprakash is fully aware of such dangers, and the strategy of total revolution that he suggests is of setting up student and people's action committees in all parts of the country. M.N. Roy's influence on Jayaprakash's line of thinking in this respect is quite obvious. In M.N. Roy, Jayaprakash finds the answer that "ultimately, the problem of democratic political practice is that of decentralisation."[64] The idea gets its concrete form in people's committees, which will be basic units and also act as "standing bodies with wide powers and direct influence on similar committees for larger areas, and through them the citizens will actually be in possession of power always."[65] The result will be far-reaching decentralisation of the state, which will become a clearing house of information to co-ordinate and supervise policies, framed directly by the people as a whole.

The student and people's action *samitis*,[66] set up within the framework of total revolution, will mobilise public opinion, endorse candidates for legislature, and work for his success. If the elected representatives of the people indulge in corrupt practices, the force of public opinion, generated by these *samitis*, will make them resign. Jayaprakash approaches these *samitis* as people's organs of power, and this way, he shows preference for minimum government and maximum independent community initiative. The positive job to be done by these *samitis* will be possible when their organisation is complete and the people have effective voice. They can take up "other programmes like uplift of Harijans or the Adivasis, like land distribution, like putting an end to the practice of *benami* cultivation, like the dowry system—anything that goes against the interest of people," leading to the transformation of society "politically, culturally, economically."[67] The politics of total revolution is the politics of "Lokniti—that is, people's politics and not Rajniti or the elitist politics," and "this new politics will not be imposed from the top, but will be built from below."[68] The revolution of the New Left operates through diffusion and dispersal of power among people. Democracy "is not, in a strict sense, a single form of authority."[69] Democracy is a set of conditions which can only be approximated in real life. A key characteristic of democracy is the continuing responsiveness of the government to the preferences of its citizens as political equals."[70] Jayaprakash Narayan's people's *samitis* envisage a plural society, based on devolution of power and decentralisation of authority.

Jayaprakash's emphasis on the non-partisan character of his movement raises the question of partyless democracy, which is the ultimate but not the immediate objective of total revolution. "Present-day mass election, manipulated by powerful, centrally controlled parties, with the aid of high finance and diabolically clever methods and supermedia of communication represent far less the electorate than the forces and interests behind the parties and the propaganda machine."[71] Democracy cannot be practised through the intermediary of party-politics. Jayaprakash comes close to M.N. Roy, who believes that "so long as parties stand between the state and the people, the latter can never be the sovereign power."[72] But in the immediate context of the movement for total revolution, Jayaprakash does not insist on partyless democracy. "This is an ideal. Even the communists who criticise me forget that Marx spoke of the eventual dissolution of the state. Partyless democracy is something for the future. It is possible that a new party may emerge from the movement but that is not its aim. It seeks to give to people the power over their interests that they have been deprived of."[73] What Jayaprakash advises the students and other youth participants is that even if they belong to different political parties, they must function unitedly and give the objectives of the movement priority over the programme of their parties. The purpose of associating youth with the movement is to "work for the transformation of society without any lust for power."[74] The concept of total revolution, by making its participants non-partisans, paves the way for the evolution of communitarian democracy, in which the party system may become irrelevant and redudant. A comparative study of political parties[75] substantiates the viewpoint of the New Left that the party system is incompatible with the ideal of participative democracy.

Specific nature of a revolution, including that of New Left, would be governed by the needs of the time, the situation that exists in the country, and the forces that contend for power. In the present context, "a total revolution in India should mean a revolution from the village upwards to the largest urban concentration. There must be a total change in civic life, civic relationships, civic institutions, and as we enter larger sphere of the state of national life, we have innumerable spheres in which the changes will have to be brought about."[76] The institutions of Western Democracy far from representing living together, expresses the depersonalisation of man. Jayaprakash's proposal to invert the power pyramid suits India's immediate political needs. He outlines the form he wishes to see *panchayat raj* take on the basis of political consensus in small communitarian village societies, cooperative economic enterprises, indirect elections through tiers of representative assemblies, and the withering away of the commanding position of a centralised state. The communitarian democracy takes the form of primary community neither so small that a balanced development of communal life and culture becomes difficult nor so large that life in them becomes impersonalised. The social organisation, envisaged by Jayaprakash Narayan, offers maximum opportunities to the people, who will no longer be "an amorphous mass of human grains but organised in self-governing communities—to govern themselves."[77] Such a communitarian polity is the ideal of total revolution, leading to participative democracy and stemming the tide of totalitarianism.

The relevance of non-violence to the revolution of the New Left becomes obvious when one takes a look at the experience of violent revolutions.[78] It happened invariably that those who succeeded in taking hold of the means of organised violence usurped power for themselves, protesting no doubt that they were doing so in the name of the people and for the good of the people. They were working out the logic of violence. Talking in the perspective of participative democracy, Jayaprakash warns that "power to the people is an empty slogan without non-violence and thorough going decentralisation."[79] Thus, satyagraha becomes the social expression of the new order, born out of total revolution. Spelling out his ideas on the non-violent basis of the new social order, Jayaprakash mentions other elements of satyagraha method, such as "(a) conversion by persuasion of individuals and groups to new ways of thought and action; (b) a programme of 'constructive work' designed to serve and help the people and to act as a medium through which to touch their hearts and minds; (c) non-violent non-cooperation and resistance when necessary; (d) raising a bank of properly trained volunteers committed to non-violence and selfless service to the people to act as the conscious cadres of the revolution"[80] This is the process of total revolution to be worked through the technique of "satyagraha on a mass scale."[81]

One may appreciate Jayaprakash presenting non-violent direct action as the technique of New Left in India in the light of the changed position, taken up by Herbert Marcuse, the spokesman of the New Left in Europe. The New Left in Europe has veered round to non-violence as a technique of political and economic resistance in a spirit kindred to Herbert Marcuse that "non-violence is not a virtue; it is a necessity."[82] Like Herbert Marcuse, Jayaprakash had experienced the futility of violence in his career, and had given up that path after mature consideration. As he puts it: "Under the existing circumstances, violence will lead to anarchy. Unless the widespread discontent in the country is channelized into peaceful struggle, it will express itself in sporadic violence, and this will make it easy for whosoever is there at the head of government to clamp down a dictatorship."[83] The New Left in India has, therefore, attempted to divert popular discontent into non-violent movement for total revolution. What India needs today on its political agenda is a non-violent social revolution. This is needed not only from the moral point of view, but from the viewpoint of social peace. Mrs. Indira Gandhi failed to perpetuate her authoritarian rule by default. But for the leadership and organisation, provided by the New Left, the collapse of Mrs. Gandhi's dictatorship, might have ended in chaos. Jayaprakash's movement for total revolution projects a new image of social change. The tremendous popular enthusiasm generated by the defeat of Indian authoritarianism requires to be canalised in activities to strengthen Indian democracy. This implies revolutionary change, which cannot be brought about without the pressure and thrust of a movement. In the new context of increasing tyranny, perpetrated upon the Harijans and other backward sections, Jayaprakash has called upon them to organise for a class war within satyagraha framework. "The class struggle was inevitable with the present gap between the haves and have nots existing in society," and "this danger could be avoided only when the haves responded to the needs of the have nots."[84] Jayaprakash makes an attempt to "lift the sword of discontent out of the black sword of village destitution."[85] By making satyagraha the operative part of total revolution, Jayaprakash Narayan has turned the New Left into a resourceful alternative to violence.

Despite a specific constitutional directive against untouchability and a number of welfare schemes undertaken by the Union and the State governments since independence, the fact remains that the social and economic conditions of Harijans are far from satisfactory. It is in this context that the satyagraha concept of class struggle advocated by Jayaprakash Narayan gives a new dimension to the New Left model of contemporary revolution. This development runs parallel to the forces of New Left in the West among blacks.[86] Like the American Negroes, Harijans in India constitute apolitical sections of society, and are resource poor. As such, they cannot make effective use of constitutional remedies. It is natural that they may look to the New Left for non-violent direct action as legitimate means to put an end to centuries' old exploitation. The socio-economic reality in the villages is ugly and distressing inthe extreme. The social aspect of total revolution makes frontal attack on "the authoritarian taboos of caste."[87] Giving a call for starting the second phase of total revolution, Jayaprakash says that it should "begin from the villages where the majority of people lived and where society was ridden with casteism and superstition,"[88] and, where "the condition of Harijan families is worse. They are even deprived of the simple necessities of life."[89] The success of Harijan satyagraha may remove the danger of a violent shake-up. Thus nothing short of non-violent massive efforts to rectify economic and social injustice can prevent Harijans from resorting to the violent path.

The gospel of the New Left is the gospel of revolution which Jayaprakash has retained as a remnant of his initial phase in which he held a Marxist approach to the problem of social change. Although he has successfully liberated himself from the ideal of violent upsurge, he still retains the ideal of revolution which he expects to carry out in a non-violent manner. It remains to be examined how far revolution of the New Left, as presented by Jayaprakash Narayan, comes to measurement of various hypotheses that predict the direction and intensity of revolutionary movements. First, in this connection, is the "rise and drop"[90] hypothesis, which is an analysis of a long period of socio-economic improvement that is followed by a sharp reversal. According to this hypothesis, if the expectations of desired growth appear blocked, then frustration and revolution may occur. Second is the "rising expectations" hypothesis[91] which suggests that a period of socio-economic growth fosters expectation and desire for further improvement and, if this improvement is perceived as occurring too slowly, then impatience may lead to rebellion. Third is the "relative deprivation"[92] hypothesis, which predicts that if certain groups perceive their situation as improving but at a slower rate than other groups in society, then dissatisfaction and protest may appear. Fourth is the "downward mobility"[93] hypothesis, which maintains that when one group perceives its status as declining while other groups appear to be gaining, the imbalance between actuality and desire may lead to a social movement. All of these four hypotheses suggest that temporal changes in terms of perceived discrepancy between desired versus actual circumstances encourage the development of revolution. The fifth non-temporal "status inconsistency"[94] hypothesis proposes that if status mobility is high with regard to certain dimensions, but mobility appears blocked to other status factors, then tension, frustration, and protest may occur.

One may test the viability of Jayaprakash's total revolution as the model of the New Left by the criteria of these hypotheses, which, in general, recognise that changes in objective conditions may create a general mood in which people perceive themselves as unjustly deprived of a better life. More specifically, the rise and drop situation will be more intense than the rising expectations situation and more likely to lead to revolutionary activity than to reform. The rise and drop, rising expectations, and relative deprivation hypotheses explain progressive movements, since dissatisfaction is viewed as a result of comparing with the possible future conditions. The New Left in India is covered by the first three hypotheses as the programme of Jayaprakash's total revolution has instant and ultimate appeal for the youth, the middle class and all the exploited sections of society, including Harijans, Adivasis, and the rural and urban poor.

The downward mobility hypothesis, on the other hand, appears applicable to regressive or right-wing movements, since dissatisfaction is based on comparison of actual with past conditions. The various status inconsistency combinations may predict both intensity and direction of social movements, depending on the nature of status discrepancy. The direction taken by movements resulting from circumstances described in the status inconsistency hypothesis would depend upon the nature of inconsistency involved. Individuals who experience status inconsistency resulting from greater educational investments than income and/or educational investments will very likely attempt to reduce dissatisfaction in one of the two ways. They may bring about consonance through individual mobility. If this is not possible as in the case of supporters of Jayaprakash's total revolution, they may shift to protest activities. It is likely to be in the direction of creating an egalitarian society in which rewards are based upon universal criteria—a progressive movement. This analysis reveals that whereas the fourth hypothesis is not applicable to the New Left revolution in India, the fifth one is partly relevant.

Conclusion

In conclusion, this essay finds the New Left in India a viable theory of social and political change. It represents political anti-matter, given to struggle against freezing of any political system into establishment. As such, revolution of the New Left is the anomic equivalent of the system. As against it, the communist movement as represented by CPI and CPI-M, is engaged in a quest for legitimacy and independence.[95] Its derevolutionisation has eliminated its role in bringing about basic transformation. The Naxalites represented by various shades in CPI-ML, have proved grossly wrong on two counts. They over-estimated the revolutionary potential of Indian working class and the masses; they also underestimated the material and moral capabilities of the Indian Government. These miscalculations, coupled with poor preparation and coordination, doomed the revolution before it started. There never was any general violent uprising in India; instead, there were acts of sabotage, incendiarism, loot and murder. This could hardly lead to any social and political change.

This essay, therefore, rules out the efficacy of violent move-ment to produce revolutionary results. It is not invariably true that objective conditions and historical necessity contribute to the success of revolution. After all, man's freedom lies not in merely accepting change but putting his own stamp on the process of change. But to be able to put his own stamp, he has to visualise the forms to which the change should lead. Uto-pianism is ingrained in man in so far he is a free agent and creator. Between conception and actualisation, there is an inevitable distance. In art, the bridging of this distance may conceivably be within the power of an individual visionary. In social change, however, the construction of bridges is conditional upon many factors, the most important being the acceptance of this vision by other individuals, and their effort to actualise it. It is at this stage that the New Left in India emerges into a comprehensive theory of revolution. In Jayaprakash Narayan's conception of total revolution, man would also undergo a revolutionary change. "So, it is the totality that undergoes the change including the individual."[96] It is comprehensive as it possesses the recognised characteristics of a revolutionary process, event, programme of change and a political myth.[97] But in being non violent, the revolution of the New Left in India is yet to earn the distinction of being one among the "Great Revolutions".[98]

As a theory of social and political change, the New Left in India aspires to tame the naked force of the state. The state claims the monopoly of the use of force within its territorial jurisdiction. It is not possible to separate the persistence of physical force in any pattern in the service of the state from its potential or actual impact upon politics. Any use of force can be institutionalised into a pattern of social control, and this implies therefore that in certain circumstances it may also be used in patterns of political control. It is in this perspective that non-violent technique of satyagraha operates as a social expression of the New Left to meet the subtle aggressions of the state on individual freedom. In modern times, this pattern, raised to a high degree of sophistication in, for example, South Africa,[99] has been developed into a deliberate pattern of inhibition of the expression of interests, held by a substantial section of population. In normal circumstances, it is inapplicable as it leads to irritation and social instability. This risk, however, is one which governments still seem quite willing to take. The New Left in India, having experienced this treatment during the period of internal Emergency, had found remedy in Jayaprakash Narayan's method of peaceful resistance to fight the authoritarian behaviour of the state. Political allegiance is important as a system input, and if the political majority considers the system legitimate, this will contribute to social peace. It is in this context that the theory of social and political change presented by the New Left becomes functional in a democratic political system.

The struggle of the New Left in India is the struggle to create and strengthen people's organs of power as centres of parallel polity so that the state does not operate as the only instrument of social and political change.

REFERENCES

1 The old Left in India includes the CPI, the CPI-M, the Socialists, and the Young Turks and splinter groups.

2 V.I. Lenin, *Left-Wing Communism: An Infantile Disorder* (New York, 1934), pp 28-29.

3 The CPI in the Congress-led coalition Government in Kerala.

4 The CPI-M-led United Front Government in West Bengal.

5 The Socialists and Young Turks in Janata Government in New Delhi.

6 Communist Party of India, *Constitution of the Communist Party of India* (New Delhi, 1958), p. 3.

7 E.M.S. Namboodiripad, *Fight Against Revisionism* (Trivandrum, 1965), p.74.

8 *Contribution to the Critique of Political Economy* (Chicago, 1911); *The German Ideology* (New York, 1939; *The Poverty of Philosophy* (Chicago, 1910); *A Contribution to Critique of Hegel's Philosophy of Right* (New York, 1923); and *Economic and Philosophical Manuscripts* (New York, 1923)

9 Karl Marx, *Poverty of Philosophy* (Chicago, 1910), p. 53.

10 Bertall Ollman, *Alienation: Marx's Conception of Man in Capitalist Society* (Cambridge, 1971), p. 31.

11 Ibid., p.134.

12 Herbert Marcuse, *Eros and Civilization* (Boston, 1955), p. 63.

13 Herbert Marcuse, *One Demensional Man* (London, 1964), p. 70

14 Herbert Marcuse, "Repressive Tolerance," in Robert Paul Wolff, Barrington Moore, Jr., and Herbert Marcuse, *A Critique of Pure Tolerance* (Boston, 1965), pp. 95-96.

15 Marcuse, n. 12, p. 174.

16 Mohit Sen, *Communism and the New Left* (New Delhi, n. d.), p. 10.

17 Mohan Ram, *Maoism in India* (Delhi, 1971), p. 59.

18 M.K. Gandhi, *Constructive Programme* (Ahmedabad, 1948), p. 21.

19 Jayaprakash Narayan, *Face to Face* (Varanasi, 1970), p. 2.

20 Sumant Sen, "Portrait of a Naxalite," *The Statesman*, 15 August 1971.

21 Jayaprakash Narayan, "Naxalite Revolt—I: The Gun is not in the Hands of People," *The Hindustan Times*, 29 November 1970.

22 Narayan, n. 19, p. 14.

23 Jayaprakash Narayan, "Naxalite Revolt—2: Alternative Strategy," *The Hindustan Times*, 6 December 1970.

24 Narayan, n. 19, pp. 15-16.

25 B.C. Nag, "Future of Maoism in India," *Assam Tribune*, 21 June 1969.

26 V.N. Giap, *People's War, People's Army* (New York, 1962), p. 34

27 Che Guevara, *On Guerilla Warfare* (New York, 1961), p. 17.

28 Daniel James, *Che Guevara* (London, 1970), p. 235.

29 Normen F. Cantor, *The Age of Protest, Dissent and Rebellion in the Twentieth Century* (London, 1970), p. 17.

30 Cohn Bendit, *Obsolete Communism: The Left Wing Alternative* (New York, 1968), p. 27.

31 Massimo Teodori, *The New Left, A Documentary History* (London, 1969), p. 22.

32 Jayaprakash Narayan, "Foreword", J. D. Sethi, *Gandhi Today* (New Delhi, 1978), p. xi.

33. Ajit Bhattacharjea, *Jayaprakash Narayan: A Political Biography,* rev. ed. (New Delhi, 1978), pp. 172-73.

34 Ibid., p. 173.

35 Herbert Marcuse, *Essay on Liberation* (London, 1973), p. 11.

36 "J. P. on his movement in Bihar," *The Radical Humanist,* BC 5, 1975, p. 11.

37 Jayaprakash Narayan, *Prison Diary : 1975* (Bombay, 1977), p. 21.

38 Ibid., p. 23.

39 John R. Wood, "Extra-Parliamentary Opposition in India: An Analysis of Populist Agitations in Gujarat and Bihar," *Pacific Affairs,* 1975, p. 326.

40 Ibid.

41 "J. P. on his movement in Bihar," n. 36.

42 *Asian Recorder,* 9-15 July 1975, p. 12671-73.

43 Vasant Nargolkar, *J P Vindicated* (New Delhi, 1977), p. 54.

44 Narayan, n. 37, p. 83.

45 Ibid.

46 Janata Party, *Election Manifesto, 1977* (New Delhi, 1977), p. 8.

47 "J. P. urges fresh mass movement," *Indian Express,* 6 June 1978.

48 Ibid.

49 "J P reiterates 'revolution' call," *The Hindustan Times,* 16 June 1978.

50 Ibid.

51 T. Goertzel "Generational Conflict and Social Change," *Youth and Society,* 1978, pp. 327-52.

52 S. N. Eisenstadt, "Archetypal Patterns of Youth," E. H. Erikson (ed.), *Youth, Change and Challenge* (New York, 1963), p. 24.

53 E. W. Bakke and M. S. Bakke, *Campus Challenge* (Hamden, Conn., 1971), pp. 25-41.

54 Karl Mannheim, "The Problem of Generations," *Essays on the Sociology of Knowledge* (London, 1952), p. 301.

55 Ibid., p. 303.

56 Marcuse, n. 14, p. 100.

57 Narayan, n. 37, p. 34.

58 Ibid., p. 67.

59 Ibid., p. 87.

60 Ibid., p. 21.

61 Allen and Windy Scarfe, *J.P.: his Biography* (New Delhi, 1975), p. 348.

62 Jayaprakash Narayan, *A Picture of Sarvodaya Social Order* (Tanjore, 1975), p. 52.

63 Robert A. Nisbet, *Quest for Commnity: A Study in the Ethic and Freedom* (New York, 1953), p. 98.

64 M.N. Roy, *Politics, Power, Parties* (Calcutta, 1960), p. 86.

65 Ibid., p. 57.

66 Nargolkar, n. 43, p. 35.

67 "J.P. on his movement in Bihar," n. 36.

68 Nargolkar, n. 43, p. 36,

69 Robert A. Dahl, *After the Revolution ?* (New Haven, Conn., 1970),

p. 59.

70 Robert A Dahl, *Polyarchy* (New Haven, Conn, 1971), p. 1.

71 Jayaprakash Narayan, *Socialism, Sarvodaya aud Democracy*, ed., Bimla Prasad (Bombay, 1964), p. 215.

72 M.N. Roy's letter to Richard L. Park, dated 2 April 1951 (Dehradun, M.N. Roy Archive, Indian Renaissance Institute), Document No.3, Subject: Individual Correspondance Foreign, Richard L. Park, File No. 1 C-FOR/RLP-1.

73 "J.P. on his movement in Bihar," n. 36, p. 11.

74 "J.P. renews call for total revolution," *The Hindustan Times*, 7 March 1978.

75 Kay Lawson, *The Comparative Study of Political Parties* (New York, 1976), pp. 4-20.

76 Jayaprakash Narayan, *Towards Total Revolution*, vol. 4, ed., Brahmanand (Bombay, 1978), p. 198.

77 Jayaprakash Narayan, *A Plea for Reconstruction of Indian Polity* (Varanasi, 1959), p. 43.

78 Erik H. Erikson, "In Search of Gandhi," in Dankwart A. Rustow, ed., *Philosophers and Kings: Studies in Leadership* (New York, 1970), p.44.

79 Jayaprakash Narayan, "Gandhi and the Politics of Decentalisation," Sibnarayan Ray, ed., *Gandhi, India and the World* (Bombay, 1970), p. 273.

80 Ibid., p. 230.

81 Jayaprakash Narayan, *Total Revolution* (Varanasi, 1975), p. 9.

82 *Marxism, Religion, aud the Liberal Tradition*, Lecture delivered by Herbert Marcuse in Temple University, Philsdephia, 17 April 1969.

83 Nargolkar, n. 43, p. 137.

84 "JP's plea for have-nots," *The Hindustan Times*, 10 March 1978.

85 Allen and Scarf, n. 61, p. 375.

86 Armed L. Mauss, "The New Left and the Old," *Journal of Social Issue*, vol. 27, no. 1, pp. 40-62.

87 L. P. Sinha, *The Left Wing in India* (Muzaffarpur, 1965), p. 33.

88 "Call for 2nd phase of total revolution," *The Hindustan Times* 6 June, 1978.

39 "JP blames Nehru for neglect of villages," *The Hindustan Times*, 22 June 1978.

90 James C. Davies, "Toward a Theory of Revolution," *American Sociological Review* (February 1962), pp. 5-18.

91 Ibid., p. 9.

92 James A. Geschwender, "The Negro Revolt: An Examination of Some Hypotheses," *Social Forces* (December 1964), pp. 248-56.

93 William Kornhauser, *The Politics of Mass Society* (Glencoe, Ill., 1959), p. 181.

94 James A. Geschwender, "Continuity in Theories of Status Consistency and Cognitive Dissonance," *Social Forces* (December 1967), pp. 615-67.

95 Bhabani Sen Gupta, *Communism in Indian Politics* (New York, 1972),

p. xiv.

[96] Narayan, n. 76, p. 198.

[97] Peter Calvert, *A Study of Revolution* (Oxford, 1970), p. 4.

[98] Lyford Paterson Edwards, *The Natural History of Revolution* (New York, 1965), p. 23.

[99] David E. Apter, *Introduction to Political Analysis* (Cambridge, Mass. 1977), p. 316.